"To organize communities and workers, you have to listen to them. Jon Melrod's many stories show he did just that—and had a blast, too, as they turned their creativity and solidarity against the boss. Yes, there's a lot to be learned from Melrod's tales, but they're also a joy to read."
—Ken Paff, cofounder of Teamsters for a Democratic Union

"Brother Melrod's book *Fighting Times* provides firsthand insight into the valiant struggles waged in the early to mid-1980s in the contentious struggle between rank-and-file auto workers and the four US auto manufacturers. Concession fever, pushed by both the auto companies and their partners in the UAW International union, swept the industry and threatened to decimate decades of hard-fought gains won by the rank and file since breaking down the nonunion shops in the 1930s. For any young activist just entering the labor movement, *Fighting Times* offers inspiration, guidance, and insight on how to motivate the rank and file to identify its own interests and stand up to corporate attacks and, in some cases, union sellouts who do the bidding of the owning class. The book is a must-read for all aspiring labor activists."
—Peter Kelly, former president, UAW Local 160 GM Tech
Center, UAW National Bargaining Committee 1985

"Long before Kenosha, WI, became a flashpoint in Black Lives Matter protests in 2020, this blue-collar city was the scene of intense shop-floor campaigns against racism and for militant unionism in the auto industry. Jon Melrod's account of his workplace organizing and reform caucus building in the 1970s and '80s is full of useful lessons for younger radicals trying to revive organized labor today. *Fighting Times* illustrates the importance of resisting contract concessions, defending free speech on the shop floor, and democratizing the United Auto Workers, a key rank-and-file struggle to this very day."
—Steve Early, labor journalist, former international representative
at Communications Workers of America, author of *Refinery Town:
Big Oil, Big Money, and the Remaking of an American City*

"Jon Melrod's *Fighting Times* tells the story of a '60s-era student radical who was one of thousands of young revolutionaries who left the campus and headed for mills, mines, factories, and battered neighborhoods. It was a learn-as-you go migration that was as challenging and exciting as it was chaotic and dangerous. Much ink has been devoted to Weatherman's stuttering attempts to attack the system. What's missing from those accounts is the organizing these onetime SDS activists did in the coal miners' right-to-strike movement, the postal workers' wildcat strikes, and—in Melrod's case—Kenosha's American Motors factory. American youth everywhere were inspired by the freedom fighters of the Black Panthers, Vietnamese NLF, and the Chinese Revolution. It was an exciting time, and Jon Melrod's extraordinary book puts you there."
—Tommy Amano-Tompkins, English professor at LA Harbor College and onetime arts editor at the *San Francisco Bay Guardian*

"*Fighting Times* is an excellent example of a militant rank-and-file caucus taking up the battle for women's equality. The Fighting Times caucus at the American Motors auto plant in Kenosha, WI, took up the battle against discrimination of women on the shop floor, within the union, and in the broader community. When Jon was elected chief steward his election slate consisted of newly energized women activists. Under his leadership, half the steward body were women. I recommend any young person looking to become active in the union movement read this book, which is vital for building today's movement in support of women's fight for equality and the fight for social justice."
—Laura Drake, senior organizer at Chicago AFSCME Council 31

"Jon Melrod, now in his seventies, has been an activist all his life, starting in second grade. His book, *Fighting Times,* is a remarkable document that shows us how one dedicated person became a leader who helped build a movement that improved the lives of industrial workers. *Fighting Times* is a blueprint for anyone who seeks to bring justice to the workplace."
—Stephan Shames, photographer

"For too long the dominant narrative of Sixties radicalism has been one of unrealistic idealism giving way to desperation, capitulation, or despair. Missing are stories of those who became radicalized in that time and went 'to the working class' as a means to effect fundamental change. Now Jon Melrod brings us one of those stories, one that is both unique—his having been a catalyzing force in key struggles— and far more representative than what we have been led to believe. His is an essential story of someone who emerged from the Sixties maelstrom intent on taking things in further liberatory directions."

—Aaron J. Leonard, author of *Heavy Radicals* and *The Folk Singers and the Bureau*

Fighting Times
Organizing on the Front Lines of the Class War

Jon Melrod

Fighting Times: Organizing on the Front Lines of the Class War
Jon Melrod
This edition © 2022 PM Press.

ISBN: 978–1–62963–965–9 (paperback)
ISBN: 978–1–62963–980–2 (ebook)
Library of Congress Control Number: 2022931968

Cover by John Yates / www.stealworks.com
Interior design by briandesign

10 9 8 7 6 5 4 3 2 1

PM Press
PO Box 23912
Oakland, CA 94623
www.pmpress.org

Printed in the USA

Due to space constraints, sections of the original manuscript had to be cut but have been posted to my website, www.jonathanmelrod.com, along with primary source material supporting the book, including portions of my FBI dossier.

Fighting Times is dedicated to my sons Eli and Noah, whose questions about my life, during the period I battled pancreatic cancer, inspired me to write this book. It is my deepest hope that they will continue to find their own ways to better society as they proceed along their lives' paths.

WARNING: Language in this book is racist

Fighting Times focuses extensively on the topic of racism and confronting real-world bigots and white supremacists. Readers will find certain language to be ugly, demeaning, and utterly abhorrent.

I thought long and hard about whether to include racial epithets. Racism, I believe, must be exposed in all its ugliness and aggressively opposed. Rather than sanitize the language, I chose to quote individuals in the context of their most distasteful and hateful utterances, which at the time, and today, make me cringe in disgust and despair.

I first experienced racism in its most despicable form as a ten-year-old growing up in apartheid-like Washington, DC. The amusement park my buddies and I visited—Glen Echo—in nearby Maryland was forced to desegregate by courageous and persistent young Black students, who faced not only arrest for trespassing but harassment from counterprotesters from the American Nazi Party.

I remember later in my childhood seeing a Black chain gang working under the blazing summer sun on a Virginia road under the glare of white guards with shotguns cradled in their arms. That indelible scene of American racism in action turned me into an antiracist at a young age.

I joined the Student Nonviolent Coordinating Committee in 1965 after three young civil rights workers were murdered in Mississippi by the Ku Klux Klan. Around the same time, I joined my first picket line in front of the South African embassy in DC to protest apartheid. From then until now, fighting white supremacy has been at the heart of my political organizing.

As one cannot live life in America without observing and experiencing racism, I decided not to disinfect the language of the book, as I want readers to see the world as I did in my many years of organizing. I hope you will understand.

Contents

Acknowledgments

Hundreds of people have directly and indirectly influenced my life and thinking over the past seventy-two years. If one is an observer of the human condition, there are no limits to what can be learned from others and their experiences. They are our guideposts for understanding our mandate for change and how to go about it.

Sadly, quite a few partners in crime and close political comrades have already departed, many from the protracted ravages of the Vietnam War and others from the effects of spending one's life working in dangerous, often toxic factories.

I owe special thanks to those who have provided invaluable assistance in the lengthy process of writing, editing, researching, and designing this book and my website. Much credit is due to my wife, Maria Isabel Melrod, who has been my rock over the past eight years, nursing me through numerous health crises and always being there for me in good or bad times. I also owe my brother Joey Melrod much thanks for being available for me through thick and thin.

Much credit is due to Tod Ohnstad and John Drew for putting up with me over the years at American Motors and without whom there would be little to write about. Also, I owe a shout-out to now-deceased Rudy Kuzel and Robert Fletcher, my Local 72 mentors, friends, and veteran union militants from whom I learned so much.

There are many more to whom thanks are due, including Martha Gruelle, Casey Goodwin, Noah Melrod, Ethan Young, Mara Yokohama, John Kaye, Mat Callahan, Tommy Tompkins, Max Elbaum, and Darryl Vance, my invaluable graphic/web designer. I sincerely apologize to those I've left out.

Finally, I pay tribute and offer encouragement to newly minted activists who are ready to devote themselves to the struggle for a just and humane world. All power to the people!

Introduction

I wasn't looking forward to the call, but it felt inevitable. Just the day before, I'd undergone an emergency scan to ascertain the cause of the incessant, nagging pain in my abdomen. Most days, I reported to work at Rock River Music in San Francisco but found myself resting my head on my desk for hours, overcome by debilitating pain and nausea.

Though I knew the phone would ring, the piercing sound triggered a visceral reaction.

"Hello, Jonathan. Dr. Abel here."

"Good morning, Dr. Abel. I guess you have news."

"I do, Jonathan, but it's not what we hoped. The scans indicate a tumor on the tail of your pancreas. It appears malignant. We need to immediately get you into surgery. This is quite serious, but we'll do our best."

"Do our best." That didn't seem very reassuring.

A quick Google search left me gobsmacked. Odds of surviving pancreatic cancer ranked among the lowest of any cancer, particularly for the aggressive variety that afflicted me. Only about 2,750 pancreatic cancer patients out of 35,000 survive five years. There were *no statistics* available for how many survived beyond those five years to lead a cancer-free life.

Why me? Why was a nice Jewish boy, raised in all-white, middle-class Northwest Washington, DC, a terminal cancer statistic at fifty-four? I needed to understand genetic factors and behaviors I had engaged in that might explain my 2000 intestinal surgery and now my diagnosis of terminal pancreatic cancer.

At twenty-one, after high school and college years consumed as a radical activist in support of student rights and the civil rights movement, in opposition to the criminal Vietnam War and in support of the struggle for Black liberation and women's liberation, I had chosen to continue organizing by working in a factory.

Along with thousands of other student revolutionaries, I believed that our generation could organize workers and poor people to fight for an end to exploitation, racial oppression, and sexual discrimination, and to bring to birth a new world in which hunger, poverty, inequality, and environmental destruction were forever banished.

Little did I realize that the choice I made then—to take factory jobs to organize workers in those plants and help them get the justice they deserved—might end up killing me decades later.

In the spring of 1972, just months out of college, I took my first job as an hourly wage slave at a small plastic injection-mold factory in South Milwaukee, Wisconsin. I soon found myself at the bottom of a large concrete vat, rushing frantically to clean the toxic residue of trichloroethylene (a cancer-causing chemical) used to degrease the oil on metal paint trays. When I asked for protective gear like a respirator, the straw boss let me know that respirators were for girls and sissies. "Juan—are you a sissy?" he asked.

In May I landed a job at the large United Auto Workers–organized American Motors Corporation (AMC) plant in Milwaukee. Within months, I led young workers to fight forced overtime and a speedup of the auto assembly line. The FBI, hot on the trail of student radicals taking factory jobs, met with AMC management to orchestrate my discharge.

Unemployed and likely blacklisted, I took a job at the lowest rung of the industrial hierarchy, a nonunion shop populated entirely by workers of color, except for me: Phister and Vogel tannery, where thousands of stinking, maggot-infested cowhides were turned into luxury leather. At P&V I experienced exposure in my groin area to the acidic industrial-grade solvents used to waterproof leather, which made me wonder if I would ever have kids.

Later I worked at Crucible Steel, manufacturer of Mack Truck axles. Nightly I choked on welding smoke, while tiny particles of silica dust swirled around me. When red-hot molten steel was poured from the overhead ladle into a sand mold in the shape of an axle, a byproduct was crystalline silica dust, the cause of silicosis. The FBI tracked me to Crucible, and again I was discharged.

Then Pressed Steel Tank in West Allis, just outside Milwaukee, hired me as a general laborer in 1975. At PST, I wore asbestos mitts to offload red-hot, high-pressure tanks as they exited roaring blast furnaces, spewing hot air that singed eyebrows. All around me floated feather-like particles of asbestos that had burned off my mitts.

On another job at PST, I climbed into a four-foot-high pit under a "blaster" to shovel metal pellets—tens of thousands of metal pellets. After I emerged from the pit, I coughed and sneezed black, crystalline soot, protected only by a rag tied around my mouth and nose. Again, no company-issued respirator.

While I was working in industry, I didn't focus on toxic exposure but instead on building solidarity and militant resistance among coworkers to capitalist exploitation. Before I left PST, the Unity caucus, a group of young rank-and-file militants I had pulled together in our Steelworkers local, led a bitter eight-week strike. We flattened the tires of trucks crossing our picket line to transport strikebreaker-made tanks. When GMAC (GM's financial arm) used the court system to repossess a striker's car, we barged en masse into a staid GMAC office, causing a disruption until the executive manager returned the striker's keys and apologized.

The National Labor Relations Board (NLRB), after an appeal by American Motors to the Seventh Circuit Appellate Court, ordered the nation's number-four automaker to reinstate me after 1,008 days, with restored seniority and back pay. I reassembled our rank-and-file caucus, Fight Back, in time to organize resistance to the takeaway of hundreds of jobs. Pinkertons, perched on rooftops, filmed us picketing the AMC employment office, resulting in two-week disciplinary suspensions for four of us.

The NLRB administrative law judge ordered American Motors to remove the suspensions, which was my second of seven NLRB wins in forcing American Motors to reverse decisions punishing me for my organizing efforts. When I transferred with 350 other Milwaukee workers to AMC Kenosha, I joined with other activists to help organize the Fighting Times caucus in United Auto Workers (UAW) Local 72.

Over the next nine years, our caucus grew into a militant, class-conscious organization of shop-floor activists, and we led relentless day-to-day resistance on the assembly lines and joined broader political struggles.

As a consequence of the caucus publishing the highly popular, bold, and irreverent *Fighting Times* newsletter, supervisors at the behest of (and funded by) the company sued three of us for defamation (John Drew, Tod Ohnstad, and me), alleging damages over $4 million. The NLRB intervened after the civil trial, finding AMC in violation of our protected rights and ordering the company to pay over $300,000 in legal fees and lost wages.

Despite incessant red-baiting and periodic physical attacks, I steadily moved up in UAW leadership. I held the positions of line steward, department chair, education committee member, chief steward, and international union delegate, and eventually I was elected to a top position on the executive board, which also was the bargaining committee.

While I was chief steward of the trim department, my desk sat within breathing distance of an open barrel of trichloroethylene used to wipe grease off car bodies. Despite the skull and crossbones warning on the barrel, bare-handed repair workers dipped rags into the barrel, slopping toxic chemicals over themselves, the floor around us, and onto car bodies. It required a battle of the first order to force the company to move the barrel and eventually substitute a less virulent, noncarcinogenic chemical.

In 2004, Dr. Abel mentioned to me that Ashkenazi Jews experienced a statistical propensity to suffer from intestinal and pancreatic cancer. I arranged for a state-of-the-art genetic test at UCSF medical center to determine if my cancer had been the product of an Ashkenazi genetic abnormality. The answer came back negative. As the clinician interpreting the test results explained, "There is no evidence of genetic-based causation for your cancer. Based on your employment history, the most likely explanation is that the disease resulted from prolonged exposure to industrial toxins."

In July that year my thoughts had turned to my two sons, Eli and Noah, ten and seven, when I received the prognosis that I needed to put my affairs in order and had only six months to a year to live.

Somehow, some way, I promised myself, I would beat the odds. I had two young boys, and I wouldn't leave them without a father.

Later, as my sons were growing up, they asked about my life before them. As they grew older, their questions turned increasingly to my political activism. I shared many stories you will soon read. "Dad," they asked, "why did you pull a shotgun on the FBI when they wanted to talk with you?"

> In college, were you really a bodyguard for a Black Panther?
> Why did you go to work in a factory after graduating from college?
> Why did you go to an Indian reservation when you could have been killed by police?
> Did you get cancer from working in factories? What kind of factories did you work in? Was it dangerous?
> What is a union like? Did you really get sued for $4 million?

So many important questions to answer, including the ultimate: would I do it all over again knowing I would contract cancer from toxic factory chemicals?

The first thing to say is that hardly anyone else working in those factories had the choices I did. Most didn't have the option of safe and healthy careers, and, if they did, it would have been at far too low a wage to support themselves, much less a family.

Whether or not I would do it again, there were strong reasons for my choices. I am convinced of the need for revolutionary societal change, and that certainly won't happen on its own, particularly the long-term goal of a socialist society.

I've seen again and again what disempowered people—students, community members, women, people of color, and workers—can do when they join forces. That is awe-inspiring, whether in day-to-day struggles on the shop floor or political campaigns like confronting the KKK or fighting with the Menominee Warrior Society to break a police blockade of their armed siege to win a medical clinic for their deprived reservation, as I did in 1975.

And I must be honest: we had a blast—a total blast. There is little that rivals the spiritual high of joining with coworkers to take on a pompous, autocratic boss who needs a slapdown, or walking off the assembly line to launch a wildcat strike.

Two people who were an essential part of organizing at AMC deserve special mention: John Drew and Tod Ohnstad. They were my compatriots, fellow activists, and codefendants in the Fighting Times defamation trial. My stories mostly center around what happened in my own department, in Building 40, and John and Tod worked elsewhere in the plant. But keep in mind as you read about Fighting Times that I was one of a trio.

Not knowing if there would ever be enough time to answer my sons' queries, I started writing a memoir some fifteen years ago. The chapters that follow, I hope, will answer many questions, point today's new generation of organizers in the right direction, and maybe inspire a few young people to join the struggle.

CHAPTER 1

Apartheid in My Backyard

My world as a young child in the mid-1950s was an all-white, largely Jewish enclave in a largely Black city: Chesapeake Street in Northwest Washington, DC, adjacent to Rock Creek Park. I walked about a mile through all-white neighborhoods to an all-white public elementary school; rode bikes with other white kids who lived on my cul-de-sac; played basketball at the Jewish community center; and enjoyed shoestring fries, ketchup, and cherry cokes at a drug store counter staffed by young white waitresses.

Outside the Northwest quadrant, however, the city transformed into a bustling Black metropolis. In the 1950s, DC remained as racially segregated as any Southern city.

My naive, mostly color-blind view of the world was transformed one summer day when a roadside scene, just beyond the borders of DC, imparted an indelible imprint on my young mind. My father had taken the family for a weekend drive on back-country roads in nearby Virginia. I peered out the window and noticed a line of Black men chained together. As we neared them, clad in white-and-black striped uniforms, I noticed that each wore heavy metal shackles around his ankle and waist, causing the line to shuffle awkwardly, the men tethered by twos.

Perched atop imposing horses, as the chain gang labored with pickaxes and shovels, slouched large, potbellied, uniformed white men cradling scary-looking rifles. I felt sad for the unhappy-looking men chained together. Puzzled, I wondered why they were all Black.

For perhaps the first time, I experienced a disquieting inkling of the racial divide in which I lived. That vivid childhood memory has long remained with me, particularly the black and white stripes and the imposing white men on horseback with rifles.

My parents grew up in Newark, New Jersey. In search of opportunity, my father, Leonard, left Jersey with five dollars in his pocket and moved to Washington, DC, in the late 1940s. He pulled himself up by his boot-straps from selling shoes to become a self-educated attorney. Having no money for tuition, he sat on the floor in a hallway listening to evening law school classes through a transom. Weekends he spent in the library reading volumes on court decisions.

After passing the DC bar, no law school degree required, he hung out his shingle. My mother soon joined him from Newark. I arrived in 1950, and our family moved from a small apartment to Northwest DC about six years later.

In the torrid heat of the DC summer, we often escaped to Glen Echo Amusement Park in Montgomery County, Maryland. As I frolicked with friends, it never occurred to me that the ornate merry-go-round with its gaudily painted wooden horses, towering Ferris wheel, white wooden roller coaster, and expansive swimming pool were the exclusive province of white kids.

For Black kids, Glen Echo's pool and rides were a mirage. They glimpsed the park through a chain-link fence, but the pool's cool waters were off limits. Glen Echo in the 1950s enforced a whites-only admission policy. Black kids, banned from the park, might open a fire hydrant to cool off when temperatures topped one hundred degrees.

Summer 1960, students from Howard University organized a picket line and demanded Glen Echo be integrated. On a steamy summer day, Black students made it into the park and refused to disembark from the carousel. A security guard approached Laurence Henry, a divinity student from Howard, and challenged, "What race do you belong to?"

Henry responded, "I belong to the human race, sir." He was promptly arrested.

Riots ensued as white bigots furiously tried to hold back the tide of history. For days, we heard scary rumors of whites attacking Blacks at the park. From my eleven-year-old perspective, I couldn't understand the fuss. Why couldn't Black kids enjoy the rides and pool with us? They were, after all, members of the human race, as Laurence Henry had eloquently pointed out. Even as a kid, I was aware that some of those who had attacked picketing students at Glen Echo Park were members of George Lincoln Rockwell's American Nazi Party.

By summer's end, the conflict dissipated. The next season Glen Echo opened on a nonsegregated basis, but I never returned.

Racial tension over the integration of Glen Echo was merely an opening salvo of a contentious battle in Washington. Black residents of the capital and its environs were emboldened by a newfound awakening, while many whites resisted encroachments on their protected sanctuaries—an incursion on their racial pride and privileged white supremacy.

In 1962 opposing racial camps faced off at the "City Title" high school football championship, played each Thanksgiving between the DC public school champions and the Catholic school champs. Considering the racial makeup of the public schools versus the Catholic schools, the matchup was incendiary—gasoline awaiting a spark.

Excitement welled up in me when my father announced he and I, father and twelve-year-old son, would be going to DC Stadium to join the crowd of fifty thousand fans watching St. John's College High School play Eastern High School.

In the fourth quarter, the ferocious athletic battle turned nasty after a tussle between two players, and the Black player was removed on a stretcher. Tension in the stands was already high, as cheers were replaced with racial epithets. My father grabbed my arm and rushed us out of the stadium before the final whistle blew and verbal aggression exploded into raging violence.

Numbers of injuries reported ranged from forty to five hundred. One thing for certain, the racial divide, inflamed by the game, engulfed the city, and the title games were canceled forever.

My parents were not particularly political. They were upwardly mobile, middle-class Jews who religiously voted for the Democratic Party. Early 1960s Democrats were good liberals, as were my parents: fair, honest people. I grew up with a deep-seated sense of justice.

It came as a shock when my mother suggested I apply to Putney School on Elm Lea Farm in Vermont for ninth grade. No one I knew attended boarding school; the very concept seemed foreign. To my surprise, I was admitted.

My parents and I flew to the tiny airport in Keene, New Hampshire, rented a car, and traveled an hour to the town of Putney—population under one thousand—and then continued up the mountain until we spotted the Elm Lea Farm sign.

I hoped my parents would realize they'd made a mistake and return me home. As we moved my few belongings into the Noyes boys' dorm, the highly intellectual conversations I overheard sounded foreign. I'd arrived in an alternate universe.

I inquired about weekend activities. "On Friday night we all gather to sing madrigals," a student volunteered with a smile. What, I wondered, were madrigals? And would I be required to sing them? Sure enough, after

Friday dinner the entire student body moved en masse to the nearby Main Building.

For the next two hours, two hundred students sat packed together, shoulder to shoulder, sweaty thigh to sweaty thigh, on backless wooden benches, in an airless hall, singing Mozart, Bach, and Beethoven. The conductor, Norwood Hinkle, who I learned was an esteemed classical music teacher, worked himself into a frenzy, waving his wooden batons. I squirmed on the uncomfortably hard bench.

As my student life weaved through transformative political, cultural, and social events, I remained sealed-lip silent at Friday Sing. It wasn't my thing. One Friday I sat, head bent, shoulders hunched, engrossed in a book by Aldous Huxley. Startled, I heard a furious clanging of the wooden batons on the metal lectern. The hall fell deathly quiet. I continued reading.

"Mr. Melrod!" Hinkle bellowed, clearly exasperated. "Do you have something better to do than join us?"

I responded with a nonchalant yes. I was barely sixteen but felt certain this man, despite his reputation, had no right to force me to sing. Hinkle's voice ratcheted up a few octaves, "And what could that be? Do tell what has your rapt attention."

"An excellent book by Aldous Huxley." In defiance, I lowered my gaze and resumed reading.

Completely flummoxed, Hinkle yelled, "Mr. Melrod! Put down that trash immediately and join us."

Slowly raising my head to meet his incensed gaze, "I don't think so, Norwood. (At Putney we addressed teachers by their first name.) I'm thoroughly enjoying my book."

Utterly beside himself, he sputtered, spewing spittle on the first row of students: "Leave the hall immediately. Wait for me in the Social Room."

Immensely pleased with myself by the unexpected outcome of being released from mandatory Friday Sing, I squeezed through the rows of students.

I plopped comfortably into an overstuffed chair in the Social Room and was soon engrossed in my reading. I hadn't noticed the singing had ceased when the door flew open. As if possessed, diminutive Norwood barged in, barely able to control his anger.

"Mr. Melrod, since I've been here at Putney, students have sung madrigals every Friday night. I will not tolerate your flouting of our traditions. I expect you will rejoin us and surely participate."

"Nah, I don't really think that's gonna happen."

With my unequivocal and rude rebuff, Norwood flew into a rage, clenched his fists, and seemed poised to hit me. As the distance between us shrank, I jumped up, grabbed each of his flailing fists, and held him immobilized.

"Norwood, I'm going to say this once and only once. Don't you ever, ever try to hit me."

He shot back, "Melrod, you're banned from Friday-night madrigals. I don't want to see your face again." At that, he turned and stomped out, breathing hard.

How very perfect, I thought, proud that in the school's thirty-two-year history, I had achieved the dubious distinction of being the only student expelled from Friday Sing. For every ensuing Friday evening until I graduated, I lounged in my dorm room reading science fiction.

When Norwood raised his voice to belittle me and his fists to hit me, I intuitively understood for the first time that authority is only as powerful and commanding as one allows, a most valuable lesson that would serve me well.

I arrived on Putney Mountain a political neophyte, conscious that there were Democrats and Republicans, a president, Congress, and a Supreme Court.

But political turmoil swirled around the country from coast to coast, even on our mountaintop in Vermont. I searched for answers to explain the dramatic events unfolding in the world beyond Elm Lea Farm. I needed to understand why inequality, injustice, and racism seemed so rampant in America.

A fellow student suggested I read *Red Star Over China* by Edgar Snow. After reading it I composed a handwritten letter on three-hole, loose-leaf notebook paper:

> Dear Mao Tse-Tung, Chairman of the Communist Party of the People's Republic of China:
>
> I am a high school student in the United States. I don't believe that we are living in a fair society. Daily I read about horrible racial inequities and unfair economic disparities. Our country is perpetrating an illegal war of genocide in Vietnam.

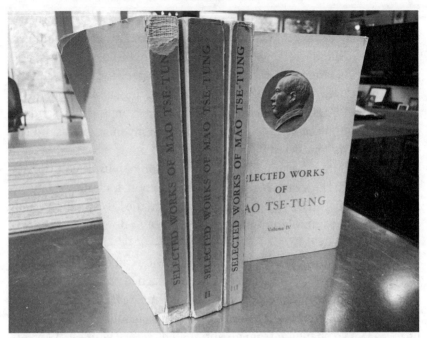

A few months after writing to Chairman Mao in Peking, China, to inquire about "socialism," I received this four-volume *Selected Works* in my high school mail cubby.

I would very much like to find out more about socialism. Could you please send me your writings, as I would like to understand for myself what socialism is all about and how your system works?

Sincerely,

Jonathan D. Melrod

Putney School

Months later, after I'd forgotten the letter, a package arrived. It was surprisingly heavy and postmarked Peking, China. I couldn't contain my curiosity, ripping open the wrapping to discover four volumes of *The Selected Works of Mao Tse-Tung*.

Nearing the end of freshman year, I resolved to act on my newfound political ideas. A fire of activism had begun to burn within me. Among civil rights organizations at the time, I felt the most affinity with the Student Nonviolent Organizing Committee (SNCC) and its young, militant leadership.

In DC for summer break, I sought out the SNCC headquarters, located across the city, two buses and a long walk away from the familiar confines of the Northwest quadrant.

The woman at the battered reception desk peered at me, puzzled. I timidly asked, "Is there anything you need me to do? I'm here to volunteer."

In the headquarters' windowless basement, I folded, stuffed, and stamped thousands and thousands of letters reciting details of the Schwerner, Chaney, and Goodman murders, soliciting support both moral and financial. Their three faces, staring up at me from the thousands of letters I folded, became indelibly imprinted on my memory, as did the ominous words "murdered by the KKK."

Back at Putney, reading Mao's writings, along with revolutionary authors like Che Guevara, Malcolm X, Frantz Fanon, and others, I began to see links between US racism, the Vietnam War, the US capitalist system, and our nation's unrelenting imperialist drive to dominate countries throughout the world.

Bay Area antiwar groups issued a nationwide call for Stop the Draft Week in October 1967. A small group at Putney signed up to block buses at the military induction center in nearby Manchester, New Hampshire. As we arrived in working-class Manchester, I glimpsed a banner reading "BETTER DEAD THAN RED" hanging from an antiquated factory window. Workers hanging out the windows yelled, "Commies, get out of town! We support our boys! You're a bunch of longhaired hippie traitors!"

Damn, I thought. *I sure wish we had those guys on our side. I don't get it. Their sons are the ones fighting and dying.*

Putney tradition dictated that every Sunday night the student body listened to an outside speaker, someone well known. A scheduled guest in February 1968 was Senator Robert Kennedy. The student body and faculty were abuzz with excitement over the opportunity to hear the prestigious senator in an intimate, informal setting.

Senator Kennedy opened with friendly banter and told the crowd: "Young people have, of course, been playing a greater and greater role in the political efforts and political life in the United States. Goethe once said that the future of nations is determined by the opinions of young people under the age of twenty-five."

He continued by listing the myriad of daunting challenges young people faced in solving the problems of humankind—hunger, poverty, illiteracy, and disease. He spoke about the problems faced by "Negroes" in a racially divided America. He touted the young men and women in the Peace Corps. He finished to thunderous applause. He knew his audience and delivered a message they readily embraced.

Then came time for questions. I stood up. "Senator Kennedy," I said, "you quote Goethe on young people's role in changing society. With all due respect, you've completely circumvented the most important issue facing people under twenty-five—the Vietnam War. How can we sit here listening to you speak eloquently about the role of young people in America while the US government is at this very moment bombing, napalming, and killing the people of Vietnam under the orders of the government you serve in the Senate?"

As I concluded, I looked around the hall for support. A few students clapped half-heartedly, but the room was bathed in deafening silence. I later came under biting criticism from the entire faculty and some of the student body for having embarrassed Senator Kennedy and for not having shown proper deference.

Graduation came and went. I rolled my diploma into a cardboard tube and stored it, a relic of a past that I was prepared to leave behind. Next stop: University of Wisconsin, Madison.

CHAPTER 2

Madison on Fire

I n August 1968 I headed to Madison, Wisconsin, for the very first time, the start of a new phase of my life. I arrived on campus primed to join the fight against the US war machine. I was a natural recruit for Students for a Democratic Society (SDS.)

By 1968 national SDS had grown to over one hundred thousand members, with many tens of thousands more identifying with its antiestablishment message. My hopes were high. Madison SDS did not disappoint. Our collective sentiment held that campus ROTC was a direct manifestation of the war and had to go.

First step: disruption of the ROTC orientation classes that were required of every male freshman. I was assigned to a Monday morning session.

After the second lieutenant leading the class had prattled on about the benefits of ROTC, I stood up. All eyes focused on me, wondering who I was and what I planned to do.

I raised my voice, glancing around the room at mostly blank faces: "What we're hearing is a lot of *bullshit*. ROTC is trying to recruit us to be part of their military war machine. I say fuck the Vietnam War and fuck ROTC."

I turned to face the officer, who had been taken by surprise at my outburst. "Let me ask you a question. Why aren't you telling us about how many officers are being fragged, offed by their own soldiers?" I continued. "I'll tell you why. The US is fighting an unjust war of aggression against a people fighting for their liberation. I side with self-determination and liberation and don't plan on sitting here listening to your tired propaganda!"

On cue, thirty of us disrupters, out of a class of around three hundred, walked out chanting antiwar slogans. As I walked out, I couldn't help but smile inwardly. I had come to Madison to fight the war machine and within

A much longer version of this chapter appears at www.jonathanmelrod.com/madison.—Ed.

week one had already made ROTC orientation class difficult, if not impossible, to conduct.

At a September 18 meeting, about seven hundred SDS activists committed to focus on organizational and educational activity to win over broader numbers of students.

The successful battle to dislodge ROTC was merely an introduction to how I would spend my next three and a half years.

The war was the single issue for many on campus. I aligned with a growing number who saw it in the context of a universal fight against all oppression, foreign and domestic. One fall day, I noticed a poster, adorned with a bold black stylized eagle, stapled to a telephone pole. The poster announced a speech by Jesus Salas, a representative of the Wisconsin farm-workers' union Obreros Unidos. He would lead a discussion on workers' rights and the farmworkers' strike and grape boycott launched a few years before in Delano, California.

I thought I might be interested. Yet I couldn't escape my own prejudice stemming from prior experience with blue-collar workers, like those in New Hampshire who had hurled accusations of "traitor!" when we tried to shut down the military induction center. Regardless, I decided to check out this Jesus Salas.

On the appointed evening, a couple dozen students gathered to hear Jesus, who spoke passionately about the years-old, bitter struggle in the grape fields of California, to form a union to protect the mostly Latino and Filipino workers from inhumane working conditions—like toxic pesticides in the fields, and the absence of toilets or water to drink. The United Farm Workers (UFW) campaign to boycott grapes (pending union recognition) brought the public into the fray and put pressure on the growers to recognize the union.

His words struck a chord—and after the speech I hustled to the front of the hall to volunteer to assist the grape boycott.

Jesus was thrilled to have solicited at least one seemingly enthusiastic volunteer. He introduced me to his older brother Manuel, who ran the day-to-day affairs of Obreros Unidos. I immediately took a liking to the soft-spoken Manuel with his messy mop of black hair and bushy Pancho Villa mustache. Despite our vastly different backgrounds, Manuel and I bonded, so much so that Manuel virtually adopted me.

I might have backed out of my union organizer apprenticeship if I had known it required endless hours of listening to ranchero music, hanging out night after night in bars where no one spoke English (and I spoke no

Spanish), and driving Manuel around unpaved country roads, to meet with migrant workers, in a vehicle that could barely pass DMV inspection, let alone hit 60 mph on a downhill slope.

I continued my organizing with Obreros Unidos—Friday picket lines at Kroger's grocery, printing "BOYCOTT GRAPES" bumper stickers, and leafleting students to spread word of the boycott. More than that, I was becoming a full-timer in something much broader—a revolutionary movement that covered many battlefronts.

When I arrived in Madison, only about four hundred students were Black, out of a student population of around forty thousand. A group of students had formed the Black People's Alliance (BPA).

By the fall 1968, the BPA had repeatedly demanded that the administration address the historical disparity faced by Black students. Frustrated by the lack of response, an angry squadron of Black students roamed classroom buildings exhorting other Black students to join a class boycott, while pulling fire alarms to disrupt business as usual.

Many white students, including in SDS and the Wisconsin Student Association, supported the BPA's thirteen demands. On Monday, February 12, 1969, roving groups of Black and white students interrupted classes, saying, "We're here to let you know that the university is being shut down as of today. Classes will not be allowed to function until the administration grants the Black People's Alliance's thirteen demands."

Picketing began, day by day our picket lines expanded to more campus buildings, and the university ground to a halt.

Momentum extended beyond the ranks of committed activists. Black athletes on Badger sports teams risked their athletic standing and even their enrollment. Six Black athletes boycotted an indoor track meet against Michigan State University.

On February 12, more than two thousand students blocked entrances to major campus buildings with "impenetrable picket lines." We had finally shuttered the entire liberal arts campus.

The governor mobilized the National Guard. Upwards of one thousand troops, in full battle gear, with fixed bayonets, as if dispatched to the jungles of Vietnam, marched onto campus. Military units, combined with the entire Madison police force, forcefully opened safe pathways into classrooms.

The BPA and SDS issued a clarion call for a mass march on the domed state capitol—home to the Wisconsin legislature and the seat of state power. According to news accounts, twelve thousand students—over one-third of

The Black People's Alliance upped the ante by organizing *"impenetrable"* picket lines to physically block classroom building doors during the February 1969 Black student strike. (Author in parka third row from bottom on the right.) The governor activated the National Guard to force open classrooms at bayonet-point, dispersing our picket lines after a two-week strike.

the student body—gathered as the sun set, skies darkened, and cold wind whipped through our ranks. With tectonic force, thousands surged into the streets with homemade placards and banners supporting the Black liberation struggle and the BPA's demands. Never had such a powerful force of humanity gathered under one banner in Madison's history.

Black student leaders held flaming gas-soaked torches aloft, turning the night skies orange. We marched up State Street, a mass of humankind on a singular mission to disavow white supremacy and support the BPA.

From the front of the march, I looked back at the seemingly endless flow. The sheer expanse of humanity was both humbling and inspiring. Never would I have predicted or allowed myself to imagine that twelve thousand would stand solidly with the BPA and Madison's Black students. For that moment, revolution was in the air, and racial justice appeared over the horizon.

Like a tornado that arrived with thunder and fury but dissipated after having spent its massive energy, the gargantuan march marked the pinnacle of the student strike. The National Guard had placed the campus under a virtual lockdown. Before we could close ranks, unsheathed bayonets and machine gun–equipped jeeps forced us to disperse. The National Guard had regained control of our streets and our campus.

By February 18, student support had dissipated, and the BPA suspended the strike. On February 27, the *Daily Cardinal* said of the Black student strike two weeks earlier: "Students were more in control of the UW-Madison campus than the administration was by Feb. 13, 1969."

The most significant concrete achievement of the strike was the establishment soon afterward of UW's Department of Afro-American Studies, launched in the fall of 1970.

Yet a more profound point is that those many thousands of white students, mostly Wisconsin kids, took an unprecedented stand. They jeopardized their educations to support demands that expressly and solely addressed the historical disparity faced by Blacks at UW Madison—and across the nation. Collectively we proved that despite years of racist division and countless decades of white supremacy, thousands could leave behind the barriers of history and march forward as one.

I had fled the dorms before the end of my first year, moving into a third-floor walk-up apartment in the center of the student ghetto, the 500 block of Mifflin Street. For blocks in all directions, thousands were packed into wood-frame houses needing fresh paint, long neglected by absentee landlords.

I often walked up the block to the Mifflin Street Co-op. I'd pause just inside the front door, helping myself to free peanuts from a wooden barrel, and talk with other students—shelling and tossing—about politics and culture.

That spring of 1969, folks meeting at the co-op decided to organize a block party on the first weekend of May to celebrate our community and the coming of spring.

While the never-ending Vietnam War was on everyone's mind, the block party was to be a celebration, though with a rebellious overtone. The flyer read, "Why don't we do it in the road? Off the PIG! Roll your own reality. Bring share, Food, Fun, Drums, Dogs."

Predictably, Madison police denied permission to hold the party. Of course, denial by the authorities only fueled our determination.

On a sunny afternoon, kids gathered near the intersection of Mifflin and Bassett Streets. Clean-cut students in Greek-lettered tees came from fraternity row on Langdon Street. Young, innocent kids from the farmlands of Wisconsin ventured over from the Ag School dorms. Sounds of rock and roll could be heard for blocks. By midafternoon, the pungent smell of marijuana filled the air.

Once sidewalks, balconies, and porches filled, kids with long hair in brightly colored tie-dyed clothing circle-danced in the street, hippie-type dancing emanating an aura of youthful innocence.

Late in the afternoon a squad car ominously arrived, creeping slowly down the 400 block of Mifflin, then stopping in the middle of the street. Several others followed closely behind—a snake.

Police Department inspector Herman Thomas arrived with about twenty officers decked out in full riot gear. Inspector Thomas later was quoted: "We're going down there . . . we're going to crack some skulls." It was a head-on collision of two opposing cultures, and the intersection for that inevitable encounter was Mifflin and Bassett.

Suddenly the cops barked an order to open the street. Kids continued to frolic and dance. Then came the announcement echoing loudly through the bullhorn: "You are ordered to immediately disperse. This is an illegal gathering."

Still, music and dancing, as many of the kids didn't pick up on the menacing tone in the police command. On a predetermined signal, lines of police swept down the street, wildly swinging riot-length billy clubs like baseball bats. They pushed, shoved, and hit unsuspecting students at random, with each swing of a club a blow for the sanctity of their status quo and perceived authority.

Hours of intense street fighting followed. The police charged repeatedly. Squad cars raced erratically down Mifflin Street, scattering students in their wake like bowling pins. Police chased fleeing students onto front porches and around the sides of homes.

Kids fought back, throwing rocks and bottles. Canister after canister of tear gas rained down. Shocked and angered, we'd duck into the alley to gulp fresh air and then run out into the street again to battle. Groups pushed garbage cans and parked cars into the streets to block the police. The cops, increasingly pissed at our fortitude, started coming down harder on unprotected, vulnerable heads. Dozens of bloodied and broken students were whisked away in ambulances, sirens blaring.

Fighting lasted until around midnight, when an unofficial, undeclared truce descended.

The fire of the street had tested my courage. I felt pleased with myself and my fellow students—my comrades. Under unprovoked attack by riot police, we built barricades, held our ground, and engaged in relentless battle.

The following night saw another confrontation, this time without the music and dancing and with no pretense that the police were there to open the streets. The battle spread to Fraternity Row on Langdon Street.

On the third night, battle lines again formed. Our spirit, however, had begun to dissipate, and classes had resumed. After the third night, both sides fell into an undeclared truce. In all, over seventy were seriously injured, and more than one hundred students were arrested. Although quiet outwardly prevailed, battle lines had been drawn.

Looking back, some might see young lawless miscreants acting out antisocial impulses, blowing off steam. This is a mistake. On one side of the barricades was the system and its defenders in blue riot gear, and on the other side were thousands of students who aspired for a better world, a new world, although most couldn't exactly define what it would look like, only what it wouldn't.

The violence of May 1969 had its impact on the participants. The hippies began withdrawing from politics to pursue alternative lifestyles, while political activists increasingly rejected claims that lifestyle had any meaningful effect on politics.

We charted our future direction—no going back. Along with like-minded others, I chose the political road, opting to dedicate myself to the struggle for revolutionary change.

That summer of 1969 I wholeheartedly devoted myself to working with the Salas brothers, organizing the fledgling farmworkers' union in the canneries and growing fields of rural Wisconsin. Proudly armed with a newly laminated Obreros Unidos card (stamped "ORGANIZER"), I permitted myself to daydream that I had roots in the militant 1965 strike by Filipino workers in Delano, California, that launched the UFW. My commitment to help launch the new union brought on an adrenaline rush.

I lived in a house that headquartered the Obreros Unidos organizing efforts. One of the adjacent lots sat empty, cluttered with unsightly debris, broken bottles, and garbage. Community members decided to clean it up. We worked tirelessly under the blazing summer sun and turned it from an eyesore into a makeshift People's Park. We used the park for fundraising efforts for Obreros Unidos and for a visit by UFW's legendary leader Cesar Chavez to solicit support for the California grape boycott.

We served plate after plate of Mexican food to hundreds of students and community members. Cesar spoke about the importance of the grape boycott and union organizing efforts among Latino and Filipino farmworkers, even though the efforts were transpiring thousands of miles away in the fields of California. For many, Cesar's speech marked the first time they had been exposed to the idea of supporting workers struggling for dignity and a decent life.

We had hoped Obreros Unidos would develop into a statewide local that might affiliate with the California-based UFW. Mexican American workers populated the yearly migrant stream that traveled to Wisconsin in the summer for the harvest and back to Texas for the winter, trying to survive on the meager wages earned during the harvest.

One of the early organizing events of Obreros Unidos that summer had entailed a visit to the School for Workers, where union representatives and rank-and-file union activists visited the Madison campus to learn the history and practice of trade unionism. A bit apprehensively, I accompanied Manuel to a class filled with members of the United Steelworkers of America (USW).

Looking out at the mostly white steelworkers, my stomach knotted. A bunch of redneck-looking guys—all white men—sporting union T-shirts and close-cropped hair filled the room. These USW members looked ominously like the guys hanging out the windows in Manchester, yelling epithets and hurling anticommunist tirades when we had tried to shut the induction center.

Despite my study of exciting tales of heroic union solidarity through the decades, I just couldn't imagine these crew cuts giving a damn about Chicano farmworkers. I couldn't shake my prejudice. Images of hard hats in New York City violently attacking antiwar demonstrators flashed through my mind. What was I doing here?

Manuel opened with a brief history of the farmworkers' strike, which had begun in 1965. Why the boycott? He laid it out. After decades of long hours under grueling sun, working for little more than a dollar an hour, thirty thousand Filipinos in the grape fields had gone on strike. Cesar Chavez's fledgling farmworker union pledged support, and the strike spread to include Chicano and Mexican workers. After years of stalemate, a nationwide grape boycott had been organized to pressure growers into recognizing the UFW.

I looked out at the steely faces in the audience, trying to read their take on Manuel's message. Inwardly, I hoped to escape the room as soon as possible. As Manuel concluded, however, a hand shot up. "Brother Salas—how can we help? How can the USW support the fight?"

"Brother"? What is this "brother" stuff? I wondered.

"Thank you, brother," responded Manuel, as if he were privy to some language I had not yet learned. "Every Friday we picket Kroger's grocery to pressure the chain to take nonunion grapes off the shelves. We would be greatly appreciative if you would join us Friday."

Another hand shot up. "Okay, boys—I move that we support Brother Salas and his union and join the picket line at Kroger's this Friday, but we'll make it a real picket line! As if on cue, all rose and sang the traditional union anthem—"Solidarity Forever."

When the union's inspiration through the workers' blood shall run
There can be no power greater anywhere beneath the sun
Yet what force on earth is weaker than the feeble strength of one
For the Union makes us strong
In our hands is placed a power greater than their hoarded gold
Greater than the might of armies magnified a thousandfold
We can bring to birth a new world from the ashes of the old
For the Union makes us strong

I tingled listening to the words. I looked out again at the crowd and wondered, "Maybe these guys aren't so redneck after all. This is some really cool shit." This line played over and over in my mind: "We can bring to birth a new world from the ashes of the old."

My first union picket line impressed me. I felt real camaraderie as we walked in a small circle of about fifty, carrying signs demanding that Kroger stop selling scab nonunion grapes. I joined enthusiastically in singing of "Solidarity Forever," while stammering over the lyrics.

On a cue that I hadn't been aware of, we all marched into Kroger's. Each steelworker nonchalantly filled a shopping cart to capacity, groceries spilling over the sides, and walked to the checkout aisle. Upon reaching the cash register, each steelworker abruptly walked away, jamming up checkout lanes with overflowing, abandoned shopping carts. As the lines backed up with aggravated shoppers, we marched out signing "Solidarity Forever."

Maybe, just maybe, I had something to learn from these rednecks in their nylon USW jackets.

Students streamed back for the 1969 fall semester, anticipating what the school year might hold. I shifted focus back to campus, rejoining the student movement. Over the summer, while I had been bumping up and down the back roads of rural Wisconsin in a beat-up old Valiant, a small, dedicated, and analytical group within Madison SDS—the Woody Guthrie Collective—formed to meet the challenge of the upcoming year.

But while antiwar sentiment was strong, national SDS convulsed. Three warring factions within SDS hatched contradictory plans based on distinctively disparate approaches. SDS splintered at its national meeting in June 1969. Of those factions, the one that came to be called Revolutionary Youth Movement II was the most pro-worker and pro–Black Panther Party, so it won the allegiance of most in the Madison chapter.

The kickoff was to be the year's first mass SDS meeting, where members of the Guthrie Collective would lay out goals to concretely advance the struggle against the Vietnam War: (1) Reserve Officer Training Corps (ROTC) off campus, (2) Army Math Research Center (AMRC) off campus, (3) Land Tenure Center (LTC) off campus. The AMRC did research for the US military's war efforts. It would shortly become a major focus for SDS antiwar actions. The Land Tenure Center conducted research aimed at "pacifying" rebellious indigenous populations in Third World countries from Guatemala to Vietnam.

Our fall meeting was to be the first since the national SDS split.

The quite effective student rumor mill carried word that a crew from one side of the national factional conflict, the Weathermen, who had no influence in our chapter, was headed to Madison from Chicago to take over the meeting.

The hundreds of returning students cramming into the Great Hall were not ideologically rigid for the most part. They came as members of this new movement, determined to turn capitalist America upside down. As the meeting started, about a dozen Weathermen stormed the stage, grabbing the mic: "You don't see no motherfucking students at no motherfucking university. Everyone up here on this stage is a stone communist revolutionary!"

The dozen Weathermen, waving Vietnamese National Liberation Front (NLF) flags, exhorted the crowd to storm outside, trash campus buildings, and "tear up the country!"

Max Elbaum, a seasoned local SDS leader (as much as one can be seasoned at such a young age as he was), described what happened:

> The first few rows began to stir and start hollering that if the Weatherfolks did not get off the stage willingly, there were more than enough people prepared to throw them off.

Suddenly the microphone in the hands of the Weatherman spokesperson went dead. The room went quiet and a couple seconds later everyone heard the crackle of static. Then a voice came from the newly turned-on microphone in the back of the room. [The voice was that of Allen Hunter, another of the Madison SDS leadership.] "OK, everybody… turn your chairs around and we'll continue the meeting." Allen introduced the next speaker and gave him the live microphone to get on with the agenda.

The reckless disruption by the Weather squad had been thwarted but dissipated much of our initial energy.

At a minimum, our SDS leadership had been able to put the three demands in front of the attendees.

Another historic event, in nearby Chicago on December 4, 1969, drove home the degree of violence and mayhem that law enforcement was capable of unleashing against those deemed, in the FBI's words as contained in my surveillance file, "potentially dangerous because of background, emotional instability or activity in groups engaged in activities inimical to U.S."

On the night of December 4, Chicago police, in league with the FBI, assassinated the charismatic Illinois chairman of the Black Panther Party, twenty-one-year-old Fred Hampton. Fred was riddled with bullets as he lay drugged (surreptitiously by a police agent), unconscious in his bed. The uniformed hitmen grinned as they dispatched his lifeless body.

Chairman Fred had assumed an esteemed standing in the Madison activist community. He had spoken twice to overflow audiences. Each speech packed a large lecture hall, creating a sense of revolutionary purpose and fervor for those in attendance.

Many who heard Fred's speeches, including me, departed the hall feeling transformed. If one attended his speech questioning the system, one came out indicting the system. While speaking in his rapid, rhythmic, staccato style, Fred locked eyes with each of us, issuing what felt every bit a personal challenge. Looking back, I can safely say that the short life and premature death of Fred Hampton turned thousands of 1969 radicals into 1970 revolutionaries.

Fred's words demanded that each of us rise to the occasion to do more than question the system. I recall thinking as I left his second speech, *Fred is right! There is a fundamental unfairness inherent to the capitalist system that can't be covered over with a bandage.* I pledged to rededicate myself to fight for a new society devoted to the betterment and well-being of all people. Fred's words triggered my metamorphosis from student activist to committed revolutionary. Making such a commitment would now largely determine my life's path.

Fred's words also acted as a stern admonition about the dangers inherent in rebelling against the system. No one who attended his speeches could ever forget the chillingly premonitory message that had become his revolutionary refrain,

> I am a revolutionary
> I believe I'm going to die high off the people
> I believe that I will be able to die as a revolutionary in the international proletarian revolution
> Remember comrades—
> You can kill a revolutionary—but you can't kill the revolution!

While self-defense had once been an academic question, the murder of Fred and our unceasing, frequently violent battles with the authorities had impressed upon many students the need to arm themselves. By the summer of 1970, many of those who lived in the Mifflin/Bassett neighborhood were armed with handguns and long guns, having gained proficiency in their use.

Only about four months after Fred's murder, his partner in leadership of the Illinois Panther Party, Deputy Minister of Defense Bobby Rush (later a longtime US representative), was scheduled to speak at the student union. I was tasked with providing security. I accepted with trepidation, aware, at least in the back of my mind, of the personal danger involved.

If I had given thought to agreeing to such a potentially life-endangering event, I might have questioned the wisdom of such a weighty obligation. Providing security for a Panther leader, particularly after Fred's death, was a sobering commitment, as every Panther leader now walked with a target on their back. Such were the times, however, that I stepped forward out of a sense of responsibility, consequence be damned.

At the last minute, the Chicago office informed us that Bobby Rush couldn't make it and that Illinois Black Panther captain of defense William Calvin would fill in. I borrowed an old Chevy from a friend to transport Calvin from the airport.

On the appointed day, I dressed appropriately—black leather tam, black leather coat, and black leather pants that my girlfriend, Anne, had sewn for me. (Looking back, it may have appeared that I had been hired out of central casting, uniform and all, but it reflected how seriously we took solidarity with the Panther Party.)

I had parked the Chevy in front of my apartment on Mifflin, hoping not to attract attention when stashing my Mossberg pump shotgun with eighteen-inch barrel in the trunk. The old Chevy had trouble starting as the bitter Wisconsin winter cold had chilled the decrepit engine.

At the airport, it wasn't hard to pick out the Panthers even though I had never met them. Among a crowd of deplaning white passengers, three Black dudes, all in leather, screamed "Black militant!" I opened the passenger door to let them in.

As I slowly pulled away from the terminal, each Panther took out a pistol from a briefcase and bullet clip from their carry-on luggage. (At the time, carrying an unloaded handgun onto a plane wasn't prohibited.) My earlier trepidation morphed into stark paranoia.

As planned, we pulled up to a side door along a narrow street next to the student union. I asked Calvin and bodyguards to hang for a few seconds as I retrieved the shotgun. I took a deep breath and escorted the three through the door and onto the stage where the speaker's podium stood, decorated with a poster of Huey Newton in black leather, black beret, and clutching a sawed-off shotgun—a rather auspicious marker for the program.

Calvin raised a clenched fist and, with a powerful, commanding voice, began—"All Power to the People," to which the audience responded, "All Power to the People." From my post next to Calvin, I surveyed the hall packed with mostly white students. Despite trying to keep my mind clear and focused, I couldn't help but think, "Any one of them could be FBI. I really hope that today isn't the day they decide to take out the Illinois captain of defense." In the wings, visible to those in the hall, stood the Panther bodyguards eyeing the crowd.

Calvin continued, "We're not using rhetoric anymore. You have to practice what you preach and not preach any more. You're never going to get any peace talking about it. We're going to bring liberation to the colony [the Black community] and revolution to the mother country."

As Calvin spoke, my mind wandered. What if shooting breaks out? What if I actually am called on to protect Calvin? My thoughts wandered more: *There's no way this university is not going to kick me out tomorrow. You just can't stand in front of hundreds of students with a shotgun on your hip and expect to get away with it! Shit!*

Finally I detected that Calvin's speech was concluding. "We don't want war, but we understand that people with no guns have been compromising with people with guns. We don't believe in murder; we believe in protecting the people we love." I let out a deep sigh—I'd done my job and nothing bad had happened. I just had to hope that the university didn't serve me with walking papers.

Telephone contact with the Chicago Black Panther Party to arrange Calvin's speech, and other collaboration (such as Panther newspaper sales), put me on the FBI's radar.

CHAPTER 3

United Front against the War

As 1969 bled into 1970, one of the most explosive political flashpoints, both nationally and in Madison, was the trial of the so-called Chicago Seven. Demonstrations at the 1968 Democratic Convention were turned into a bloody melee by Chicago police. Eight "co-conspirators" were indicted for planning to incite a riot, a number that became seven after Black Panther leader Bobby Seale's case was severed.

At one point, Judge Julius Hoffman ordered Seale bound and gagged for allegedly calling him a "fascist dog" and a "racist," as the Panther leader demanded separate counsel.

In Madison, I had been tasked by SDS to help develop the propaganda effort to build defense support for Bobby, who we feared faced many years of incarceration or worse. At the time, I led a squad selling the Panther newspaper on and around campus. At our high point, we sold over three hundred copies of each issue at a quarter apiece, reflecting a high degree of support among students for the party.

At the time, I didn't know that I had appeared on the FBI's radar. It wasn't until years later, after repeated Freedom of Information Act requests, that I would come into possession of my extensive surveillance file. In a memorandum dated June 10, 1971, the dossier reveals that my telephone calls to and from the Chicago office of the Black Panther Party had been monitored as early as July 1970.

Coordinating sales of the Panther paper may have been what first called FBI attention to me, as the earliest entry in my thousand-page file tracks a phone call from my apartment on Mifflin Street to the Panther office in Chicago to coordinate paper distribution.

Emory Douglas, Panther artist, created an iconic image of Bobby, barefoot, in prison garb, strapped to a stark wooden chair. Framing the graphic was the caption, "The fascists have already decided in advance to murder Chairman Bobby Seale in the electric chair." I personally felt an awesome

Every month, our distribution team sold roughly three hundred copies of the Black Panther Party newspaper at twenty-five cents each. Many students expressed solidarity with the Panthers, and we encountered very little negative reaction from the predominantly white student body.

responsibility to position Bobby's case as prominently as the Chicago Seven case. I composed a flyer, including a lengthy synopsis of the historical oppression suffered by Black people in the United States.

Perhaps my convoluted text didn't matter, as the stark message above the image of Bobby gagged and strapped in the chair delivered our warning:

"If he's bound up tight, we'll hold back the night, and there won't be no light for days." Not so subtly, the message foretold a violent response to a conviction.

For many of us at the core of Madison SDS, the battle to maintain the chapter as a viable campus organization entailed political bickering that drained our collective energy.

A grouping of seventy like-minded activists, after intense discussions, set up a new organization, the Mother Jones Revolutionary League (MJRL)—the name to pay tribute to the role of women and to the struggle of the US working class to whom Mother Jones had devoted her life. We organized around work groups and cadres, not mass meetings. We planted our roots in painstaking, day-to-day organizing and militant mass actions, believing that history is made by broad masses of people taking collective action. Those principles soon led many of us into industrial workplaces.

On April 30, 1970, then-president Richard Nixon announced that a joint force of US and South Vietnamese troops had invaded Cambodia to root out "Communist sanctuaries." Spontaneous demonstrations erupted over the weekend on far-flung campuses. On Monday, May 4, four student protesters were killed by National Guard troops at Kent State University.

Quickly, a broad spectrum of Madison political organizations formed an all-inclusive united front to develop a coordinated, collective response. The call for the united front read:

> In light of the crisis provoked by the intensified war in Vietnam, Cambodia and the rest of Southeast Asia and the intensified repression in this country[,] a national general strike of university communities has already begun. In Madison the United Front has been formed to aid in implementing this strike.... We demand:
> 1. immediate withdrawal from SE Asia
> 2. [that] all political prisoners be set free and that the University of Wisconsin pay $30,000 ransom for the Milwaukee 3 [three Panthers framed for attempted murder of police]
> 3. An end to university participation in the war machine
> 4. An end to oppression by U.S. corporations of workers and peasants at home and abroad

On Monday, May 4, the united front convened an evening rally to kick off the strike. An agitated crowd of three thousand gathered on the student union terrace.

Thus began more than a week of intense confrontation on and around the Madison campus—kids versus cops, rocks versus gas, bare skulls versus riot sticks. Students with our youthful mobility outmaneuvered police and National Guard with their armored vehicles.

The Army Math building and the T-16 ROTC training building were targeted repeatedly: walls spray-painted, windows smashed, trash cans burned, desks and cabinets upended. Nothing could bring back our four dead comrades in Kent, Ohio, but destroying T-16 symbolized our rage.

Governor Warren Knowles mobilized the National Guard, eighteen hundred troops. Caught up in the ongoing melee were not just demonstrators but also bystanders who felt the sting of tear gas in their lungs and at times received riot stick blows to the body.

I remember being on the Library Mall the first night of the student strike. The images would leave a lasting impression. All around me thick clouds of tear gas hung in the air. Kids yelled for their affinity groups—small groups organized for mutual protection—to reassemble. Folks issued warnings to anyone walking alone to be careful. The area was pitch dark with the exception of hazy headlight beams, the gas refracting the light. The ground was strewn with spent gas canisters, lying next to shattered glass and rocks of every size.

I watched, flabbergasted, as squad cars, sirens blaring and lights flashing, veered from city streets, violently bouncing over the curb, bottoming out on concrete, and heard the sound of scraping metal adding to the cacophony. Despite considering myself a veteran, I watched in horror at the fury with which squad cars gave chase to demonstrators running pell-mell in all directions. Deputy sheriffs, under cover of darkness, made no pretense of being there to enforce the law. Rather, they were there to crack skulls and kick ass.

National Guard troops deployed CS gas, stronger and more long-lasting than traditional tear gas, and began to fire canisters from mortars, out of the reach of our thrown rocks. We shifted to mobile hit-and-run tactics, circling behind the Guard, unleashing attacks with Molotov cocktails and rocks, then fading away.

As we tried our best to hide and outmaneuver police and guardsmen, Guard helicopters took to the sky, shining down super-intense "block lights"—bright enough to light an entire city block.

The war had come to Madison.

With campuses across the nation in an unabated uproar, the Madison rebellion settled into a routine. Daily in the streets and in front of campus buildings, demonstrators waged battles with local and county law enforcement, supported by the eighteen hundred National Guard troops. Predictably, strikers fanned out across campus, setting up obstructive picket lines to close classroom buildings.

Violence and frequent fires broke out nightly across campus and the city, and 242 faculty members stopped teaching to support the strike, as did most teaching assistants.

There was serious escalation by police, particularly in the Mifflin and Bassett area. According to the campus paper, the *Daily Cardinal*, "Thursday, police gassed the area thoroughly several times and moved into houses in which forms were seen, searching for rock throwers and barricade builders." Police acted out their aggression, no longer observing fundamental rights and legal protocol for search and seizure. In their minds, they were bringing the war to us.

New fronts sprang up like mushrooms, with barricades erected in far-off dormitory areas and on Fraternity Row. An ad hoc committee of fraternities issued a statement: "While we leave the question of violence or nonviolence to the individual, we are in complete support of the strike sponsored by the United Front. We pledge to organize our respective fraternities and sororities to demonstrate solidarity with our fellow students *against American imperialism and racism.*"

Reflecting how broadly the rebellion permeated campus culture, the Campus Crusade for Christ circulated a hand-printed flyer: "Medical Info Bulletin." When I saw the flyer, I felt that all the nights of rapping in the dorms and educating fellow students had paid off. We were all in this together.

During the first week of the strike in Madison, the number of university buildings firebombed exceeded twenty-seven, with an additional forty firebombed in the city in a single night. The National Guard, traveling in a caravan of twenty-five machine gun–equipped jeeps, positioned a machine gun nest in front of the Army Math building, strategically placing sharpshooters.

At 8:00 p.m. on Monday, May 11, two thousand protesters gathered on the Memorial Union Terrace. By an almost unanimous vote, attendees decided to move out, dispersing teams to dorms and neighborhoods. Despite a week of striking, those of us in Mother Jones still considered it our mission to win over undecided students and continue to increase the numbers of those boycotting classes.

Despite our determined organizing efforts, the next day's rally drew only about five hundred students, a far cry from the thousands that had previously stormed the campus. The solid unity of the prior week slowly dissipated, as energy drained from the strike.

While remaining active on campus throughout the strike, I had also joined one of the nonstudent united front organizations, the Community and Labor Relations Committee, in reaching out to local factories and the working-class community. Pauline Lipman of the committee explained in the *Cardinal* that since the strike had begun on May 5, daily leafleting had been going on "in 16–17 Madison working places," including the large Oscar Meyer plant, Gisholt machine shop, battery maker Ray-O-Vac, and the city's main hospitals. The committee had also been going door-to-door soliciting residents to sign petitions against the war.

In conversations with workers on their way into factories, I found almost overwhelming opposition to the war. Many eagerly welcomed our flyers and embraced our antiwar stance.

Management mobilized to isolate us as outsiders and troublemakers. At Ray-O-Vac, management threatened workers that if they signed our peace petition they would be discharged. While some workers backed off, fearing reprisals, antiwar sentiment remained; it was their sons being sent to the jungles to do the fighting and dying.

Finally the semester ended. Many had missed more class time than we had spent in classrooms. The faculty pressured the administration, and final exams were canceled in most courses.

During the academic year there had been more than nine thousand protests across the country, including eighty-four major acts of arson and bombings. During the first week in May 1970, thirty ROTC buildings across the country were burned or bombed, and National Guard units were mobilized on twenty-one campuses in sixteen states. Approximately four million students and 350,000 faculty took part in the May strike.

Henry Kissinger was quoted as saying, "The very fabric of government was falling apart."

It seemed time to look beyond Madison to learn from the experiences of other political organizations. My then-girlfriend Anne and I headed for the summer to Oakland where we immersed ourselves in organizing led by the nascent Bay Area Revolutionary Union (BARU).

At the time, BARU had become a leading force among a new, expanding constellation of local and regional collectives striving to organize workers on the job and in their communities, arising from the same political strain as MJRL but more developed.

BARU was positioning itself to lead a new Marxist-Leninist wave nationally. BARU studied Mao's writings oriented toward workers' revolution. Born in the Bay Area, BARU was inspired by the Black Panthers and often allied with Panther leaders. The organization considered itself "preparty"—that is, it aspired to lead but was still learning what that involved with regard to the developing "the workers' movement."

I traveled frequently to working-class Richmond, just north of Oakland, to help BARU members publish the debut issue of *People Get Ready*, a monthly newspaper aimed at the working-class community.

BARU activists impressed me. The staff of *People Get Ready* consisted of some former students working in industry, young factory workers, and community members. They had come together to create a paper that spoke to conditions in local factories and described the struggles being waged by unions and militant workers in the Richmond area. *People Get Ready* was a strong voice supporting local struggles against discrimination and police attacks on people of color.

BARU members working on the paper were genuine and blended well with other local activists. We all shared the excitement of producing a new vehicle for organizing the nascent worker's movement.

It had been an exciting few months. I joined thousands, distinguished by all-inclusive ethnic diversity, in front of the Oakland Panther headquarters in a solemn memorial for Jonathan Jackson, who had been shot down after holding a judge at gunpoint to demand freedom for political prisoners, including his nationally prominent brother George.

I also participated in the Los Siete de la Raza Defense Committee. Seven young Latinos in San Francisco's Mission District had been ensnared in a police altercation resulting in the death of a cop. Panthers and others built support, through education and marches through San Francisco's streets. All seven were eventually acquitted.

Young BARU cadre members, none more than a year or two older than me, held a weekly Marxist study group in which I participated. The theory, we hoped, would guide our still politically immature movement to successfully fight for liberation and an end to the capitalist system.

While the level of political discussion was elementary, we followed a long tradition of learning to apply scientific socialism to conditions in the United States. We had grandiose goals. Along with countless others in the country and around the world, we believed that, by devoting our lives to the cause, by fighting the good fight, and by fearing no sacrifice, our movement would change the world for the better.

The short summer wound down, and we got ready to return to Madison. We had no idea the summer was soon to end with a bang—a very big bang.

Early in the morning on August 27, I lay in a deep sleep. No sound invaded my slumber until I felt a vigorous shaking as if I lay atop a shifting California fault line.

"Jon—you have a call; it sounds urgent! Get up—you need to answer the phone."

I stumbled to the phone in the front room. Despite no introduction, I recognized Michael Rosen's voice, which conveyed a sharp edge of apprehension and dire warning. "Melrod—you need to get back."

"Hear those sirens? Someone took out Army Math. Shit's going down big time!" The urgency in Michael's voice dispelled any lingering hope of going back to bed.

"Wow! Someone finally did it!" It had been only a matter of time. The words "took out Army Math" came as no surprise, as if a ticking time bomb had inevitably struck the deadly hour. It came as no shock that someone had taken matters into their own hands and that the explosion was loud enough to awaken me in Oakland.

Tragically, the bombing resulted in the death of a researcher, Robert Fassnacht. It injured three others and caused significant destruction to the Physics Department. The four young bombers—Leo Burt, David Fine, and two Armstrong brothers—had meticulously observed the building in advance of the night, but Robert Fassnacht happened to work late.

Describing the period, Madison mayor William Dyke was quoted as saying that the leadup to the summer of 1970 had been "nine months of guerrilla war" on campus and on city streets. In Clara Bingham's *Witness to the Revolution* (2016), one of Madison's top law enforcement officers, Tom McCarthy, described the authorities' war footing: "We [were] going to bring the war to Mifflin Street . . . so we went down there and bombed the shit out of them [with tear gas]. We took their bicycles and threw them in a pile, and burned them. The protesters hated me and I hated them."

Rumors swirled that the FBI had compiled activists' names via their network of informants. The Mifflin/Bassett community waited apprehensively for the feds' hammer to drop.

One Saturday morning, as I lay in bed, I suddenly heard a major commotion. My front window overlooking Mifflin Street was wide open to allow in any slight breeze that might relieve the end-of-summer Wisconsin heat and high humidity.

I jumped up and ran to the front window. Zero hour had inevitably arrived: gathered on the corner of Mifflin and Bassett near the co-op were dozens of feds distinguishable by their almost identical uniforms of mirror sunglasses, buzz cuts, and cop shoes. Standing opposite them was a steadily growing and boisterous crowd, heckling and chanting for the FBI to get out of "our neighborhood."

I knew feds would soon be banging on my door. Fearing how aggressive and violent they might be after such a high-profile bombing, I carefully positioned my Mossberg 12-gauge by the door, propped against the wall—assuring myself I would never use it unless my life absolutely depended on it.

As I waited for the inevitable knock on the door, I felt a deep foreboding. After the cold-blooded murder of Chairman Fred, each of us knew that the government was fully capable of eliminating anyone they considered dangerous or threatening to the established order. I glanced again at my shotgun, repeating my solemn mantra to never use it unless my life were endangered.

The wooden stairs to my third-floor walk-up creaked under the feet of at least two people. As the sound of steps grew louder, I consciously tamped down the fear that had welled up in me. I steadied my breathing, trying to maintain a modicum of calm.

A sharp banging on the door focused my attention. I silently waited—"Maybe they'll leave if I remain quiet and they think I'm not home."

An authoritative, increasingly ominous voice—"Jonathan Melrod—we are agents with the Federal Bureau of Investigation. We'd like you to open the door so we can have a brief talk—nothing serious, just a conversation."

"We have nothing to talk about," I calmly responded in a determined voice that I hoped betrayed no hint of apprehension.

"We think we do. Just let us in and we'll be brief—just a few quick questions."

"I have nothing to say. We have nothing to talk about—*absolutely nothing!*"

OPTIONAL FORM NO. 10
MAY 1962 EDITION
GSA FPMR (41 CFR) 101-11.6

b6
b7C
b7D

UNITED STATES GOVERNMENT

Memorandum

TO : SAC, MILWAUKEE (157-1530)(P) DATE: 6/10/71

FROM : SA [ ]

SUBJECT: JONATHAN MELROD
RM - BPP

Re Chicago letter to Albany, 3/16/71, captioned,
"BLACK PANTHER PARTY (BPP), CHICAGO DIVISION."

By relet, Chicago advised the below-listed
individual was called from either telephone number
[ ] all of which
numbers are connected with the Chicago BPP Chapter.
These calls were made during the period July, 1970 to
February, 1971.

JONATHAN MELROD
506 West Mifflin
Madison, Wisconsin
Telephone: 608-257-9889

Milwaukee indices are negative re subject.

LEAD

MILWAUKEE

At Madison, Wis.

Conduct background investigation to identify
subject, and contact logical sources to determine subject's
BPP or other extremist associations.

2 - Milwaukee
JBG:rab
(4)

109-20447-3
157-1530-2

INDEX/RQ
SERIALIZED FILED

3010-108-02

Telephone contact from my apartment on Mifflin Street with the Chicago
office of the Black Panther Party initially landed me on the FBI's radar.
Surveillance continued for at least the next seven years.

Again there was banging—this time conveying a sense of urgency and increasing intimidation. "We'd like you to open the door so we can speak."

"Do you have a warrant to enter my apartment?"

"We don't need a warrant to simply speak with you. Now cut your messing around and let us in!"

I glanced at the shotgun and took a deep breath. I picked up the Mossberg and pumped it—chambering a 12-gauge shell. The metallic sound rang out—the unmistakable, threatening metallic sound that only a pump shotgun conveys.

"I told you—we have nothing to talk about. If you don't have a warrant, you have no authority to enter my apartment. If you come through that door—I promise, we'll both be unhappy."

While I tried to sound confident, my heart beat against my chest and beads of sweat pooled on my forehead. After what felt like an eternity, I heard steps descending the stairs, the sound of the old creaking wood under their feet never so welcome. I let out a deep sigh, glad that was over, at least for the time.

I am white. Had that not been a factor in an FBI inquiry into a deadly bombing, the consequences of such defiance might very well have been drastically different. Looking back, I readily admit my white skin acted as protective armor.

A confluence of events—the vicious assault on the student body conducted by police and National Guard during the uprising protesting the bombing of Cambodia; a high-stakes rent strike and armed confrontation with local slumlord William Bandy over housing rights in the student neighborhood; and the intimidating FBI invasion after the bombing of Army Math—shook the Madison movement to its core.

Some turned inward, focusing on personal lives and future careers, forsaking the student movement. Others continued to see the ongoing need to build the antiwar movement on campus, but their efforts were an uphill struggle. The most dedicated and committed departed Madison for working-class communities throughout the Midwest to pursue organizing efforts. We had witnessed the pinnacle of the organized, mass student movement; never again did the numbers of active students on campus come close to the period before the bombing of Army Math.

Many dedicated activists concluded that, with the ebb of the campus movement, the time had come to leave Madison to transition to factory and community organizing. As the Mother Jones founding document had laid out, "Cadre may eventually leave Madison to work in the cities, army, etc." For many, that eventuality had arrived.

I moved to Milwaukee to join other comrades. I planned to sink the deep roots necessary to galvanize the formation of a class-conscious, radical, working-class movement with the goal of fundamentally remaking society.

CHAPTER 4

My Introduction to Wage Slavery

I packed my Volvo wagon and left bucolic, snow-covered Madison, perched between two pristine lakes, for the gritty North Side of inner-city Milwaukee. Separated by only ninety miles along I-94, the cultural and political divide between the two cities stretched far wider.

I was ready and anxious to leave the ivory tower behind, to swap my typewriter for a black lunchbox and steel-toe work boots. I found an apartment, and my roommate Mike, a vet, and I moved into the ground floor of a two-flat, badly neglected by years of absentee landlords.

Milwaukee winter temperatures hover in the low teens; the only source of heat was an antiquated, noisy space heater in the dining room. My bedroom and the bathroom were cold. But the rent was cheap, and no references were required, at least not for two white guys.

I was impatient to land an industrial job, preferably one with a union. Daily I scoured the *Milwaukee Journal* and *Sentinel* want ads. I circled the city's industrial sections, scoping out the factories making up Milwaukee's still-booming 1970s industrial landscape. At least ten times a day I stopped to fill out job applications.

Within days, EZ Paintr hired me in their St. Francis plant. EZ manufactured painting hardware such as trays and plastic handles for paintbrushes and rollers. When business associates asked my father what line of work I had pursued after graduation, he referenced a line from *The Graduate*, saying, "Jonny has gone into plastics."

Having slogged his way up from a poor background, my father wondered what sane person would voluntarily work in a low-wage factory, but he was generally good-natured.

I looked forward to my first day at EZ with the excitement of a kindergartener on the opening day of school. I bought a metal lunchbox with a silver thermos. In an unopened box sat my steel-toe black work boots. I wanted to fit in, worried that I would stand out because of my student background.

I hired on to the graveyard shift, which started at 11:00 p.m. and lasted until 7:00 a.m. I was paid the princely sum of just under two dollars an hour. I had never worked all night and slept during the day, but I approached the new experience with the wide eyes of a youthful romantic joining Marx's proletariat.

EZ turned out to be the perfect venue to launch my new career. It was low-paid but equally low-pressure. Most employees were women, traditionally paid less for working in a "woman's factory."

At the shift's start, I stood in the damp cold of the unheated factory under the haze of dusty, glaring lights, engulfed by the strong smells that pervaded every factory I was to ever work in. The supervisor issued a list of assignments. I looked at mine and froze. I panicked. How could I possibly get all my responsibilities completed in eight hours?

I began by mixing colored powder into hundred-pound barrels of plastic pellets the size of BBs. The pellets were to become fodder the next morning for huge injection molds, which formed molten plastic into roller and brush handles.

Awkwardly, and with much straining (I weighed only 120 pounds at the time), I maneuvered the first barrel of pellets to the color-mixing station. I measured out colored powder, poured it into the barrel, and locked it into a machine that violently shook it to disburse the powder. The pellets fed into the injection mold emerged as red, green, white, yellow, and blue plastic handles.

I soon transferred to second shift and left behind the isolation of graveyard. Second shift buzzed with activity. Tentatively I became more comfortable and began to integrate with coworkers. I groused along with others about how cold the plant was, how pitiful the pay, and how weak the union. Complaining about lousy working conditions and how we were treated by shitty bosses made me feel right at home.

Once I no longer felt like an outsider, I contemplated how to begin organizing. I enjoyed the camaraderie of day-to-day chatter, but I felt the compelling need to raise political issues. I didn't really know how to start. It's not like the job came with an organizer's manual, nor were there any veteran comrades to provide guidance. I lay in bed thinking how to launch myself as a political activist.

The Vietnam War had begun to wind down, despite continued combat. As many of the women in the plant had sons of military age, I decided to wear a button, "U.S. OUT OF VIETNAM—NOW." I felt unsure of myself, but what the hell; I had been in training long enough.

I prepared to face controversy. Little ensued, however, and I even heard a supportive "hell yeah—get our boys home." By late winter 1972, focus had turned to the peace negotiations, and few supported the war. Regardless, in my own mind I had taken my first baby step to identify myself as a political radical.

While I gingerly stepped into activism in the factory, on the streets the transition was less smooth. I returned home one night after work to discover my front door wide open, my TV on its side in the doorway. "Shit—I been ripped off!"

Reluctantly, I dialed 911, not sure whether someone might be waiting nearby with a weapon. Squad cars arrived, lights flashing and sirens blaring. In rushed six of Milwaukee's finest—all beefy and white. Two drew service revolvers and headed into the back alley, flashlights casting beams of light that cut through the darkness.

The four in the flat were polite and friendly, and it occurred to me that I was white in an all-Black neighborhood. I must have appeared as one of their own.

Their friendly demeanor reversed the instant they spotted a two-foot stack of Black Panther newspapers. The cops pointed to the papers, nodding knowingly to each other, their eyes now ablaze with contempt. Time stood still then. I was surrounded by very pissed-off cops, all glaring disdainfully at me.

My roommate owned a 9mm semiautomatic Browning. I worried it might have been stolen, so I went to his room to look for it. The police followed me, saw it, and confiscated it as "evidence." I thought better of mentioning the sawed-off Mossberg stashed in my bedroom closet behind some boxes.

It came as no surprise that the cops treated me like an enemy after eyeing the Panther papers. The Panthers and the Milwaukee police had been locked in a long-running, vicious street war. Soon after the chapter's formation in the late 1960s, the Milwaukee Panthers challenged the rampant police brutality inflicted on the Black community.

Members of the infamous, all-white Milwaukee Police Department Tactical Squad were notorious for their racist intimidation and punitive violence. The squad routinely cruised the inner city, three or four officers to a vehicle, their windows down and their shotguns and high-powered rifles pointed toward Black pedestrians.

Before moving to Milwaukee, I had briefly experienced the Tactical Squad's intimidation. On weekends, I traveled with other politically active students to join demonstrations supporting the Milwaukee 3. The Milwaukee 3—Booker Collins, Jessie White, and Earl Levrettes—were Panthers arrested in September 1969 for supposedly attempting to murder a police officer. The charges were widely believed to have been politically motivated.

After settling into Milwaukee, I joined in actively supporting the Panthers. I visited their Third Street office to pick up papers to hawk on street corners. Quite a few of the Panthers were Vietnam vets who imparted a militaristic aura to their office. Members were often armed, some displaying Mao's Little Red Book in their back pocket.

Reflecting back, it doesn't seem coincidental that a 1974 FBI investigative summary read, "Melrod originally associated with the Black Panther Party (BPP) in Milwaukee."

The robbery at my flat had most likely prompted the Milwaukee Police to confer with the FBI.

At EZ, I frequently worked with an older Chicano named Miguel. Miguel had accrued seniority and often acted as my surrogate boss. One afternoon, Miguel was waiting for me at the time clock. "Hola, Juan, I have an especial assignment for tu tonight. Mucho fun!" I was savvy enough by now to understand he meant the opposite.

My "fun" assignment took me to the punch press area. Before pieces of metal are fed under a press, they are coated with oil. The oil prevents the metal from sticking to the dye when the press stamps out the product, in this case a shiny aluminum paint tray.

After the dye stamped the metal into form, a thin coating of oil remained. A worker hung each tray on an overhead line, very much like the chain link line at the dry cleaners. The line, loaded with hanging paint trays, traveled slowly through a large degreaser vat. Stacked next to the degreaser vat were hundred-gallon barrels of trichloroethylene (TCE), an industrial solvent that burned oil off the trays.

Every few months, the degreaser vat required cleaning. Miguel's special assignment required me to clean the vat. The degreaser vat looked like a five-foot-deep witches' cauldron from which toxic fumes rose in a swirling plume before being sucked up by a wheezing exhaust fan.

"Juan—climb over the vata and jump to the bottom," Miguel instructed in Spanglish. He handed me a broom to sweep the toxic particles from the vat floor. Man, did I not want to do that job, particularly after I saw the skull and crossbones on the TCE barrels. But, without seniority, I'd certainly be fired if I balked. This is what it's like to be in the working class, I thought. No ditching assignments.

I climbed a ladder and jumped in, immediately overcome by a heavy, sweet smell. The fumes burned my nostrils and irritated the inside of my mouth. Within minutes my head pounded, and the vat walls spun. I clambered out, gasping for fresh air like a fish on land. In the midst of a gasp, I croaked at Miguel, "What the hell—you *puto!*"

Miguel chuckled. "Sorry, hombre—somebody gotta do it!"

"Don't you think I need protective gear like a ventilator or something?" I asked.

He smiled mischievously, the way a senior worker smiles at a rookie about to be subjected to an endurance test. In a thick machismo voice, "Amigo, I been cleaning that vata for muchos years and never needed no chinga ventilator. Nada. Ventilators are for senoritas." Completing the assignment had become a virility test. My pride took charge as I descended again into the "vata."

My head pounded as a sickening dizziness overcame me. I worked as fast as possible, desperately trying to complete the cleanup. Within moments, I became confused and dazed. I jumped up for air. I repeated my hopping in and out of the witches' cauldron like a frog, trying to hold my breath for as long as possible. Finally I swept up enough toxic crystal-like debris to consider my "especial assignment" completed.

Years later, again exposed to TCE at the American Motors Corporation, I learned that TCE exposure is like alcohol intoxication and causes symptoms like dizziness and confusion that lead to unconsciousness. In the worst-case scenario, respiratory and circulatory depression from TCE result in death. Research by the National Cancer Institute has shown that trichloroethylene is carcinogenic, producing liver cancer in mice and kidney cancer in rats. I can't help but wonder whether it might also cause cancer in humans. Did the TCE fuel my pancreatic death sentence thirty years later?

My job at EZ only lasted a few months. It turned out to be a good place to acclimate myself to factory life, but I had set my sights on a more strategic employer. In April, I received a call to interview for the job I coveted at the American Motors Corporation plant on North Richards Street.

CHAPTER 5

American Motors— Welcome to the Bigs

L anding a job at a car factory meant joining the United Auto Workers, the mass industrial union founded in 1935. In school I read virtually every book I could put my hands on depicting the history of the UAW and the formation of the CIO.

Many UAW pioneers were socialists, anarchists, or communists. Many were American by birth, but others had recently arrived at Ellis Island. These twentieth-century radicals rallied tens of thousands to the union cause through their courage to defy beatings, firings, and blacklisting and endure weeks-long sit-down strikes. Their tenacity and dedication forced concessions from Ford, GM, Chrysler, and second-string AMC.

Following my dreams and vision for radical change, I set my sights on the AMC factory on Richards Street in Milwaukee. AMC came into being in 1954 from the merger of Nash-Kelvinator and the Hudson Motor Car Company. After the merger, AMC closed the Hudson plant in Detroit and moved production to the Nash plants in Milwaukee and Kenosha, Wisconsin.

The merger left five main automobile companies. The Big Three— Ford, GM, and Chrysler—towered above the others financially. That power allowed them to dominate the landscape in terms of production, marketing, and technological innovation. The other two were AMC and Packard-Studebaker-Kaiser.

By landing a job at AMC, I would be embracing a long and venerable tradition in the auto industry. In fact, while still working at EZ, I had heard stories about union rowdies at AMC who spent more time striking than building cars. In fact, during the week of October 7–14, 1969, there were thirteen wildcat strikes in the Milwaukee and Kenosha plants. Those stories called out to me like Mecca beckoning the faithful.

So, in early May 1972, I was excited to find an envelope in my mailbox with a return address simply displaying AMC's red, white, and blue logo.

Dear Prospective Employee:

If you are interested in employment with the American Motors Corporation—please report to the personnel office on Wednesday morning May 17th.

A home run! AMC might not be Ford, GM, or Chrysler—but auto it was.

At the designated time and place, I lined up with a motley gaggle of young women and men, Black, white, and brown—all eyeing each other nervously. The employment interview turned out to be a mere formality. Anyone not severely crippled or hopelessly derelict received an employee ID and instructions to report. AMC was on a production roll, and workers were desperately needed to populate the assembly lines.

My group of thirty or so new hires gathered at 7:00 a.m. the following Monday.

"Listen up, rookies! I'll be escorting you to the department where you'll be working. Once assigned—that will be your job unless you don't make it through your sixty-day probationary period."

Our group's first stop was the cavernous press room. The floor shook, and hot stale air rushed past as the huge two-story presses repeatedly cycled—spitting out auto parts.

Oh, my god, I worried, as I watched the presses crash down inches from workers' fingers. Were it not for the safety straps yanking back the operator's arms as the presses cycled, fingers and hands would easily have been fodder for the enormous stamping dies. Years back, before the union, there had been no such safety measures, and the loss of body parts had been routine.

Five of the six guys from our group assigned to the press room were Black. The other, my soon to be close friend and comrade Wincy Roman, was Puerto Rican. Glancing around, I noticed that the vast majority in the press room were Black men. Clearly, the press room smacked of a low ranking in the workplace hierarchy.

Our group continued up the old creaky stairwell; I was assigned to the fourth-floor trim line. Thank goodness. The trim line looked like a piece of cake compared to the dungeon below, with its unceasing pounding of gigantic green presses. In trim, workers dressed in street clothes, rather than oily coveralls, affixed clean, new parts to freshly painted Matadors, Ambassadors, and Javelins—AMC models then popular.

"Hey, Melrod—get over here," my supervisor barked. "Putting in taillights is your job, and Bill will teach you the ropes. The job's a breeze—even fucking drunk-ass Bill can handle it."

Bill looked a mess. He was clearly having trouble installing the taillights and was drenched in sweat even though it was still early morning and cool. When I got near him, the stale smell of alcohol filled my nostrils. I glanced down at his shaking hands that held a silver screw gun with a spiraled, orange air pressure hose attached. Bill appeared a stone-cold alkie.

"What's your name, kid?" Bill asked. "You're kinda skinny and need a haircut, but I guess you'll do. No matter, just get over here and fucking help. I got hammered last night and feel like shit. I really need the hair of the dog that bit me, but it ain't lunch for a goddamn couple of hours. You gotta help me make it till then."

What the fuck? I thought.

"No problem, Bill," I muttered. "What do you want me to do?"

"Pick up a taillight and do what I do. Simple enough?"

Bill threw a grimy, weathered shop apron my way, its front pockets filled with bolts. He handed me a screw gun, much heavier than it looked. I watched as he bent over into the trunk, his back contorted in an arch, and affixed six bolts to a taillight .

"Come on, kid. You got the next car."

I had barely managed to install the right-side taillight when I bumped into the next guy down the line. As I struggled to affix the left taillight, he threw an uninstalled trunk rubber into the car and scoffed at my intrusion into his work area.

"Gotta move faster, kid, or you won't be here long," he said with a smirk. From the expression on his face, I figured he was gaming me. He could have installed the trunk rubber but used the excuse of me being in his way to chuck it into the car and score a thirty-second break.

Bill—breathless and drenched in sweat—called out, "Melrod, you get the next two. I'm headed down to grab my spot for lunch. I'll save you a place." Many Local 75 members ate (or drank) their lunch in one of the bars across the street.

The line abruptly stopped as I finished the two bodies that still lacked taillights. "Damn!" I said. The line came at me much faster than I expected. It took finesse. Shame on me for not anticipating the difficulty and skill of a trim-line job. My back was killing me.

After I finished the two cars, I walked down to lunch. Bill, now grinning like a Cheshire cat, had saved the bar stool next to him. I noticed his lunch consisted of a couple of shots of whiskey with a Pabst Blue Ribbon to chase it.

"Here, brother—have a shot on me," he said.

"Thanks, Bill. I'll pass. I'm having a tough time keeping up as it is."

"Don't worry, by contract you've got three days to learn the job. I been here twenty years—the Motors is my living hell, and this dulls the pain," he said pointing to his lunch. "I live in a room by myself, and all I got is this fucking job, and now the bastards want to take it away! You know, kid—you're already turning into a company man. Have a shot, for Chrissake."

Like lemmings heading to the sea, everyone jumped up, crossing the street before the line cranked up for the final stretch of the shift.

My supervisor called me over. He was wearing a heavily starched, white short-sleeve shirt, marked by years of indelible stains, permanently yellowed under the armpits from profuse sweating, and emblazoned with the AMC logo on the breast pocket. It was a shirt I would get all too used to seeing.

"Hey, Melrod: a piece of advice. Don't listen to a word from that loser Bill. He's on his way out again for boozing, this time for sixty days to dry out. If it weren't for the goddamn union, he'd be outta here for good. He won't be here tomorrow, so you gotta stand on your own feet. None of this three days to learn the job—that's a load of shit. You ain't in the union for sixty days, and I can fire your ass at any time. Understand?"

As I hustled to keep up, I found myself sweating in tandem with Bill.

No matter what, I had to make my sixty days. It'd be too fucked up to land a coveted job in auto and not even make it off probation. This was only one of the many, many times over the ensuing years that I found myself pushing beyond what I thought were my physical limitations.

But sixty days later I made it and joined the ranks of UAW Local 75.

Fridays were paydays. The glorious end of the painfully long workweek just a mere eight hours away. I had assembled a tight group of buddies. We religiously reserved Friday and Saturday nights for getting hammered and clubbing till late, fruitlessly endeavoring to hit on girls.

In our early twenties, with no families to support, we were flush with cash and time on the weekends. Of course, my weekends also required political meetings with fellow activists in the Revolutionary Union, the national organization that grew out of BARU. I learned, however, to accommodate both obligations, although the latter suffered due to routine weekend hangovers, necessitating "criticism/self-criticism" sessions intended to render me a better revolutionary.

One Friday, while my mind flirted with visions of hitting the streets, I realized I hadn't received my morning break. Although a break only meant having a relief worker jump in to cover five cars, it was a highly welcome time to hit the bathroom, snack, or grab a smoke.

I searched for my relief worker. Seeing none, I called out to my supervisor, demanding my now-past-due break. Suddenly, much to my chagrin, the issue of my break, or lack thereof, became a source of ribald entertainment to the otherwise bored workforce on the monotonous assembly line.

"Hey, Melrod—don't you have the balls to take your break?" someone yelled. "The contract gives you the right. Fuck that punk-ass supervisor—he ain't paying you no attention. He knows you're a fucking pussy and won't dare walk." My ears burned.

What to do? Only days before, I had been a probationary employee with the rights of indentured servitude. I now belonged to the almighty union. But would that really protect me, I wondered, if I just upped and walked off the job? Meanwhile, the chorus up and down the line intensified into a collective chant: "Walk! Walk! Walk!"

"If you've got the balls—walk!" someone yelled. "Maybe he doesn't have balls down there. Has anyone ever seen his balls?" Collective laughter greeted his jibe, and I felt my face flushing as my untested union creds were challenged.

Another guy piled on. "Hey pussy, show some guts! Yo, Melrod—you a company man?"

Fuck it! I admonished myself. *If I'm going to be a badass militant, it's time to throw down!* I chucked the next set of taillights into the trunk of a Javelin and walked away to rousing cheers and rowdy catcalls. Head held high, I strutted to the lunchroom to await my fate.

Before I even fired up a Camel, I spotted my outraged, white-shirted supervisor headed in my direction. As the distance between us shortened, my heart beat ever faster. *Stay cool,* I urged myself. *You're in the union now. What can he do?* As the distance closed, I drew on my harsh, unfiltered cigarette.

"Melrod, you're fucking fired!" he yelled, out of breath. The Matadors and Javelins running down the line with circular holes where taillights should be looked like jack-o-lanterns at Halloween. Workers past my workstation, seeing that taillights hadn't been installed, threw their various parts, like trunk rubbers and taillight bulbs, into the trunk under the pretext that they couldn't do their job without my taillights. Like kids opening a fire hydrant on a stifling summer night, everyone joined in on the fun, while simultaneously striving, in good humor, to make my plight worse.

"Melrod, who do you think you are? What gives you the right to walk off *my* line and let my units go by without taillights? Look at the mess you've made. There's fucking car parts everywhere."

Locked in a Kabuki dance of my own making, I played to my audience, knowing that my actions over the next few moments would do a lot to define me within the Local 75 ecosystem.

"I know my rights!" I fired back. "You didn't give me my break, so I had the right to take it. I want my steward. I gave you the thirty minutes the contract provides for you to get me my steward."

Again: "You're fucking fired, Mister Thirty-Minute Contract Man! Sit here, and don't move your skinny, longhaired ass!"

Not that I had anywhere to go. A growing gaggle of onlookers watched in rapt anticipation. Nothing was more entertaining, particularly with boredom the operative state of affairs, than to watch a new guy squirm.

Soon, and much to my relief, I spotted my union steward, Dick Wakousky, headed my way in lockstep with my crimson-faced supervisor. My defiance had directly challenged the boss's authority. While I wasn't yet fully aware of the stakes, I was becoming party to the age-old battle under industrial capitalism: Does ultimate power rest solely with the company? Or could rank-and-file workers flex their muscles to challenge the balance of power and act in outright defiance of so-called work rules?

With Dick sitting next to me across from the supervisor, the dance resumed.

Dick pulled a well-worn black book from back pocket and opened it to the appropriate provision in the all-important Working Agreement. As I soon learned, the Working Agreement between AMC and Local 75 governed *all* interactions between the company and its union workforce, down to the most picayune detail.

The power of Local 75 was such that the company, and its army of white-shirted supervisors, were narrowly circumscribed as to their every move on the shop floor. The Working Agreement codified years of class struggle. Rank-and-file workers and Local 75 had bitterly battled to establish procedures that pushed back against the company's unchallenged authority over its workforce.

Dick quoted page and verse guaranteeing employees a morning break. "Why," Dick queried the supervisor, "wasn't Melrod provided with his break?" The supervisor stammered that he had no option since staffing was insufficient because of high absenteeism.

Dick retorted, "Not Melrod's problem." I'll never forget my surprise when Dick didn't equivocate but admonished my boss that I had every right to take my break as management had failed to provide it in a timely fashion.

"Back to your job, Melrod," Dick instructed me, as the supervisor sat like a pillar of salt melting in the rain.

That's what I want to be, I thought. *A blue-button union steward.*

A roar of approval greeted me. My daring had established my standing as a kid with the balls to assert his rights. Still, as the supervisor walked past, he muttered, "I'm not done with you Mr. Big Shot. Your time will come." I said nothing but didn't look away.

Dick had given me a copy of the Working Agreement, which I soon committed to memory. (Local 75's Working Agreement was unique in the industry. None in the Big Three had anything close to it. Much of our day-to-day power and interaction with management grew out of our venerable Working Agreement.)

The next Thursday, the supervisor, accompanied by my steward, walked the line issuing twenty-four hours' notice that we would all be required to report for an eight-hour overtime shift on Saturday to meet demand for Ambassadors, Matadors, and Javelins. *Saturday?* A 7:00 a.m. work call after Friday night partying?

I turned to my Working Agreement, wondering if it could be true that we were in fact obligated to work overtime. If so, Saturdays would become the downfall of our celebratory Friday nights. Thumbing to the page on overtime I read, "All overtime shall be voluntary and at the discretion of the employee."

The next morning, I headed to the lunchroom before the 7:00 a.m. buzzer. I gathered my posse, showing them the provision stating that overtime was voluntary. Our scrum enlarged as more young workers gathered around to ponder the little black book I held up. I did not just want to highlight the provision on overtime but also to illustrate that the contractual provision existed as a time-honored mechanism to force the company to hire *more* workers, creating *more* jobs, rather than work us harder and longer.

Clearly, many did not want to work on Saturday. As the line cranked up, one after the other we demanded to see our steward within the thirty minutes provided by the agreement. Almost every young worker told their steward they weren't working on Saturday. The collective nature of our refusal felt empowering. On a day-to-day, hour-by-hour basis, the company dictated the rules of the game. But now, in this moment, we exercised our power.

After lunch, supervisors walked the line accompanied by stewards. "Bernie Lepianka, Local 75 president, wants you to know that he has an agreement with the company that you are expected to report on Saturday. We need you here to fulfill back orders."

Phrases like "No way!" "Not me!," and "I ain't coming in!" echoed, and the chorus of rebellion swept up even those who might otherwise have welcomed the overtime to make a little extra money.

Within an hour, supervisors again walked the line with stewards in tow. "Saturday work has been canceled due to lack of adequate staffing." Then the unofficial notice: "A few have screwed it up for all."

My supervisor shot me a portentous dig: "Melrod, this is your bullshit. You're high up on the company shit list. You better watch your step, brother. Lepianka's got your number."

My supervisor appeared to be threatening on behalf of both company and union. While I hadn't individually shut down Saturday, I had planted the idea. The cancelation of Saturday work meant the loss of hundreds of vehicles. Worse, Bernie Lepianka had been left with egg on his face, as he couldn't deliver the Saturday workforce he had promised the company.

I had to learn not to go it alone or play the hero. I was in a precarious position as an individual. Next time we take on the company, I thought, we need a well-thought-out plan and a disciplined team to collectively actualize it. My only protection, our only protection, lay in our numbers, particularly if, and when, the union sided with the company, as Lepianka had shown himself willing to do.

A strategy began to take shape in my mind. We needed to pull together a more formal group of young workers into a rebellious caucus to plan our future defiance and strategy for fighting back. My prior research on the UAW had made me aware that caucuses in the union were long-established ways to effectuate joint action.

CHAPTER 6

Fighting Speedup

After the emotional high of collectively beating back the company's attempt to force overtime, the doldrums of the assembly line set back in with a vengeance, car after car, taillight after taillight, screw after screw—interminable monotony. Eventually I moved to installing seat belts. My new operation required using a mega-heavy torque gun, at least three feet long, to affix three massive screws to the right-side doorpost.

After torquing the top screw in, I moved in a single fluid motion to the bottom screws, never wasting a second. The job required sitting on the sharp metal edge of the car body. My blue jeans provided little padding, and my butt turned raw. Luckily, my partner Bill Wolfgram, on the left side of the car, noticed my growing discomfort.

Bill, a middle-aged white guy steeped in years of militant unionism, taped together thick pieces of discarded foam packing material, three inches thick. He added a makeshift string belt, and, voilà, I had a foam tail like a beaver flapping behind me. Admittedly, I looked stupid; my butt remained forever grateful.

This small act of unsolicited kindness taught me an early lesson. Management couldn't care less about my physical discomfort or the physical impact of any job. But working together day in and day out, packed together on a constantly moving assembly line, we experienced an organic camaraderie, regardless of race, sex, ethnicity, age, or political differences. We took care of each other, sometimes via collective action, like refusing forced overtime, and at other times through simple but meaningful acts of friendship.

The intraplant grapevine carried warnings of an increase in line speed to crank out more production, a speedup. When break arrived, I eschewed my normal smoke. I moved up and down the line, hitting up those who had participated in the pushback against overtime to gauge resistance to the pending speedup. Despite our small numbers, we agreed to hatch a plan.

While the core of our group were workers of color, a South Side white guy named Dave Lamb volunteered his apartment as a meeting venue and offered to provide pizza and beer. Everyone was up for that, even if it meant driving across the city from the predominantly Black north side.

The initial group included Dave, Bill Roby (a Black Vietnam vet), Willie Williams (a Black brother recently up from the South), Kitty and Gail Gaillard (African American women from the trim department), Wincy Roman (my Puerto Rican buddy and Vietnam vet), and a few whose names I no longer recall.

Wincy had earlier caught my eye wearing a Young Lords Organization (YLO) button on his shop coat. The Lords had morphed out of a Chicago street gang, adopting much of the Black Panther ten-point survival program.

While our group hadn't yet defined exactly who or what we were, I proposed we hand out a flyer—"WORKERS—FIGHT BACK!"—focused on the looming increase in line speed.

Large bold letters screamed: "FIGHT SPEED UP." We reprinted a cartoon from the left-leaning United Electrical workers union in which a management person declared, "In this plant we haven't had to lay off a worker in years! We just work them to death."

We hit the plant gates on the morning of March 15. While we were pretty nervous distributing our first flyer, much to our satisfaction we encountered hundreds reading it when we entered the plant. Dozens had cut out the cartoon and posted it on workstations.

Glancing up the line, I observed my supervisor accompanied by an industrial engineer (IE), armed with his obligatory clipboard with two stopwatches affixed to the top; a utility worker, assigned to jump on any of our jobs; and my steward, Dick Wakousky. The entourage stopped at every workstation, as the utility worker jumped on the job, as the supervisor spoke with each worker, depositing an official-looking document on each workbench. (The contract required that a steward accompany company personnel interacting with a worker.)

"Melrod, I have your new assignment. In twenty-four hours [the time required by contract to alter a worker's job assignment], the line speed will increase. You will work on three more cars per hour. Javelins are hot, and dealers are backed up. IE has determined that you have available time."

Fuck IE! I thought. IEs stood out as the most hated cog of management, as their job consisted solely of making ours harder.

At the punch-out line, there was much grumbling about the new line speed. "I can hardly keep up as is," someone said. "Let IE do my job for eight hours and see how exhausted they are," added another. "The union should do something to stop this damn speedup." A last person added, "We need to fight back like we did with their overtime."

That night, I perused my Working Agreement to review the section on job assignments (a "man assignment," as they were called, listed each tiny component of a job and how much time, down to the second, a worker was allocated to perform it). I searched for options to resist the impending speedup.

I learned that the union had our own time-study reps that an aggrieved worker could call on if they couldn't keep up. If union time-study couldn't resolve the dispute with IE, a grievance could be filed to protest the work pace. An idea began to gel that we could replicate our struggle to oppose mandatory overtime. But we needed to get more organized.

On March 19, after the requisite twenty-four hours, stewards notified us that the line speed was being upped from 576 bodies a day to 600. The company intended to derive greater profit by producing more cars with fewer workers. Yup—that's how capitalism works.

If you think completing three more cars an hour seems a small burden, you've never worked on an assembly line. The additional work made it difficult to complete the job in the boundaries of one's work area. When that couldn't be done, one had to either push the worker at the next station down the line or just throw the uninstalled parts into the passing car for repair workers to install later.

After unsuccessfully trying to keep up, I fully got the disgust and anger with which veterans spat out the dirty word "speedup." I shouted to Bill over the din of air guns, "What the hell, man—this is ridiculous! What do you guys do about this shit?"

"We work at a normal pace and ride the line" he responded. "The contract stipulates that you can't be disciplined for working at a normal pace."

"What do you mean 'ride the line'?" I asked.

"Well, it takes unity to pull it off. Basically, you refuse to work faster and only work at a normal pace. 'Riding the line' means that you stay in the car working until you complete your entire operation. Guys end up halfway into the next work area, which pushes the next guy further down the line."

He kept going. "Contractually, you can't be disciplined if you maintain a normal pace. If you get so far out of station that your gun runs out of hose, just throw the parts in the car and move to the next body. It's that simple, but the company will try to intimidate us by threatening discipline."

"I get it," I said. "You end up with a clusterfuck of half-built cars. Does it work?"

"We done it before. All we can do is give it a shot and see what shakes out. It'll depend on whether the union backs us up. If you're in, guess we'll see."

I scrounged up as many Working Agreements as I could find, having decided to start by educating others on our contractual rights. I passed out copies at Dave's that night. The meeting acted as an introduction on our contractual rights with regard to production standards.

We also backed into our first conversation about who we were and why we were meeting. I threw out the idea of us being a "rank-and-file caucus" to push Local 75 to be more responsive to members' needs. As hundreds of young workers had recently been hired, we agreed we had a big job ahead to pull the young people together.

Many six-packs and pizzas later, we settled on dubbing ourselves the Fight Back Caucus. We assigned ourselves the task of getting more contracts into people's hands and committed to spreading the word that we could resist the speedup and not be forced to work faster than a normal pace.

We weren't the only ones riled up about the line-speed increase. The next morning, conversations were almost universally bitching sessions about how hard the new jobs were. Those of us with copies of the Working Agreement, particularly those of us who had met the night before, were like the town crier drawing attention to contractual provisions on working at a normal pace. Soon, talk of "riding the line" became top news, with many vowing to resist.

As if by osmosis, disparate individuals began to act in unity. Soon those riding the line drifted farther and farther out of their workstations, pushing everyone after them down the line and out of their respective stations. Car bodies no longer passed assembled but were filled with random car parts that workers had thrown into the body for repair workers to piece together. What I had referred to as a "clusterfuck" morphed into a demolition derby of half-built cars being manually pushed off the line, jamming already overflowing repair areas.

Supervisors, with stewards in tow, requested repair workers to work an additional four hours, in the futile hope of clearing out the parking lot of half-built cars, many of which had been trucked to the roof. Every few seconds, the line stopped for repair to patch up unfinished work. Every time the line paused, a loud victory cry spread through trim. At day's end, there were few fully built cars.

Our little Fight Back Caucus had begun to function as a support group in the midst of the ongoing struggle. At a copy store, I reprinted the relevant contract pages, giving extras to caucus members. They in turn spread copies around to other young workers, many of whom were in a union for the first time and were first experiencing collective action.

Caucus members stood out as leaders, as others sought our advice on their rights.

After days of production chaos, disruption spread out of trim like a virus. Word spread that folks who couldn't keep up should file "standards grievances" demanding that IE and union time study adjust their jobs. Loud calls erupted: "Get my steward! You've got thirty minutes to get my steward, or I walk!"

In a provision unique in the auto industry, and a tribute to the militant, left-wing unionists who founded Local 75, the Working Agreement mandated that the supervisor make a steward available to a worker within thirty minutes of the request. The most militant interpreted the provision to mean that if that didn't happen, the aggrieved worker could simply down their tools and walk off the job to await the steward. That day, well, just imagine the chaos of workers up and down the line walking off their jobs thirty minutes after requesting a steward, with no utility workers available to cover their operations.

That night we convened at Dave's with a larger group. Inspired by the shop-floor action, we decided that we needed to up the ante by penning a hard-hitting flyer urging resistance.

Our drafting process unfolded like an infant standing on two wobbly legs. Everyone threw out random ideas. I had brought my old Smith Corona typewriter; the metal strikers punctured the green waxy stencil that we fitted to a mimeograph machine drum containing ink. A hand crank turned the drum that squeezed ink onto a sheet of paper. A slow, time-consuming process, it was state-of-the-art, at least for us.

The collectively chosen headline read "Are You Dead Yet!" To make the title pop, we used a pen to scratch large letters on the stencil. The flyer was impactful but not for all the right reasons:

Are You Dead Yet!

Now is the time. Are you happy? No? Where is your steward. See [them] now. Tell it like it is?

Distributing the first Fight Back Caucus flyer at the Richards Street entrance to the Milwaukee AMC plant. The flyer called for mass resistance to the line speedup, leading to "clusterfuck" of half-built cars as workers implemented a rigid "work to rule" slowdown.

Last month 5 brothers had a heart attack. 3 died. Why? Machines are only made to run at the speed. Hitler didn't ask that much.

Yesterday we filed grievances. Work ran down the line undone. People were walking all over one another. Don't let [the supervisor] bribe you with phony promises. We must keep on fighting.

Brothers and Sisters Let's Get It Together, Unite.

Fight Back Caucus Local 75

(I shudder as I read the reference to Hitler. At the time, I explained that a speedup couldn't be equated to Hitler's execution of six million Jews in World War II. But, much to my chagrin, I got voted down. Democracy is democracy despite bad results at times!)

A few felt intimidated by the idea of publicly handing out a flyer. We discussed how it was our right, as free speech, to hand out a leaflet at the gates. Bill Roby, in his typically quiet but forceful voice, jumped in. "Damn you guys—I just served my time in 'Nam. The hell if a fucking bunch of cracker supervisors are going to tell me what I can and can't do!" Wincy, also a Vietnam vet, threw in a "right on!" and we were off, dividing into teams to meet at 6:00 a.m. to distribute flyers at the two plant gates.

The flyer unleashed a virtual tsunami. As I hurried up the line before the buzzer, every head was bent over reading. Once the line started, the majority commenced riding it. Soon yells erupted asking for stewards to file production standards grievances.

Wolfgram and I continued to work at our normal pace; after a few cars we found ourselves drifting past our workstation. Now, however, we attracted a gaggle of managers. They were staring at me, aware that I had orchestrated the "Are You Dead Yet!" flyer.

Eyes bore down on me, watching for any evidence that I had purposely slowed down. Maintaining a slow-but-steady pace for eight solid hours—not rushing while not obviously dragging my feet—was exhausting.

As Bill and I screwed in seat belts, he half-jokingly whispered, "How'd I end up with you as my fucking partner? I didn't expect an audience. Sure hope Lepianka doesn't unleash the company on us as payback for your morning stunt at the gates!"

I gulped and continued at a normal pace, agreeing with Bill that our flyer certainly had unleashed a shit storm.

Normally, auto bodies from Milwaukee were trucked to Kenosha (about fifty minutes away) for motors to be installed. In the afternoon, word spread that workers in Kenosha had been sent home early, as there weren't enough finished bodies to fill the engine lines.

On a break, I checked in with a worker named Al Guzman I'd heard was being harassed for not keeping up. His supervisor rushed over to threaten me with discipline for "interfering with production."

Next break I headed out to check in with guys in another section. I got into it with another supervisor, who likewise kicked me out of his section under the threat of charging me with interfering with production. Taking incoming from all sides confirmed that our "Fight Speed Up" campaign had gained momentum.

And with that momentum, we got the caucus back together. I opened, "We need to fan the flames to keep it up. Plus, we need to spread this out of trim. Any ideas?"

Wincy jumped in to suggest a third flyer: "Not everyone knows how to use the Working Agreement to legally fight back. There are hundreds of young people we don't know, and we need to get them on board. Let's explain the contract in a leaflet."

A subcommittee was tasked with drafting a flyer, and this time I made sure to be one of the drafters, hoping to avoid references to Hitler.

Bill Roby added, "How 'bout we make T-shirts?"

Being a recently returned Vietnam vet, Roby exhibited a sense of organization and discipline, a legacy of his military training. Like countless other vets, Roby had returned from Vietnam with a burning contempt for authority and a deep grudge against the system. He had been sent to fight in Vietnam's jungles only to return home to a country in which he was treated like a second-class citizen. Roby's militancy and "fuck the company" attitude derived in large part from his Vietnam experiences.

His suggestion was greeted by supportive comments. "Roby rocks!" "Let's do it!"

Not sure how T-shirts would be received, I suggested we silk-screen them at my house the next night but only make twenty-five to test the waters. I agreed to draft a third flyer with Dave and promised to present it while we screened shirts.

None of us had ever silk-screened a T-shirt, which turned out to be challenging. Our first shirts ended up with splotches of red ink dripping everywhere. Finally we got the technique down and printed about twenty, leaving them to dry overnight, with a plan for me to sneak them in the next morning.

Dave read a draft of the flyer. It described "round one" in the struggle against speedup and our impact on production. Then we explained workers' right to see a steward and file a standards grievance. "Local 75 knows how to get our grievances settled," we wrote. "If we stand strong in our fight, we will surely win."

The next morning, I entered the plant surreptitiously carrying a bag stuffed with T-shirts. We met in the lunchroom and put them on. The front of each T-shirt bore an eye-popping red stop sign with "FIGHT SPEED UP" in the center.

I had barely picked up my air gun before there had assembled a line wanting shirts. Not just young workers but also older Blacks and even a few older whites who had been standoffish before. I had almost sold out when Labor Relations and my supervisor jumped me. They confiscated the bag despite my protests that the shirts were my personal property. In response, my supervisor issued a verbal warning for violating a "no solicitation" rule.

That night we rushed back to my apartment. We were assembly line workers, so we knew about mass production: the first person unpacked the shirt, the next flattened it, the third laid the screen on it, and the last threw on a glob of red ink, using a squeegee to turn out a red stop sign with "FIGHT SPEED UP" in the center.

A chill had set in, and we used it to our advantage. Afraid the guards would have been instructed to frisk us for T-shirts, we planned to wear bulky jackets to hide our contraband.

The next morning, at least a half dozen smuggled in shirts, but the guards pegged me and confiscated my shirts, which led to a heated exchange. Despite my demand to see a steward, the guards refused to budge, telling me I could retrieve the shirts at Labor Relations after work.

Shirts began sprouting like weeds, as all we had produced again sold out. Our original timidity morphed into cocky boldness as we felt the exciting power of intensifying resistance.

When I headed to Labor Relations after my shift, they claimed to be holding my shirts as "evidence" and said they were considering whether to charge me with violation of the "no solicitation" rule or the more serious charge of "concerted action" (a dischargeable offense). I located my steward, and, after a heated exchange, Labor Relations relented and gave me the bag of shirts. Dick had come through again. "Melrod," he said, "You're keeping me busier than I been in years, but you got guts."

Years later I learned why supervisors were losing it, feeling their authority eroded. According to the National Labor Relations Board (NLRB) transcript: "Employees in the plant began wearing T-shirts on which was printed by a silk screen process a large red stop sign with the words printed in white therein 'Fight Speed Up.' [Plant manager] Zorn promptly gave orders to the supervisors to stop that practice. In fact, one supervisor, at least, admittedly threatened disciplinary action against an employee for wearing such a T-shirt. Soon thereafter, Zorn rescinded this order."

In their conversations, Zorn and Ray Martin, director of industrial relations, recalled the experience AMC had had some years before, "when T-shirts bearing the words "Black Power" appeared in the plant. At that time [AMC] found these 'Black Power' T-shirts to be so 'inflammatory' that *with the assistance of the Union* [emphasis added] the employees were persuaded ... to forego wearing them."

Expecting that we'd cave in, management let it be known that anyone wearing a "FIGHT SPEED UP" T-shirt the next day would be discharged. Rather than intimidate, the threat sparked more anger. Demand rose for the T-shirts we had been producing nightly.

"FIGHT SPEED UP" T-shirt silk-screened at the author's apartment by caucus members. Hundreds on the line wore shirts defying company threats of discharge.

A few in union leadership got off the fence, bought shirts, and publicly committed to wear them the next day. The line buzzed. News that local vice president Bauman and head steward Kojak would be wearing shirts passed rapidly along the grapevine and allayed some of my fears that union leaders might all side with the company. Many openly wondered if the company dared to discipline them.

Little did I know that President Lepianka was at that moment in cahoots with top management. Lepianka saw our rebellion as a challenge to not just the company but also to his authority.

Bauman and Kojak approaching me to buy shirts gave me pause. My view had been that all union leaders were the same. But both Bauman and Kojak were taking a principled stand for militant trade unionism and free speech. While the scuttlebutt was that Lepianka collaborated with management, and was a lackey for the international, clearly Kojak and Bauman were willing to buck the company-union cabal and take an independent, public stance siding with the resistance.

Donning T-shirts didn't mean Kojak and Bauman were planning to join the Fight Back Caucus, but it certainly turned them into tactical allies. With their tacit endorsement, some stewards stepped forward to wear shirts.

The rapid proliferation of T-shirts pushed a panic button on the company's dashboard. A known company man passed by and mumbled, "Hey kid. You're going to end up just like Roy Webb. Watch yourself on the steps—they're slippery."

I jumped in the next car. "Yo, Bill," I said. "Some company suck-ass just snipped I'm gonna end up like Roy Webb. What's up with that?"

"Melrod, take him seriously. Roy Webb was a red—a commie who was a tough union guy. He caught a lot of shit, but there were a lot of radicals in them days. Webb was a steward, but he got in trouble during the Korean War for passing a petition against the war. One day a bunch from the cushion room jumped him on the stairs and pushed him down a couple of flights. He broke his back."

The "commie" branding did not arise out of a vacuum. I had recently begun selling the Revolutionary Union's newspaper, the *Milwaukee Worker*, in the shop. I needed to link our struggle against forced overtime and speedup with the struggle of other autoworkers, which the *Worker* did.

I also wanted to set our day-to-day struggles into the global tableau of bosses versus workers, people of color versus racism, and the struggles of countries all over the world to free themselves from the yoke of US economic imperialism. Selling the *Worker* may not have been the most prudent strategy so early in my employment; it definitely put a target on my back. But I sensed that younger workers, especially Vietnam vets, were open to wider political ideas and valued the right to free speech.

The paper made no secret of its political orientation. Its self-description: "The *Milwaukee Worker* is an independent monthly paper written by and for the working and oppressed people of Milwaukee.... Some of [our staff] belong to the Revolutionary Union, a national communist organization. We stand together solidly behind our class, the working class, against the day to day attacks against us from our employers."

The clock hit 3:25 p.m., and the line stopped. I carried a stack of *Milwaukee Workers* under my arm as I lined up to punch out. I heard a loud, antagonistic voice, "Hey, fucking Melrod. You think you're a tough guy. You won't be so tough when we kick your commie ass. You best stop handing that shit out at the gate and stop selling that commie paper. I ain't bullshitting."

I recognized the guy as being from the cushion room, which was technically part of trim but its own separate world. The jobs were offline and cushy. I had heard stories that the union packed the cushion room with loyalists—all white. I had also heard that they were all conservatives.

I stood silently in line, feeling under the gun. Another guy, I assumed also from the cushion room, chimed in. "You fuckin' commie. I did my duty in Korea. Guys like you need a good ass-kicking."

By now, the eyes of some hundred people were on me. A tall, imposing Black guy, in tip-top shape, hair in cornrows, stepped out between the cushion room guys and me. Suspense gripped the line. I hoped for the best.

"Listen up. I just did 'Nam, and one thing I know is that you ain't gonna fuck with nobody's politics. The government sent me over there to fight commies, and I ain't figured out why I was there or who I was shooting at. Now that I'm stateside, I ain't gonna have you fuckin' with my man over some political-ass bullshit. He gots his rights to free speech. Back off. We understand each other?"

Silence from the cushion men, and nothing but thanks from me.

I walked over to my defender. "Hey, bro—my name is Jon. Thanks for having my back."

"I'm Graham. Don't worry, my man—you got free speech as long as I'm around. I didn't dodge incoming in 'Nam to put up with bullshit back here. One lesson I learned over there—we best all stick together, or we get picked off one-by-one—you understand me?" (That was almost fifty years ago, and I still periodically call Graham to check in.)

The next morning, we hit the gates with our "WE'VE JUST BEGUN TO FIGHT" flyer. Most took a flyer, and many greeted us with a welcome nod. Suddenly, I felt something warm and gooey hit my head and splatter over my face and jean jacket. When I looked up, the shit ran into my eyes. It burned like a hot poker. I looked down and found myself standing in a puddle of what appeared to be some sort of gelatinous cleaning fluid.

Enraged, I handed off my remaining flyers to Roby and ran up four flights of stairs to the cushion room. "Which one of you chickenshit, backward motherfuckers dumped that shit on my head?" It looked like I had walked into a VFW meeting of Korean War vets. Nobody said anything, but all broke into a shit-eating grins.

Meanwhile, all hell broke loose on the shop floor. Hundreds wore our T-shirts, rode the line, demanded to see their steward, and filed standards grievances. It felt like a pitchfork moment, with management losing dominance over its workforce.

Higher-seniority workers spread the word that we should vote to strike if the company didn't settle the grievances or slow the line. (Thanks to the founders of Local 75, AMC was the only auto company left whose unions still had the right to strike over grievances—a serious hammer we held over the company.)

The bucket of cleaning fluid dumped on my head didn't scare people off. Handing out leaflets became a sign of resistance, as more people looked to fight back.

Although we had dubbed ourselves a caucus, no one but me really understood the concept, so we spent time getting on the same page. I explained that through my study of labor history in Madison I had learned that militant rank-and-file union activists throughout history had formed caucuses within unions to push them to fight harder and function more democratically.

I appreciated the reaction. A motion was made that we choose a chairperson, a secretary, and a treasurer. Kitty said she was treasurer at her church, so she was entrusted with our meager funds. Roby became secretary, and I was chosen to be chair. That gave me the opening to introduce a bit about my politics, beyond being a union militant:

> Hey, you guys. I'm 100 percent down with the caucus. You know
> how you hear backward guys calling me a commie? That's because

I think the capitalist system deals workers a shitty hand. I think the system's gotta change in a big way. So I'm not afraid when people call me out for being militant and for wanting a fairer system for working people. Believe me, you're gonna hear more of the same. Also, back in Madison I hooked up with the Black Panthers, and you can bet management and their flunkies are gonna use that to try to make me, and us, look bad. No matter, we're all here because we're into pushing the union, and it don't matter what anyone's politics are.

Everyone nodded their heads. Dave announced he was a Republican, a bit to my surprise. I needed to get deeper into politics, but that was enough for the time. I had just scratched the surface.

The next morning, we handed out our fourth flyer. We demanded that AMC hire more workers if they wanted to produce cars faster.

Since a lot of people in the shop had been asking who we were, we added: "This leaflet is being put out by a group of people who want to make our union, Local 75, stronger. The more we are willing to stand up and fight, the stronger our union will be. We call ourselves the Fight Back caucus of Local 75. You met some of us at the gate. We are Black, Latin, and white, men and women, young and old—joining together to build the workers fight back movement."

I walked into the plant excited to see people reading the flyer. Even though Lepianka had pledged at the Saturday union meeting to support the hundreds of grievances being filed, we knew he was just playing to the members who had shown up to push for a strike vote.

Now supervisors were walking the lines, painting me with a nasty brush. "Melrod's a commie. He's gonna get you all fired." "Listen to Lepianka and the union—not Melrod, who's only been here a few months." "Melrod's a member of the revolutionary hate group the Black Panthers."

At Lepianka and the international's urging, stewards tied to Lepianka picked up the company's rhetoric and outdid themselves talking trash.

I later learned of the levels of research behind the vitriol being leveled against me. For instance, Ray Martin, director of industrial relations (the forerunner of today's human resources), admitted in an NLRB hearing that since January 1973 AMC had "made extensive use of private detectives." Martin also said, "[I] asked other people [managers] in other factories . . . if they had ever been involved in this kind of thing and got a couple of positive answers. I looked at the literature that had been handed out at their plants. It was almost identical in format, the printing was similar, the content was very similar, the cartoons that had been mentioned were almost identical." He added that Briggs and Stratton "had had a problem with the Revolutionary Union."

Management had also engaged with the Federal Bureau of Investigation in checking out employees. A March 26, 1973, FBI memo records that AMC had called the Milwaukee FBI about "a group of new employees who are banding together" and in that conversation stated that I was attempting to organize a caucus. The FBI (undercover agent "MI T-6") responded to AMC: "Subject [Melrod] and several other individuals have been attempting to recruit workers at the American Motors plant ... and have created labor problems such as work stoppages and sit-down strikes. . . . MELROD ha[s] been identified as the leader of the group at American Motors. . . . He indicated he worked for the revolutionary peace movement in Madison."

Weeks later, internal FBI correspondence categorized my activities as "potentially dangerous because of background, emotional instability, or activity in groups engaged in activities inimical to the U.S." and determined that "in view of the subject's involvement with the Revolutionary Union newspaper, 'Milwaukee Worker,' it is felt that the subject should not be interviewed, in that an interview ... could lead to publicity in the newspaper and possible embarrassment to the Bureau."

What followed were the code numbers, with names redacted, of ten informants, some of whom appear to have been working at AMC.

While behind-the-scenes corporate offices were awash with FBI memos and reports from three private detective agencies, heat on the shop floor rose by the day. Right-wing workers kept ambling by my workstation to drop hints of my imminent demise. Supervisors gathered at my bosses' desks to shoot me the evil eye and talk trash about me.

I heard a steady din: "He's with the Black Panthers." "He's a leader of SDS." "Lepianka says the union is okay with him being fired." Even my loyal partner Bill expressed foreboding. "Man, seems like they got your number. Don't worry, though. You ain't done nothing wrong but fought to have work taken off our job and told other guys to file grievances. The company admitted our job was too tight. We forced them to take work off. You can't be fired for that!"

I appreciated Bill's effort at comforting words, but I could feel the vultures circling. Lest I show any weakness, I continued selling shirts and

SAC, MILWAUKEE (100-16234) (P)   March 27, 1973

SA[redacted]

REVOLUTIONARY UNION (RU)
IS - RU

   On March 26, 1973, [redacted] American
Motors Corporation, Milwaukee Body Plant, 3880 North
Richards, Milwaukee, Wisconsin; telephone number [redacted]
Ext. 238 or 275, telephonically contacted the Milwaukee
Office.

   [redacted] stated that there is a group of new employees who are banding together and are trying to create
work stoppages, etc. [redacted] stated that he believed these
individuals may possibly have some connection with the RU.

   On March 26, 1973, [redacted] advised that JONATHAN
MELROD is employed at American Motors and is attempting to
organize a caucus at that location.

LEAD

MILWAUKEE DIVISION

  AT MILWAUKEE, WISCONSIN

   Will contact [redacted] for available information concerning possible RU activity.

b6
b7C
b7D

100-20447-20
SEARCHED_____INDEXED_____
SERIALIZED___FILED___
MAR 27 1973

4 - MILWAUKEE
 (2 - 100-16234)
 (1 - 100-20447) (JON MELROD)
 (1 [redacted]
RSB/dgl
(4)

March 27, 1973, FBI memorandum noting detailed outreach by AMC
management to the Bureau raising alarm at the author's formation of
a "caucus," including allegations that Fight Back was instigating work
stoppages.

hanging with folks in the caucus, some of whom were a bit spooked by swirling rumors of my impending discharge.

On April 2, 1973, at 2:15 p.m., I spotted Dave Turrie of Labor Relations heading down the line at a rapid clip along with my supervisor, Bartoshevich, and three plant guards. The hammer was about to drop, and hard.

Bartoshevich ordered me off the line.

"Melrod, you're suspended, pending a discharge hearing tomorrow."

Without warning, guards grabbed me under my armpits, hoisting me off the ground. I tried to plant my feet, as workers around me started hollering for the guards to get their hands off me.

My steward inquired what was going on. The response: "Nothing." Still unable to walk on my own, I found myself dragged toward the four flights of stairs leading out of the plant. The rising cacophony of workers haranguing the guards, some yelling in favor of sitting down, faded as my captors dragged me down the stairs, confiscated my plant ID, and rudely deposited me on the sidewalk.

From the sidewalk, I looked up at the fourth floor and muttered, "Mark my words, motherfucker: you'll see me again."

CHAPTER 7

Campaign to Rehire Al Guzman and Me

We had scored some victories over forced overtime and speedup and in the process pulled together the beginnings of a militant rank-and-file caucus. But, at least for now, I found myself on the outside looking in.

I wasn't the lone casualty. On April 4, local 72 vice president Bauman approached Al Guzman while he was working. He notified Al that he was being discharged for "falsifying his employment application." Al later told me he felt blindsided. He had no idea the company was gunning for him.

Unfortunately, Al was collateral damage. To make my discharge appear less targeted, management fired him for an innocuous omission on his application.

In an unfortunate twist of fate, AMC's Ray Martin had picked up erroneous information that a Briggs and Stratton informant had reported that Briggs experienced a "problem with the Revolutionary Union," the National Labor Relations board would find. "They [Briggs and Stratton] understood that one of [their] employees that had used to work for them was involved in a political type movement [that] may have been associated with the Revolutionary Union and may have gone to work for [AMC].... That happened to be Guzman."

In truth, Al didn't know the difference between the Revolutionary Union, Western Union, and the credit union.

On April 3 I headed to the employment office with Bauman and Kojak. The kangaroo court took a mere fifteen minutes to reach the disposition: "Melrod is discharged."

Bauman filed a grievance demanding that Al and I be reinstated. The odds were bad. Together, AMC, Local 75 president Lepianka, the international, and the FBI (as it turned out) had no intention of letting me ever again set foot into the Richards Street plant.

Exiting my perfunctory grievance meeting left me in a quandary. Kojak and Bauman told me to go home, collect unemployment, and wait "patiently" as my grievance crawled through the steps of the procedure. But I've never been one to wait patiently.

Despite their assurances that the local would process my grievance, the road ahead looked bleak. AMC and union officialdom were in cahoots, and behind them, manipulating their puppet strings, loomed the FBI.

My way forward was determined by how much support I had engendered over the past eight months among the Local 75 rank-and-file members. Rather than stay home, I hung around the plant waiting for lunch breaks, when hundreds of workers would stream out to nearby taverns or eat while sitting on the sidewalk.

I commenced my lunchtime rounds with a group of mostly Black workers from the press room. The press room crew had a reputation for not taking shit. They had a history of sit-downs, slowdowns, and walkouts led by radical African American head steward John Collier and militant African American steward John Thomas.

Both Johns warmly welcomed me. They introduced me to a long line of young Black guys huddled on the sidewalk and assured me that no Local 75 member had ever stayed fired for being militant. "We always protect our own," they agreed. They encouraged me to stand strong and slipped me a twenty-dollar bill, which I later gave to Al, who had a family to support.

Some days I had to push myself to keep at it, approaching folks I didn't know and initiating countless conversations. Whether hanging out during lunch in one of the bars, or squatting on the sidewalk, I received mostly encouraging words. Quite a few said that they'd be willing to strike to win my job back if the grievance wasn't resolved in my favor. Each time I made my rounds, I felt encouraged, despite feeling pretty alone.

Being out of the shop, I energetically undertook selling the *Milwaukee Worker* to the thousands headed in or out one of the two gates. Some of the politically backward shot me nasty stares, and a few made anticommunist comments. Most, however, offered a friendly nod or "Right on—keep fighting for your job." Being at the gates regularly helped keep my face and grievance in front of the members, who might ultimately decide my fate should they decide whether to vote to schedule a strike vote in order to win my job back or at least as a way to pressure the company to settle the grievance.

Once the initial shock of discharge settled in, we pulled the caucus back together. I brought a new button press, and, assembly-line style, we stamped out bright orange buttons: "REHIRE AL & JON." Caucus members took buttons into the shop, and soon hundreds of orange buttons adorned

After being dragged down four flights of stairs by plant security and discharged, Fight Back Caucus members maintained the movement demanding reinstatement by selling "REHIRE AL & JON" buttons worn by many.

shirts. On my frequent lunchtime visits, I always arrived with a bag of buttons. Although I asked for a dollar to cover costs, many threw in five-dollar, ten-dollar, or twenty-dollar bills to show solidarity.

A crew of high-seniority workers inquired how they could assist. These were old-timers who barely knew me but believed I had been wronged. They committed to handing out their own supportive flyer, contingent on my assisting with the printing. "In the last few weeks we saw a group of young people fighting for better working conditions," their flyer read. "Many of us older people in the Local sat back and watched the fight without saying much.... The company fired these brothers to scare us into being quiet. We can't sit by and let this happen to our people in Local 75."

It meant a lot that senior workers, who had spent most of their lives humping the line, stepped forward to show support, risking the venom of both management and local union leaders.

While it might have been naïve to believe that the local union executive board would pursue the grievance to a successful resolution, many members still trusted the board. Not until later did it become clear that the tentacles of the international were squeezing most board members into compliance, if not outright collaboration, with the company.

A couple months after our discharge, Al and I penned an open letter. We reminded our fellow workers that we were fired for fighting for decent working conditions and asked the members to use their collective power to vote to schedule a strike vote to get us back to work. The process toward any potential strike over our grievances would start with members voting to schedule a vote on whether to strike. Any decision to strike would require another round of voting. We wrote: "We call upon our union brothers and sisters to decide our future."

It was a tough decision whether to go to arbitration or push a strike vote. My discharge might have been successfully adjudicated in arbitration, but my strong preference was to trust our fates to the membership and fight like hell to win their backing, even if it required asking them to strike for our jobs.

To my surprise, support popped up on another front. A group of high-seniority Black workers, with whom I had become friendly both personally and politically, pulled together a caucus dubbed Black+White Getting It Together (B+WGIT). B+WGIT issued their own flyer protesting working conditions and calling for a union meeting to vote on our fates, citing Local 75's "long and proud history of fighting for what's right."

Over the months-long struggle, I enlisted another vital ally, former chief steward Bill Brunton. A decade or so before I was hired, ultimate shop-floor leadership resided with the all-powerful chief steward. The chief stood for yearly elections, along with the head steward in each department and all line stewards, but the chief exercised jurisdiction over the entire workforce.

By contrast, workers under UAW contracts at the Big Three were represented by a committee person elected to a three-year term. The committee system had led to bureaucratization and severely limited accountability.

At AMC our stewards and head stewards stood for election each year. That went a long way toward preventing ossification and bureaucratization of the leadership. We had one steward for every thirty-five workers, and one head steward in each department, regardless of size. (Departments varied in size, from as few as forty to as many as eight hundred workers). Collective action depended on consensus built from the bottom up. Workers took their issues to their stewards, who then took the complaint to the head steward.

If the matter couldn't be resolved in the department and was of plant-wide importance, the dispute moved to the chief. The chief steward had the power to call for direct action as they saw fit, whether a grievance, a work stoppage, or a strike. Such was the chain of command that *no one* crossed the chief steward. To diffuse shop-floor militancy, the international had maneuvered responsibility for final resolution of grievances away from the chief steward to the local's executive board, which consisted of fifteen area reps.

For many years, ornery, unshaven, muscular, squat, hard-drinking Bill Brunton had been chief steward. Gospel in the plant at that time ran, "If you ask God, and he can't help, ask Brunton, and he'll get it done."

Bill Brunton had warmed to me, as rank-and-file support remained solid. Importantly, the ever-pugnacious Brunton *hated* Bernie Lepianka, whom he branded a company stooge and international whore.

Brunton would hear nothing of arbitration. He vehemently insisted I invest my faith and fate in the members' hands. I asked him how it was that Local 75 had the contractual right to strike over grievances. As we sat outside the plant eating sack lunches, Brunton commenced a history lesson:

> First off, you gotta understand why we got such a low local number. We are local 75 because we were an early local in the UAW. Local 75 was founded by a bunch of radicals while the Reuther boys [who led the UAW in the 1940s and 1950s] were still in training pants. From the start, we had more rights than the Big Three. Our Working Agreement provides one steward for every thirty-five guys; we got 100 percent voluntary overtime and the right to strike over all grievances. Melrod, that's why arbitration is for shit. Our members always could pull the plug on production to make shit right. Arbitration gives some outsider power to decide our fate.

Brunton and a few of his buddies put together a support leaflet in advance of the union meeting devoted to our grievance. They wrote in part,

> In 44 years Local 75 has <u>never</u> permitted the company to search back into applications after the probationary period is over to find an excuse for discharge.
>
> During the 3 months these guys have been on the streets there has been much discussion by the membership about their cases. At times the sentiment was heated about their political beliefs. But <u>most</u> members agree that they have a right to win their jobs back. These brothers were <u>good</u> union members and deserve FULL union protection. THEIR FIGHT IS OUR FIGHT!

On a Saturday morning, I headed to Serb Hall on Milwaukee's South Side where Local 75 held meetings. I was nervous. I had invested my all in my reinstatement. Al and I had engendered substantial support, but both the company and those beholden to the international were working the shop floor spreading fear that a strike would jeopardize everyone's livelihoods.

Hundreds, most of whom I didn't know, streamed in, packing the hall. It was June in Wisconsin, and the temperature inside was hot enough to make everyone sweat, adding to the already palpable tension.

Lepianka gaveled the meeting to order. My heart rate rose. The international had dispatched their only Black rep, Jimmy Lee, originally out of our local. Before the meeting had begun, I watched Jimmy Lee work his mischief with any Black member who would give him the time of day.

When the agenda opened discussion on our grievance, Jimmy Lee exercised a point of special privilege. As he rose behind the dais, groans could be heard from many of the older Blacks who considered Lee an Uncle Tom, a moniker that often popped up when his name was uttered. "Brothers and sisters," he began, "you all know me as I came out of this local. I'm here to speak on behalf of your international union." This statement was greeted with a round of boos. "Guzman and Melrod are good union boys. But are you willing to jeopardize your jobs in a futile effort to save theirs? Both have only been working at the Motors for a few months. The international has done everything it could in the grievance procedure to win their jobs back, but the company won't budge."

It was the message behind Jimmy Lee's message that counted. The international had dispatched their puppet to let it be known that they wouldn't support or condone a strike.

An older white guy, an avid supporter, took the floor. "The company has a sixty-day probationary period," he stated. "AMC has no right to extend it. If AMC truly intended to fire these brothers for falsifying their applications, they had sixty days to pull the trigger. These brothers were discharged for standing up to speedup. The company picked them out to try to scare us into keeping quiet. To hell with that! If these guys stay fired—no one is safe!"

Heated debate flowed. The majority of those taking the floor, however, spoke on our behalf. These were solid union people who for decades had squared off with AMC.

I was glued to the grey metal folding chair under me, like a spectator watching an abstract debate to which I wasn't a party. Eventually, time arrived for me to speak.

I rise to speak today on behalf of myself and brother Al. But, more importantly, I rise to uphold a basic union principle. If American Motors is successful in keeping Al and me on the streets, no union member is guaranteed their contractual rights to engage in protected union activity and exercise free speech.

The company has spent weeks trying to distract from that basic principle by engaging in a red-baiting campaign to turn members against me. As I've explained to anyone who cares to listen, I don't believe that working people get a fair shake under this system of workers and bosses. You don't have to agree with me, but I do ask you to support my right to speak out and my right to a job.

However, what is most important is that we all stick together. If we are to be able to fight speedup and protect our union rights, I ask you to vote to support our grievance being moved to a strike vote. If you vote to move our grievance to a strike vote, it will give the executive board the hammer to force the company to put us back to work. I'm not asking you to strike today but to vote to call a special meeting for the purpose of taking a strike vote. Thank you, brothers and sisters.

Feeling like a heavy weight had been lifted, I sat down to a full-throated round of applause. I hoped I had swayed a majority but knew Lepianka had other plans.

Lepianka recognized himself, ostensibly to explain the "facts." He launched into a rambling diatribe.

It's obvious brother Melrod must have something to hide because he wasn't proud enough to state on his employment application that he had attended college. Why? Melrod was a troublemaker in college, and he must have been involved in activities that he's embarrassed about. Now he wants to cause trouble for our union and our members.

Local 75 and the executive board have no problem supporting our members, we always have. But there are unknowns in Melrod's background that are suspicious. You all know that years ago we had problems with reds. If you vote yes today, you are voting to strike. Do you really want to go home to your families and tell them you're risking your jobs for someone who doesn't uphold our values? The international and I strongly urge you to vote no!

Face flush with anger, beads of sweat on his forehead, Brunton barked from the rear, "Brother Chair, Brother Chair—point of order. You ain't telling the truth. I know the Working Agreement as good as anyone. The vote today *isn't* to strike. If we vote yes today, which I damn sure hope this membership will, or we might as well give all the power to the company, we are voting to *schedule another meeting*. We never let the company tell us who's a good union man and who ain't. I say vote yes for the sake of our union and these two brothers!"

Lepianka responded, "Enough, Brother Brunton, I'm chair, and you are out of order. Sit the hell down!"

"Fuck you, Lepianka," Brunton yelled back. "We all know you're a company man."

"I'm chair, and I call the vote. All those voting no, stand." A minority then rose from their seats.

"Okay, all those voting yes, stand." It appeared obvious that yes votes had prevailed. Those voting yes included one surprise board member, plus the local vice president, Bauman. In the front row, the distinctive bald head of Kojak could be seen among those standing, as well as a few prominent stewards.

An excited buzz engulfed the hall. Banging the gavel hard to break through the chatter, Lepianka called out, "The damn hand counter is broken. I need a head count."

A rustle emanated from the back of the hall. Swiveling around, I saw that a contingent of police had entered through the rear door. My mood crashed from elation to despair. The police had been summoned to intervene in case trouble ensued when Lepianka stole the count.

The gavel slammed down, riveting all eyes back on the dais. "Those voting yes, stand." Barely waiting long enough for the count to be finished, Lepianka gaveled for all those voting no to stand.

I don't think it was my bias that made the yes votes clearly appear to hold the majority. But with the lowering of the gavel Lepianka announced, "The noes have it. Meeting adjourned."

My heart sank. Al looked dismayed. Above the chaos, I heard Brunton's voice bellowing, "Lepianka, you're a fucking low-down company whore!"

Others loudly protested that the vote had been fixed. Many, however, had already headed to the kegs of PBR, where they filled red plastic cups to the brim. Not sure what else to do, I headed toward the kegs.

Dozens approached me with words of solidarity: "Good fight, brother! You got cheated!" "What were the fucking cops doing here? You know that's a goddamn setup." "Lepianka ain't nothing but the international's whore." "Melrod, you gotta sue the damn company. We're with you!"

Despite the outpouring of support, I felt defeated and deflated. I had let myself believe we could win the vote, failing to anticipate just how dirty Lepianka and the international would play.

I poured myself another beer, hoping to drown my disappointment. One lesson I had learned when dealing with a bully like Lepianka required never showing weakness. I continued shaking hands and thanking my supporters till the beers I'd drunk needed to come out.

Lepianka turned out to be standing two urinals down. Slurring his words, he unsteadily turned to me, "Melrod, you put up a damn good fight. I gotta admire you."

"Fuck you, Lepianka, you ain't got shit to say to me," I said. "You just stole my fucking job."

As if on cue, Brunton walked in and occupied the urinal next to Lepianka. Having consumed his capacity of PBR, he wobbled. I no longer remember who threw down first, or who sparked the altercation, but soon Brunton and Lepianka were exchanging punches. Brunton caught Lepianka with a right hook; Lepianka tried to kick Brunton and almost stumbled backward into a urinal. Their yelling attracted a crowd that pulled them apart.

I left the hall. I felt like shit.

CHAPTER 8

Learning to Take the Heat but Not Miss a Beat

Lying in bed, I struggled to pry open my eyelids late Sunday morning, overcome by nagging disappointment combined with a nasty hangover.

First priority was to inform the entire plant what had gone down at the membership meeting. I rallied some core members of Fight Back who were still willing to risk the ire of the company and Lepianka—Bill Roby, Willie Williams, Wincy, Gail and Kitty, Dave, and Al (who also still hoped to win his job back).

We drafted a flyer to hand out at the gates:

WE won the vote but THEY won the count

On Saturday the discharge cases of Jon Melrod and Al Guzman came up before the membership meeting. . . .

When the question came to a vote, the motion on the floor was to authorize the Executive Board to call a *special meeting for the purpose of a strike vote.*

As everyone stood up [to vote] it looked like Jon and Al . . . had won. But after 2 votes on the motion and a broken counter, the *count* came out against fighting the grievances. Many of us have serious questions about who won.

We will be back fighting for these brothers after the changeover. They did not receive the union justice they deserve.

Regardless of being out of the plant, I continued to work with activists in the plant and to speak out on issues like the upcoming Big Three negotiations that would set the terms for AMC's agreement in 1974. A steward friend remarked, "Melrod, you're like a piece of gum stuck to AMC's shoe. No matter how hard they try to scrape it off, they can't manage to get rid of you. Commie or not, you're one badass union brother."

The time had arrived, however, to shift gears. To get back into industry to pursue my political organizing, I had to move on (temporarily I hoped) but not before I filed an unfair labor practice charge at the National Labor Relations Board's Milwaukee office. While reluctant to put my fate in the hands of a government agency, I had to pursue every possibility. Accordingly, on September 6, 1973, Al and I filed charges with the NLRB.

To our surprise, we didn't have to wait long for a ruling. On December 20, 1973, the regional director issued a complaint against American Motors. A board administrative law judge heard oral arguments and cross-examined witnesses in March. The *Milwaukee Journal* reported that testimony revealed "widespread investigations and the company's fear of young militants."

"Guzman said company officials had warned him to stay away from Melrod," reported the *Journal*. "They said Melrod was a troublemaker, that he was going to be fired and that [he] would be too, if he associated with Melrod."

Our case progressed through the NLRB hearing process through that winter and early spring. On Saturday May 25, 1974, a *Journal* headline read, "NLRB Judge Blisters AM, Orders Rehiring." I shook with anticipation as I read. "In a strongly worded decision accusing management of American Motors Corp. of 'McCarthy-like' beliefs a National Labor Relations Board administrative law judge has ordered the firm to reinstate with back pay two workers." I had hit the jackpot!

Despite the elation I felt over the judge's order and later its being upheld by the NLRB at the national level, I knew the game well enough to not expect a rehiring call from AMC.

Sure enough, a headline in the *Journal* soon confirmed my skepticism: "AM Defies Order to Rehire 2 Workers."

"An official of the regional NLRB office said the agency would file a petition in the Federal Court of Appeals . . . against American Motors for failing to comply with the order," the paper reported.

Meanwhile, I found other factory work so I could continue organizing.

CHAPTER 9

Life as a Tannery Rat

In Milwaukee, dishonorable discharge from American Motors was as if AMC and the FBI had pinned a sign on me: "Do not hire: troublemaker."

My only option to return to the industrial workforce was to scavenge for dregs of employment: the row of unorganized, low-wage, super-exploitative tanneries perched on the banks of the Milwaukee River.

Though demoralized, I did my best to cast those feelings aside. As I drove over the Milwaukee River bridge, a stench of rotting flesh engulfed my car.

Pfister and Vogel (P&V) was one of the two largest remaining tanneries in Milwaukee. Walking into P&V's shabby employment offices, I was overpowered by the acrid stench. It permeated the entire building and crept through crevices into the closed room where employment applications were handed out.

What would it be like to breathe that noxious smell day in and day out? I had worked at the most militantly unionized, highly paid auto plant in the city. Now I barely clung to the lowest rung of the industrial ladder.

I forced myself to suck it up and examine another sector of Milwaukee's working class. If nothing else, I would learn how a maggot-infested cowhide was transformed into pliant, beautifully colored leather that was used to make the stylish coats we sported for weekend partying.

After a cursory reading of my application, P&V hired me on the spot. The personnel office instructed me to report on Monday at 5:00 a.m. There being no union at P&V to bargain over the length of the workday, the standard shift was ten hours, 5:00 a.m. to 3:30 p.m.

On Monday morning, my supervisor, who stood out as the only other white person in sight, instructed me to follow, barking, "Watch your step, rookie!"

My orientation tour kicked off in the dank, windowless basement where raw cowhides were stacked six feet high on half-rotten wooden pallets. Each pallet sank under a mass of hides covered with hair, blood, fat, and decaying bodily debris. Maggots crawled in and out of the gore, and steam rose from the warm hides, filling the air with the stench of death. I held back the strong impulse to gag, lest I be deemed too squeamish for tannery work.

Putrid, filthy water mixed with rotting flesh flooded the floor. Near each pallet stood a large, muscular Black guy, his rubber boots awash with inches of muck. Heavy gray rubber aprons and gloves did little to shield the men from the blood on the hides that mixed with their early-morning sweat. I watched awestruck as they hoisted heavy, damp hides off pallets and slung them one at a time into enormous wooden barrels.

Once a barrel was filled, the operator poured in a chemical soup containing I knew not what, in addition to a large amount of lye. As the barrels spun, the mixture burned hair off the hides and killed the maggots.

God only knows what deleterious effect the chemical exposure had on the workers' health and life expectancy. A harsh reality: without a union there was absolutely nothing to prevent or mitigate the inhumane conditions of the tannery.

My tour continued as we climbed the stairs to the first floor. I sucked in the fresher air, feeling like I had escaped from hell.

The supervisor assigned me to the Flo-Coater crew, which consisted of three young Black guys, one Black woman, one Latino, and me. The supervisor instructed me to break in and was gone.

The Flo-Coater sprayed hides with a waterproofing chemical. The lead worker placed a hide on a conveyor belt, which then passed under a steady flow. I was positioned at the end of the conveyor, where I lifted the waterproofed hide off the belt and stacked it on a nearby pallet. Not being tall enough, I was provided a humiliating wooden box to stand on. The thoroughly soaked hides were heavy and unwieldy, but I dared not display fatigue or weakness.

My first day was inauspicious, though I did provide some levity for my coworkers. If I had not provided a bit of entertainment typical from a newbie, they would not have appreciated my slowing down production.

P&V had mastered the use of piece rate as a method of payment, plus control over employees' work pace. How much our crew earned was pegged to how many pieces we turned out per hour. We all pushed each other to work faster and faster to "make out"—earn the highest wage by producing the most pieces.

Nevertheless, the crew immensely enjoyed my first pile of slippery hides sliding off the pallet; additional hides continued to pile helter-skelter on the floor as the line continued to run while I frantically worked to rearrange the fallen stack.

Then, after I got the hang of the job, I felt an irritation in my crotch. Within seconds, my scrotum was ablaze, as if fire ants had invaded my underwear. I jumped back; hides fell randomly on the floor. What the hell was going on? A laughing coworker told me to run for the showers.

The crew had mischievously not told me to wear a rubber apron. As a result, the waterproofing chemical soaked my jeans and penetrated through to my skin. I wondered whether I would ever father children and feared that impotence might be the cost of my hazing ritual.

One inescapable fact about tannery work: you can *never* wash off the stink. The odor creeps under your skin, seems to permeate every cell, and clings to your hair like Brylcreem. The tannery smell is so invasive that you can taste it for hours after work. I'd vigorously wash in the showers at work and then shower again at home. Not just shower but scrub my skin raw. Maybe the smell was lodged in my nostrils; it never seemed to wash off.

The first week ended with me sore and smelling like a rotten cowhide. I flirted with the idea of quitting but thought better of it. I needed to prove to myself that I could tough it out, and on Monday I forced myself to head back.

Many of the Blacks at P&V had recently moved north from the Deep South. Some used regional vernacular and spoke with such a heavy accent that I had difficulty understanding them.

To these recent migrants, P&V offered the chance to make big money. Anyone willing to push themselves to the limit could rack up hours and hours of overtime. The company encouraged these driven individuals to work doubles—sixteen hours a day, six days a week. Paychecks ran into the thousands of dollars.

Regardless of the cultural barriers, I began to feel a great camaraderie. I was soon fully accepted despite being the sole white guy not in management. I'm sure my acceptance derived in no small degree from the fact that I never sought any special treatment.

For me, we were all equally tannery rats. We also shared the payday ritual of getting ourselves well-scrubbed, groomed, adorned, and smelling of Old Spice to cover the tannery stench. Looking fly, we'd promenade across Water Street to our favorite tavern to drink and gamble.

After a few months on the Flo-Coater, I moved up a few floors. The closer one got to the top floor, the cleaner and better the jobs got, as clean hides were transformed into finished leather. While the tannery stench still permeated the fifth floor, the individual hides weren't bad to handle.

My new job was assistant color matcher. The senior color matcher was an older Puerto Rican named Carlos who took me under his wing. I got the job because I was an educated white guy, even though I had only worked at the tannery for a few months. I felt self-conscious and guilty. But there existed no union, and no one to set fair work rules about awarding jobs.

Now the after-work scrubbing included solvent on our hands and arms to scrub off the dyes used to color the leather. (Those solvents would later be noted as a possible cause of my pancreatic cancer.)

Color matching required precise reading of formulas for mixing dyes to produce any designated color. It turned out to be a privileged job.

After working at P&V for about six months, I decided to start speaking with a few individuals about organizing a union. If there was ever a sweat-shop that needed a union, it was P&V.

I first broached the subject with Carlos. "Hey, Carlos, ever think how much better off we'd be with a union—sindicato—to protect us?"

He looked at me like a father engaging a naïve young son and nudged me into a corner where no one could overhear. "Juan, mi amigo. I got mi esposa and tres niños. I gotta put tortillas on the mesa and una casa over their heads. I can't risk nada. Por favor, no more habla union."

After that, when I had big runs of a single color and time to wander, I spoke with a few others about organizing a union. Many of the Black guys told me that they were making way more money than they ever could hope to earn in the fields of Mississippi or Georgia. They were used to working hard back home, but up here they made decent money doing it. P&V had remained union-free for 120 years for good reason. By offering those on the bottom rung a lot of overtime and a little bit of money, they protected their status as a no union shop.

I pondered the difference between UAW workers at AMC and work-ers at P&V. After decades of militant day-to-day collective battles, often led and supported by line stewards, UAW members had developed class consciousness. Local 75 members understood that their collective power as workers challenged the power of the bosses.

Unorganized workers at P&V, without any representation, had little consciousness of collective power. For them, the company held all the cards and was free to abuse, exploit, and oppress. Sure, P&V needed a union, but it would take a lot more than me talking about it after only a half year on the job.

I needed to be in a workplace with a union—even a lousy union—where people had a sense of organization. I said goodbye and scrubbed off the tannery smell one last time. Then it was hello to Welding 101 and Free Ray Mendoza.

Seeking an industrial skill to make myself more employable, I enrolled in the federal government's Comprehensive Employment Training Act (CETA) welding program. While at CETA, I was active in one of the hot political issues in Milwaukee that summer: the high-profile arrest of a young South Side Chicano named Ray Mendoza. On a hot July night, two off-duty cops had been shot and killed in an altercation in the city's Spanish-speaking neighborhood.

An all-points bulletin went out describing the suspect as a "tall Mexican with shoulder-length hair." Rogue cops rampaged through the South Side. Warrantless searches were made without any semblance of legal entry. Outrage was widespread.

Hours after the shooting, Ray Mendoza and his cousin Jesus Fiscal were arrested. In response to questioning, Mendoza told the arresting officer that his hair had been cut short two weeks before and that a laceration on his scalp resulted from falling and bumping his head on a parked car while running from the scene of the shootings. The police transcribed his words as a *confession.*

Within days of the arrest, Billy Drew, editor of the *Milwaukee Worker* and older brother of John Drew, met with Mendoza's mother. She was a veteran community activist. With Billy taking the lead, a defense committee formed with Mendoza's family at its core. The Revolutionary Union initiated a mass campaign to win support to exonerate Mendoza.

During late summer, I distributed defense committee leaflets to my fellow welding students. I also handed out buttons: "FREE RAY MENDOZA—DROP THE CHARGES." The buttons became part of our welding attire, a statement of unity.

Whether Ray Mendoza shot the cops on that hot summer night, no one will ever know. The facts were totally confused, and Mendoza repeatedly changed his testimony. He was found guilty of first-degree murder and served time but had his conviction overturned on appeal in 1978 and was acquitted in a new trial, thanks to police misconduct, mass public pressure, and a well-fought legal battle.

After Billy Drew, editor of the *Milwaukee Worker*, met with the Mendoza family, the Revolutionary Union instigated a campaign to rally the public against the arrest of Ray Mendoza and spread awareness of omnipresent police repression in the Latino community.

What I do know is that throughout the decades since that alterca-tion, similar confrontations have continued with regularity to go down in communities of color. In our fight for social justice during the Ray Mendoza campaign, we believed that we would eventually achieve a degree of equality and fairness, but as today's endless police murders attest, we are little closer.

During Mendoza's first trial and appeal, hundreds of copies of the *Milwaukee Worker* were sold in front of dozens of factory gates and on streets in the Latino community. Each time a new issue of the paper came out, I distributed it for free in my welding class. On those mornings, barely a rod was struck as heads in every booth bent over the *Worker*.

Ten weeks into the CETA program, just two weeks shy of receiving a certificate, I organized fellow enrollees to strike to demand late paychecks. We got the checks, but I got booted from the program.

I had been fired from American Motors for over a year and had begun to question whether I would win that job back. Dismayed to be contem-plating defeat, I sustained myself by dreaming about a triumphant return to AMC.

AMC had different plans, of course. In its arrogance, AMC had concluded that their corporate lawyers would convince a higher court to

The Latino community greeted with support a neighborhood march to protest the arrest of Ray Mendoza on charges of killing two off-duty cops.

disregard the NLRB reinstatement order and keep me on the street. An unnamed FBI agent in a June 1974 memo quoted an AMC official: "Melrod [will] not have to be rehired."

After expulsion from CETA, I searched for work. I focused on one of the most notoriously unsafe, low-wage foundries in the city—Crucible Steel Casting Company. Crucible had earned its reputation as a rough, dirty, and dangerous place to work. Later, after the plant closed in 1983, the company's name would appear prominently in asbestos litigation.

Stepping into the Crucible foundry was like venturing into Dante's inferno. The massive, high-ceilinged building was unheated, nearly unlit, and totally lacking ventilation.

I momentarily choked. The strong fumes and particulates that filled my nostrils and burned my lungs were a mixture of smoke from burning coke ovens and from dozens of welding rods simultaneously arcing.

I watched spellbound as molten metal poured into sand molds. The guys—all men, all Black or brown—proceeded to shake out the mold to separate the metal casting from the surrounding sand. All around swirled a dense cloud of dust.

Years later I learned that the shakeout process released deadly silica dust. I'm sure none of the guys were aware that the dust they were inhaling caused silicosis, an incurable lung disease that yearly results in thousands of industrial deaths. Crucible provided no protective respiratory masks to inhibit any of the dust from filling our lungs.

Looking back, I wonder how many of the men I saw shoveling the sand contracted silicosis. How many died without knowing the cause? Of course, because most were Black or brown, and working-class, the causes of their deaths received little scrutiny.

I was very careful to keep my employment at Crucible on the down-low, as I suspected the FBI would intervene if they discovered my new job. Nevertheless, one night the superintendent called me in to his office.

"Federal people spoke with upper management, advising that we shouldn't allow you to complete your probation. It's really out of my hands. I didn't see or hear of any problem with your work. Good luck on your next job."

The superintendent's surprisingly candid explanation was later borne out by a memorandum in my FBI dossier: "On 10/21/74 [name of Milwaukee police officer redacted] advised that he had determined that subject was currently employed at the Crucible Steel Castings Division." I lost my job on October 23.

The FBI had determined to keep me on the streets and out of work. Crucible Steel had stood for seventy-five years, but I had lasted less than ninety days. I knew my next job would prove even more difficult to land and keep.

CHAPTER 10

"Thanks, but No Tanks!"

I began scouring the classifieds for job openings, making a list of every factory accepting applications. Every day became a revolving door of ferreting out a posting in the newspaper, visiting an employment office that smelled and looked like the one before, being handed a beat-up clipboard, and filling out the form that might lead to a job.

As I searched, I constantly checked my rearview mirror, fearing that the FBI or Harry, from the Milwaukee police Red Squad, might be on my tail. Officer Harry Makoutz hovered around the activist community like a mosquito. Fucking Harry showed up at every demonstration, march, or picket line. Glance in the rearview mirror, you might spot Harry's car.

One winter night, I saw Harry following me. He pulled me over and kept me spread-eagled, with ungloved hands on the freezing trunk of my car, for nearly an hour. While Harry ostensibly checked my license in the warmth of his vehicle, my hands numbed; my fingertips tingled painfully. After an interminable wait, he handed back my license and drove off. Harry had made it clear he could exercise his authority at will. I needed to fly below his radar.

I discovered an opening for a general laborer at the Pressed Steel Tank Company (PST) in West Allis, Wisconsin. In the mid-1970s, West Allis was a booming industrial suburb of Milwaukee. I filled out my application with my phone number omitted, since I suspected the FBI had tapped my phone. I used pay phones to call PST's employment office until they knew my name by heart.

Persistence prevailed. I was told to report for an in-plant interview. Thinking that I might have a good shot at the job, I drove a circuitous route to West Allis while glancing over my shoulder to see if FBI agents or Harry were in tow.

At my interview, I didn't mention Crucible. I explained my AMC discharge by pleading a momentary bout of youthful impropriety. Mustering a sincere expression and contrite tone, I looked the interviewer in the eye, "Sir, you must have made a few mistakes sowing your oats? I'd appreciate if you'd give me a shot."

"Well, son," he said, "let's give you a second chance. Just don't screw up during your sixty-day probation."

As I walked into the factory, the antiquated machines shocked me. Many of PST's large punch presses were still powered by steam, which rose in swirling clouds each time one of the ancient presses cycled.

As a general laborer, I was assigned any lousy open job. Out of the gate, I filled in for an employee who had taken sick leave, probably to escape what I soon realized was one of the most undesirable, backbreaking jobs.

My assignment was to operate a huge green machine—the Blaster, which shot BB-like metal pellets under extreme pressure at the exterior of steel tanks to produce a shiny finish. Hour after hour, I loaded tank after tank into the Blaster's mouth. The job was hot, physically exhausting, and mind-numbing.

Every few hours the Blaster exhausted its supply of metal pellets. I then climbed into a cramped pit under the Blaster where the used pellets accumulated. I painfully shoveled piles of pellets from one side of the cavern to a hopper on the other side. Then I crawled out, my arms and back aching terribly.

My shovel kicked up countless microscopic metal dust particles. It felt as if a thin layer of sand coated my eyeballs, and each blink irritated my eyes. Wheezing, I blew my nose, filling the rag with dark mucus-encrusted particles. I hadn't been provided a protective mask or goggles. I improvised by wrapping a rag around my face, making me look like an Egyptian mummy wearing a yellow hard hat.

As the clock ticked toward the magic sixty-day marker, two fears plagued me. One was that I'd have to work my way through the worst jobs in the plant to attain a permanent position. The other was the possibility of the FBI or Red Squad uncovering my employment.

The Blaster owner's return from sick leave granted my reprieve. I raced to pass him his shovel, like an Olympian handing off the torch, although he didn't share my elation.

I moved to an adjacent building where I unloaded heat-treated tanks. Heat-treating at high temperatures strengthened the tank's metal to store high-pressure gases. The front of the mammoth furnace resembled the gaping mouth of a fire-breathing dragon.

The worker at the mouth loaded three-foot tanks onto rollers, which slowly propelled the tanks toward the white-hot gut. Minutes later, red-hot tanks emerged from the bowels of the furnace. Wearing thickly padded, heat-resistant mittens, I offloaded the tanks into a pickle basket: a six-by-six-foot metal container.

No one had trained me to safely perform the job. As I was on piece rate, the more filled baskets, the higher my pay. If I grabbed tanks at the speed they came at me, however, they were too hot to handle and singed my hands through the gloves. The trick to safely offload tanks required me to grab the tanks after they traveled a distance from the gut and had cooled enough to handle.

When I grabbed a tank still a bit too hot, little fibers broke off my gloves and floated into the air. The air around me soon filled with thousands of specks, floating dandelion hairs. I wondered, could the particles be asbestos? I banished the worry and focused: grab a tank, throw it in the basket, grab the next tank, and throw it in too, hour after hour.

I quickly bonded with my cohorts—mostly young, unmarried, muscle car–driving, hard-partying white guys. Every night we'd stake claim to the bar stools at one of the two taverns on Sixty-Sixth Street—Mr. Mort's or Jim & Nancy's—to drink boilermakers, play bar dice, and shoot pool. On Thursdays we bowled in a league. My PST team included Big Carl, Wildman, Eyebolt, and me.

All too frequently, the final frame didn't curtail the night's activity. We'd reconvene at one of the guy's places to drink more and play cards. We'd wrap up when the sun came up. PST thoroughly punished our bodies at work, and we thoroughly punished them after.

For the sixty probationary days, I lived on pins and needles. On day sixty I felt like a runner crossing the finish line with arms thrust skyward in triumph. I could resume my organizing.

My strategy of assiduously maintaining a low profile to avoid FBI surveillance paid off. I passed probation and could no longer be fired without just cause. According to a memo in my FBI dossier, written by the Special Assignment Division of the Milwaukee Police Department (the Red Squad) to the bureau's special agent in charge, they had followed me from my home to PST but only after I'd passed probation. Fuck you, agents MI 100-16566 and MI 100-15714. You were too late.

The union at PST, Steelworkers Local 1569, exercised minimal impact on our work lives. I needed a strategy to make the union relevant to our day-to-day hassles: unfair supervisors, lousy piecework rates, dangerous working conditions, oppressive heat. There were a plethora of abuses, large and small, to fight.

There was only one union rep on second shift, a rather innocuous guy nicknamed Buffer. His moniker derived from his job buffing out flaws in the metal skins of tanks. Buffer sought to be everyone's best buddy, including the company's.

Soon I got caught up in an incident that brought me into contact with Buffer and the anemic union. Our piecework rates were worse than having a bad boss. Rather than the boss exhorting the crew to work faster, the crew recklessly pushed itself to earn a few extra dollars.

Our crew operated a set of three presses. We had finished the run of one size tank and were changing the press dies to punch out a different size. Each die weighed hundreds of pounds and was secured to the press by gargantuan screws and bolts. Dick, one of the crew, had difficulty unbolting the die. The longer Dick took, the greater the tension among waiting crew members.

The crew included one Black guy—Jimmie. Jimmie grew agitated, pacing and mumbling to himself, as Dick struggled with the bolts. One of the crew griped, "Dick, you're taking money out of my pocket." Another chimed in, "Dick, I got four kids to feed." Dick became increasingly frantic. Suddenly, Jimmie flipped out. He grabbed a ball-peen hammer and started whaling on Dick.

A ball-peen hammer is easily a lethal weapon when swung with force. Jimmie felled Dick, and time froze as we watched Jimmie swing the hammer, coming down full force on Dick. I jumped down from the press and yelled, "Cool it, bro! He's doing his best!"

Jimmie kept swinging, as if possessed. I grabbed his arm, and Jimmie turned on me with blind ferocity. He hit me full on with the ball-peen hammer, and I went down hard. Five times I felt it strike me, and the last of these frenzied blows split my skull open.

I clutched my head and felt warm blood gush through my fingers. Blood filled my nostrils and mouth as I gasped for breath. Everything turned into a blur. Jimmie had backed off, perhaps shaken by the blood, perhaps broken out of his trance. I had difficulty staying conscious.

The in-plant nurse arrived and did her best to contain the bleeding. Time passed slowly as I lay on the floor, eye level with layers of grease and discarded pieces of scrap. Finally an ambulance arrived.

At the emergency room, the doctors shaved a patch of my hair and stitched up the gaping wound. In addition to the head gash, they counted four other abrasions from legs to torso.

The hospital released me with the admonition to "take it easy." Arriving home, I flopped down on my bed, floating on painkillers, and wondered what the next day would bring. I worried that things would turn ugly, racial. Jimmie counted as one of only a few Blacks at PST. I fretted over the disciplinary consequences. Might the company take the opportunity to get rid of me?

When I woke, my head throbbed where the ball-peen had dented it. I felt four tender spots where the hammer had struck. I so wanted to pull the covers over my head—no Jimmie, no Dick, no hammer. I reluctantly decided to report to work and face the consequences, whatever they might be.

Driving in, I mused over the probable reaction of my fellow workers. Obviously, disputes were the natural outcome of turning workers against each other in the mad dash to make out. I also considered the undercurrent of racism among many of the young white guys.

Before I could punch in, my supervisor instructed me to report to the superintendent's office. The superintendent seated me next to Buffer. On the other side of Buffer sat Jimmie. I glanced over. Jimmie gazed forward, face fixed in an emotionless stare, still wearing the same clothes as the night before. He looked unshaven, his afro disheveled.

Before the shift, I had spoken with a guy who knew Jimmie outside of work. Jimmie, I learned, suffered serious mental issues, triggered by catching his wife in bed with another guy.

Despite the beating, I felt Jimmie's pain and discomfort sitting in the superintendent's office. The judge, the jury, and the victim (the superintendent, Buffer, and I, respectively) were all white.

The superintendent spoke. "The company is terminating the two of you for fighting. You constitute a danger to fellow employees. Clean out your lockers and leave company property."

Stunned, I didn't believe my ears. I turned toward Buffer, expecting him to speak in my defense. He stared straight forward, not opening his mouth. Meanwhile, Jimmie continued to stare silently and blankly.

I had no intention of going down quietly. "There's no way you've got grounds to fire me. I was absolutely not fighting. In fact, if I hadn't jumped in, an employee could have been killed. The hell if I'm gonna be fired for that. The damn company's to blame for setting rates so tight and forcing us to fight each other to make out. I can promise you I'll go after the company with everything I've got!" Buffer remained silent as a rock.

The superintendent asked Jimmie to step out, then asked me, "Melrod, would you be willing to work on the same crew with Jimmie again?" I resented being put in a no-win situation. If I said no, Jimmie was out the door. If I said yes, he might again snap and hurt someone. Buffer should have come to Jimmie's defense and suggested counseling. But he just sat.

I recalled the wild expression on Jimmie's face as he swung the hammer. He had totally lost it. I loathed feeling like I appeared to side with the company, but I responded, "No, I wouldn't feel safe, but there must be a way that Jimmie doesn't lose his job."

The superintendent turned to Buffer. "Melrod can return to his job. Jimmie's discharged." I hadn't lost my job but experienced no taste of victory. I walked out past Jimmie who stared at the floor. I felt really low, like I had fired him.

Big Carl, my bowling and drinking buddy, tipped me about a job opening in the spinning room. Jobs in the spinning room paid big money. Years earlier, in a legendary job action, first- and second-shift spinners conducted a protracted slowdown, while orders for oxygen tanks outpaced production. Spinning took skill and training, so the company couldn't simply add a third shift. When the spinners' solidarity held for a month, they scored a higher pay rate.

My new assignment was spinner's helper, working for Carl. The spinner maneuvered a large, suspended arm that molded the heated, open end of an oxygen tank until it was almost closed, forming a nipple. As assistant, I pulled the red-hot tank out of the furnace with long tongs and maneuvered it into the spinning machine for Carl to mold.

I had difficulty pulling tanks out of the furnace. I just didn't have long enough arms or the required strength. As I struggled, Carl worked harder to make up the time we lost. He was skilled, applying just the right amount of pressure to force the molten metal to form a nipple without collapsing the end of the tank.

I resolved to gain Carl's respect. We had to work fast to make up for lost time. I rushed in with my tongs, in my haste moving too close to the red-hot metal. In an instant my shirt melted on both arms. Nobody had mentioned not to wear acrylic, which, I learned, melts when close to high heat. The acrylic had burned me as it fused with my skin. After the nurse applied some ointment, I worked the remainder of the night without sleeves.

I'd often heard guys referring to a Native American coworker as "the Chief." Chief was squat and barrel-chested, as wide as he was tall. Beneath his dirty, oil-stained coveralls, he was muscular and, as I soon discovered, strong as a bull.

By the time I met him, Chief had worked at PST on the same wheezing steam-powered press for almost thirty years. Chief possessed enough clout to secure jobs for his boys, Ronny and Donny.

Chief regularly held court during lunch break. He'd spin tales of the militant exploits of hard-charging unions "back in the day" and sometimes recount his own exploits as a steward. I'd soak up his wisdom, sitting at the base of his press, as I munched on a homemade sandwich.

One day Chief's son Donny confided in a hushed tone, "Melrod, don't tell anyone, but my dad has a photo of Stalin, that Russian guy, sitting on his dresser." There was more, much more to Chief than I had appreciated.

Chief was a "city" Indian, although he grew up on the Menominee Reservation in rural Gresham, Wisconsin, 170 miles north. While we were on holiday break that winter, an armed band of young Menominee seized an abandoned abbey on their reservation.

Fifty men, women, and children, the Menominee Warriors Society, demanded that the abbey, plus the surrounding 237 acres, be turned over to the tribe to be converted into a health clinic. At the time, no medical care existed within miles of the reservation.

Returning to work after the New Year's holiday, I sought out Chief.

"Hey, Chief, did you hear about the Menominee Warriors?"

He nodded but said nothing.

"Chief, the cops got those Warriors squeezed like a vise. Remember Wounded Knee? The only thing that prevented a wholesale massacre of those AIM guys was public support. If the Menominee Warriors don't get the same kind of support—and fucking soon—they're dead. They got women and kids in the abbey."

Chief didn't need me to tell him.

"Do you think I could be helpful if I headed up?" I asked.

Chief placed his hand on my shoulder. "Little Brother, one must follow one's heart and one's spirit." The buzzer rang, and Chief turned to pull the worn wooden lever to stamp out his first tank of the New Year.

Before going anywhere, I had to cover my ass by getting off work with permission so I wouldn't be fired. As fate would have it, I had sprained my wrist, when Big Carl knocked me off my bar stool with a right hook the night before the holiday break.

Dog, Eyebolt, Wildman, Big Carl, and I had been drinking boilermakers to celebrate our few days off. Carl was soon hammered. He launched into a drunken diatribe, repeating shit he had heard backward workers say about me, calling me a troublemaker and a "fucking commie." I merely answered, "Yeah, so what?" and then felt Carl's powerful right propelling me to the floor. I landed on my wrist, which had been bruised and swollen for days—resulting in PST's nurse placing me on disability.

I hoped to enlist Chief's son Donny to accompany me north, sure that I would be more readily accepted if I arrived with a tribal member. "Donny, how 'bout heading up to the rez? Just ride shotgun with me, brother. Those Warriors need support."

Donny responded quickly. "Those skins are fucking crazy, man, and are gonna get themselves killed." I sincerely hoped not, but the stakes were high.

Fortunately, a fellow activist, Doug, joined me. We headed north, armed only with our AAA map.

Local whites had organized into a self-styled Concerned Citizens Committee (CCC) of armed vigilantes. A few gunshots had been fired as the warriors escorted the caretaker's family safely out of the abbey. Shawano County sheriffs and state police rushed to the scene, forming an armed cordon blocking all access.

More than seventy local and state law enforcement officials had rushed in sharpshooters and blocked roads and snowmobile trails to thwart supporters from smuggling in supplies. But the Menominee knew the backwoods. They were able to ferry essentials to the Warriors under the cover of darkness. The scene uncannily resembled photos of combat zones in Vietnam, with white snow instead of jungle green blanketing the landscape.

Lurid comparisons to Wounded Knee filled Wisconsin newspapers, as evening TV news pumped out a steady dose of anti-Indian propaganda. Local whites, exhorted by the CCC, hysterically appealed to the police to freeze and starve out the Warriors, threatening to take matters into their hands.

Arriving at the reservation, we found the American Legion hall where Menominee gathered as they sought to support the Warriors. Menominee of all ages packed the large, sparsely furnished hall. While the temperature outside hovered around zero, the crush of bodies inside felt stifling. No one rushed over to make our acquaintance, but at least no one chased us out.

When dinnertime came, women walked around the hall serving everyone from a steaming cauldron, but they detoured around us.

Folks drifted away. We gave up, deciding to find a motel and try again in the morning.

We rose at dawn and headed back, where we again received the cold shoulder. After what felt like an eternity, a young guy with a long ponytail tentatively approached. "Hey. I'm David. I attend a nearby community college and have white friends. How come you're here?"

"To help break the police blockade before the cops massacre the Warriors," I answered.

"Do you have a plan?" David asked.

I had one shot to convince David we were for real. "Look, I've been an activist since I was fifteen. I was in the civil rights movement, the student movement, the antiwar movement, and the union movement. David, believe me, I know how to organize people. I can promise you one thing. If we don't build public support for the Warriors, they're as good as dead."

"Go on," he said.

"The health clinic is a sympathetic issue. We can rally support. Today's Friday. If the tribe agrees, we can bring hundreds up from Milwaukee on Sunday for a mass march to the police blockade. But, and this is a big 'but,' we'll look stupid if it's just a bunch of white people. The tribe needs to agree to mobilize for the march."

Before leaving Milwaukee, I'd discussed the idea of a Sunday march with some political activists around the *Worker*. They had committed to organize as many as possible if they got word that the tribe approved the plan.

While David pondered what I said, I glanced around the hall. Every so often, swaths of people reach the limit of what they will tolerate, and they collectively act, whatever the risk. This tribe had reached their limit, just as people would in Tiananmen Square in 1989, the Arab Spring of 2011, the Black Lives Matter movement of 2020.

David introduced us to the ad hoc leadership coordinating support. They listened patiently, nodding, while I ran down the proposal. Saying nothing, they walked off to huddle.

The level of tension ratcheted up. The official Menomonee Restorations Committee, who enjoyed cozy ties with local white authorities, issued a statement commanding the "militants" to vacate the abbey.

Plenty of bad blood ran between the Warriors and the Restorations Committee. Quite a few Warriors worked at the Menominee-owned lumber mill. The previous summer, mill workers had struck to demand a dollar raise, as they were making a measly two dollars per hour. The Restorations Committee refused. Lacking a support fund, strikers were forced back with a mere thirty-cent raise.

Now live fire was exchanged between the Warriors and the approximately forty sheriffs and state police holed up in a nearby barn. The police fired armor-piercing rounds, ripping up walls and shredding metal pipes like confetti, causing the building to flood. Miraculously, no Warriors were injured.

While we awaited the ad hoc leadership's decision, painfully aware that time was running out, a rumor spread. Governor Lucy had issued an ultimatum: the Warriors had to vacate the abbey by the weekend. I turned to the ad hoc leadership. "What now?"

The answer was delivered without emotion.

"On behalf of the Menominee Tribe, we agree to march but with one condition. To make sure you're not an FBI pig setting us up for a massacre, you'll be at the front of the march. If the pigs open fire, you're going down first."

I called Michael Rosen in Milwaukee to let him know he needed to mobilize for Sunday's march. It was a lot to ask on short notice, but I conveyed my commitment.

"This is serious shit. They've got these guys surrounded by sharpshooters. You need to bring every possible body. Please, get in touch with activist students in Madison." Michael promised to start mobilizing.

Word spread on the reservation that an all-out tribal mobilization was planned for Sunday.

Conversations turned philosophical. People spoke of their ancestors and the struggle Native Americans had waged to protect their lands since the arrival of Europeans. Foremost on my mind was whether enough supporters would show up. I again phoned Milwaukee.

"I don't know what will happen when we confront the police. We might be walking into a bloodbath. Please, bring everyone you can. Also, we need media. There'll be nothing between heavily armed police and us except reporters."

Leaders called a tribal mass meeting for Saturday to paint signs. More than 250 gathered, a promising sign of how many tribal members were willing to break with the Restorations Committee and stand with the Warriors.

Word reached us that government negotiators were inside the abbey. We breathed a sigh of relief. Then the mood turned grim after word circulated that negotiations had abruptly broken off. Government authorities left the abbey, clearing the way for an onslaught.

Following the departure of negotiators, Governor Lucy mobilized the National Guard to replace the local police, who were being goaded by the Concerned Citizens to clear out the occupation. We heard reports that white vigilantes on snowmobiles were firing into the abbey. In twenty hours, we would be at the police lines.

As I opened my eyes Sunday morning, I shuddered. The sick feeling of fear invaded my stomach. I didn't allow myself time to dwell on the approaching danger and headed for the Legion Hall.

Many elders had joined in preparation for the march. They gathered, many stooped from premature aging, with young Warriors in the hall. There was no sign of supporters from Milwaukee. Had I promised more than I could deliver?

Suddenly dozens of cars arrived and began disgorging groggy supporters. They had driven through the early-morning hours. A contingent from the Unemployed Workers Organizing Committee (UWOC), including a number of Blacks, had come to march. Not used to venturing beyond inner-city Milwaukee, none were wearing boots or winter clothing, even though we were soon to march on icy, snow-packed roads.

Vets belonging to Vietnam Veterans Against War (VVAW) arrived, many wearing military fatigues. VVAW members felt an affinity with the Warriors and readily organized to show solidarity.

I overheard a young Indian asking why a bunch of "niggers" were on the reservation. His words threw me. Many Menominee had done time in state prisons, where racial division was the law of the jungle. Even during shared adversity, this division ran deep. I walked over to the young guy. "Say, brother, today we're marching together; we're all here to support the Warriors. We're not red, black, or white—we're united."

The crowd swelled into the hundreds as more supporters arrived. Students from Madison unfurled their own banner supporting the Warriors.

Menominee people moved to the front.

Leadership approached me. "Hey, brother. Here's your bullhorn. You in front."

We marched down the narrow road toward the police blockade. I started the first chant. "Save Menominee lives—pull back police." We raised our voices in a united crescendo. "We support Menominee Warriors—We support Menominee Warriors!"

We snaked down the road toward the police roadblock. Squad cars came into view, small at first but larger and more threatening the closer we got. Clustered around them were dozens of trigger-happy police armed with shotguns, service revolvers, and more. They were packing automatic weapons. *Shit!*

As distance between us narrowed, my heart beat faster, and I chanted louder. Fortunately, members of the Milwaukee media were out in force. Reporters and film crews darted to the front to document our steady approach. Anything that happened would be on the record for the world to see.

Finally we were within feet of the police. Inches. Too close for comfort. We stared into each other's eyes. Our chants were met with looks of rage. How little provocation it would take for them to lay into us, I thought.

Many of the young Menominee were warriors, ready to sacrifice their lives. They were angry and defiant. Some were draped with upside-down US flags—a conscious provocation and act of disdain. Young warriors—men and women, boys and girls—danced provocatively, facing the police, daring them to react.

Despite the overwhelming police firepower, I felt elated. Lives on the reservation were colored by unemployment, alcoholism, babies born to young unwed mothers, and high rates of suicide. That day, however, all experienced a sweet taste of freedom and collective power.

Our strategy succeeded. We had mobilized enough people, including many whites, whose lives the outside world deemed more valuable than those of Native Americans. With so many cameras and reporters chronicling events, the forces of the state remained remarkably constrained, transformed into wooden soldiers.

Governor Lucy agreed to mobilize the National Guard to replace the sheriffs and state police. Lucy also agreed that the Guard would allow food past the blockade—a huge victory!

I hung around on Monday morning. The march propelled the Menominee Warriors onto the front page of newspapers nationally. Like moths drawn to a flame, celebrity leaders began arriving. National leaders of AIM, Dennis Banks and Russell Means, arrived to much fanfare. Marlon

Brando and Father Groppi, a high-profile veteran of civil rights struggles in Milwaukee, entered the abbey to show solidarity.

With all the hoopla, I was no longer needed. A bloodbath had been avoided.

Negotiations with the Alexian Brothers Order, which owned the abbey, ended with the order turning over the deed to the building and the surrounding land for one dollar.

The Warriors triumphantly left the abbey. All thirty-nine were arrested. Later, those who had been employed at the reservation lumber mill were fired, the Resolution Committee's retribution.

Back in West Allis, ice-coated cars filled the parking lot, surrounded by six-foot piles of grimy city snow.

Standing out from the other cars was Eyebolt's tricked-out, fire-engine-red Firebird Trans Am, spotless and unblemished by salt. I maneuvered into a spot between two dirty pickups and sat cocooned in my car's warmth.

As I stepped into the bowels of the plant, the stale air, heavy with the odor of machine oil, smoke, steam, and toxic fumes, assaulted my senses, and the reservation was a memory.

Among my New Year's goals, I committed to stepping up my organizing, pushing for an improved agreement in the upcoming contract negotiations. Consensus held that the Local 1569 leadership had betrayed the members in the 1972 contract. That agreement had satisfied no one but the company.

Turning around the collective pessimism, however, required a fundamental shift in the power equation between the rank and file, the entrenched union leadership, and PST.

I narrowly defined my objective: organize the young guys on second shift into a rank-and-file caucus to energize the membership. Since we already gathered at the tavern every night, I hoped to convince my group to grab sixpacks, skip the bar, and meet to discuss the upcoming contract.

To my dismay, almost unanimous negativity met my suggestion: "Meeting, fuck. I ain't ever been to a union meeting in my life." "I'd rather shoot pool than sit around and yap." And so on.

I felt gobsmacked. It all seemed so obvious. I decided that I needed a persuasive hook. At shift's end, I announced, "Listen up, I'll spring for the beer. Just do me right and see what kind of ideas come up. If we don't get organized, it will be '72 all over again, and you'll be bellyaching worse than ever. It won't cramp your style to take one night off from holding down bar stools."

I thought I had persuaded a substantial group of coworkers to check out the meeting, but a mere handful stopped at Eyebolt's West Allis apartment. The guys enjoyed the free beer but weren't accustomed to meetings. It proved challenging to keep attention focused on the contract.

After protracted and quite animated diversions about who bowled the best, had the fastest car, shot the best bar dice, could whip the most ass and drink the most shots, and which supervisor deserved the most disdain, we reached a chaotic, late-night consensus to make buttons demanding a "Good Contract." And we set a second meeting for the next week.

My clunky button press resembled an old-fashioned, stand-up orange juice maker. One of the guys volunteered to design a button. The print turned too small and the steel tank way too large, barely recognizable, but we produced buttons ourselves, and no one noticed the aesthetic shortcomings. We stamped out hundreds while downing beer.

After much prodding, Wildman, Eyebolt, Carl, and a few others reluctantly got up at six one morning to sell buttons with me for twenty-five cents to first-shift workers. We had no idea how we would be greeted. Many on day shift were lifers, having worked there for thirty years and longer, and there was a solid contingent I considered politically backward. Moreover, no one had ever undertaken an action not sanctioned by the official union leadership. To our surprise, we sold all our yellow buttons before half of first shift arrived for work. We rushed back to stamp out hundreds more.

The second shift responded enthusiastically. By shift's end, virtually every worker sported a yellow button. Even some of the backward, who had previously steered clear of me, now sheepishly approached with a quarter.

Our nascent caucus prided itself on having scored a success. The sentiment the week before: "No one really gives a damn." Now the same guys who had scoffed at meetings were anxious to reconvene.

Next we printed thousands of round white stickers—three inches in diameter—that read "GOOD CONTRACT OR STRIKE JUNE 12." This was the first time we mentioned striking. After seeing the stickers, a few older guys brought up a 1964 strike that had resulted in three months of lost wages but no gains. We had to overcome that pessimism.

In our next meeting we discussed how only a work stoppage, or the serious threat of a work stoppage, offered a shot at winning a good contract.

Unless there was a good contract proposal on the table by the date the old contract expired, we agreed that we should walk.

Workers on both shifts surreptitiously slapped stickers on punch presses, lathes, shears, furnaces, locker room walls, and even on supervisors' desks. The white stickers dotted the factory, a contagion of white in stark contrast to the grimy plant. Wherever the company assigned maintenance to scrape off a sticker, someone furtively slapped a new one in its place.

We caught the company off guard with the spirit of militancy. In years past, first and second shift were concerned only with issues specific to their shift. Individuals clung to their disparate opinions with little regard for anyone else, making it a cakewalk for the already complacent local union leaders to disregard everyone.

Our buttons and stickers fundamentally bridged the divide that separated young from old and first from second shift. Lunchroom conversations and bar time after work were filled with lively interchanges of what *we*, as a local, needed to win.

An undercurrent of rumors began to swirl around me like a funnel cloud. Company white hats (supervisors, who wore white hard hats) approached kiss-ass workers and warned them to "steer clear of Melrod." I sensed some workers talking derisively behind my back and found occasional malicious postings in the locker room.

The Local 1569 leaders, self-promoters in bed with the company, readily exploited the company-instigated rumors. The rumor campaign raised questions among some as to whether I harbored "ulterior motives." No one could quite articulate, however, what the ulterior motives might be.

While I had no inkling at the time of FBI involvement, I now assume the bureau instigated the rumors in a playbook campaign, employing time-tested 1950s-era red-baiting. A federal memorandum dated March 2, 1975, mentions a phone call from the FBI's Milwaukee office to PST's employment office.

No doubt, the conversation provided PST with enough fodder to launch their robust rumor campaign. My buddies on second shift were unperturbed, as we hotly debated politics. Every month they saw me selling the *Worker*. The second page of every issue included a statement noting that some of the paper's staff belonged to the Revolutionary Union, a national communist organization." (That group was soon to become the Revolutionary Communist Party, which I left when it later broke in half.)

Even those I had never met knew me as the guy whose picture appeared in the *Milwaukee Journal* marching with the Menominee Warriors. My politics were an open book, regardless of the sinister mystery the company rumor propounded.

Now that we had everyone talking about the contract, we needed to focus on key issues. I had learned that identifying, distilling, and popularizing primary demands would unite the vast majority, regardless of age, seniority, or politics.

When we met again, I proposed four main contract demands: better wages, improved pensions, better health insurance, and the right to strike over grievances. The first three were framed to appeal widely. A hefty wage increase was particularly important, as inflation had been climbing at a whopping 12 percent a year. Of equal import, particularly for older workers, was the demand for improved pensions since PST fell woefully short of providing a decent living standard for retirees.

I decided to broach the company's red-baiting campaign. "Listen, you guys, PST is doing whatever it can to ostracize me and split us into separate suspicious camps. I've always been straight about my belief that capitalism is an unfair, stacked system built on the backs of workers. On the immediate agenda, however, is winning a good contract. We can't let PST beat us with a divide-and-conquer strategy." None of the guys really gave a damn about the red-baiting; they knew me to be a straight shooter, and that's what mattered most.

We agreed to include a closing paragraph in our leaflet:

This leaflet was written and put out by a group of us who are all members of Local 1569. Already the company and some of their friends have been sneaking around saying we are outsiders, troublemakers, and that we want to split the union.

Everyone knows who we are. Among us are people of different political views. But the point is that we have come together because we want to unite everyone in this union to fight for a good contract.

We planned to distribute the flyer days before the May union meeting at which the membership would consider the company's "final offer." If the company's offer came up short, our leaflet advised members to tell management, "Thanks, but no tanks!"

We agreed to hang at Eyebolt's after work, grab a few hours of sleep, and distribute the leaflet to first shift. Once Carl and Wildman started drinking and playing cards, however, they ignored the sleep component.

At 5:30 a.m. everyone grumbled at having to leave for the plant. But we made it there, still in our work clothes from the night before, arriving as the sun rose at six. Most first-shifters willingly accepted the leaflet.

Hundreds attended the May union meeting at Serb Hall to consider PST's "best and final" offer. The local president, an old codger cozy with the company, feared presenting the company's proposal. He distanced himself by pushing the onus onto a United Steelworkers' international rep who had shown up.

The international rep, speaking as dryly as humanly possible, droned through the proposal point by point. When he looked up, a collective gasp, followed by angry grumbling, filled the hall. The company had guaranteed a strike with an insulting lowball contract.

Months of wearing buttons and pasting stickers paid off. The membership *unanimously* rejected the offer, leaving the local leaders with little choice but to jump on the bandwagon and embrace our demands, except for the right to strike.

As the June 12 contract expiration approached, the temperature reached ninety degrees, and the temperature in the plant often was ten degrees warmer. In a concerted action, workers flooded the nurse's office suffering from "heat stroke." Another time, workers shut their machines down early so as not to produce a stockpile of tanks. All refused overtime. These small skirmishes set the stage for the contract battle just over the horizon.

In addition to Steelworkers Local 1569, hundreds of thousands of union workers across the country were in a militant mood. The Labor Department reported fifty-nine hundred strikes in 1974. With inflation steadily eroding workers' standard of living, union rank and file responded with one of the broadest and most widespread strike waves in US history.

In other contract battles, the international had allowed the contract to expire, hoping that members would be too intimidated to walk off the job. To counter that, we handed out a flyer announcing a midnight rally. We spread word that third-shift workers should shut down their machines and walk out at midnight; we urged them to ignore threats of discipline. Would they?

When our shift ended, over 150 gathered in a warm evening breeze at the front gate. Boisterous chants of "We want a good contract!" and "On strike! Shut it down!" bounced off the factory. We wanted to ensure that third shifters heard us and could feel the collective solidarity.

The rank-and-file Unity caucus in Steelworkers Local 1659 sparked the first strike against Pressed Steel Tank in over a decade. Legendary union militant "Chief" is in the middle with clenched fist. To the right with clenched fist is his son Donny (both members of the Menominee tribe, where the author had built support for an armed takeover by the Menominee Warriors Society).

The company preemptively called the West Allis police to report that they feared violence. The local union leaders echoed the company, telling workers to stay away from the rally and saying that violence would damage the union's cause.

While our caucus initiated the rally, we invited Buffer to speak, hoping that his presence would help dispel rumors that our caucus was maneuvering to take over the strike.

I took the bullhorn, felling a surge of adrenaline. I commenced speaking in a conversational voice, forcing everyone to fall silent to hear me. Slowly I upped the volume, as well as my cadence, until the crescendo: "We're here tonight united as one union. The company has tried to paint the picture that we're a bunch of outsiders, a radical faction trying to take over Local 1569. We're not here to take over the union but to make the union strong enough to win a good contract. We're ready to walk the picket line until we win improvements in wages, a livable pension for retirees, and health insurance that truly provides for our families. This strike won't be like 1964. We'll settle for nothing short of a victory!"

To avoid disciplinary retaliation, third-shift workers reported to their workstations. They were at their stations, machines running. The moment of truth arrived as both hands of the clock reached twelve. If management succeeded in keeping third shift at work, the strike would be jeopardized. We raised the volume of our chants, imploring those in the plant: "Walk! Walk! Walk! Walk!"

After a few suspenseful minutes, a trickle of third-shift workers straggled out the gate. The rest soon followed, after shutting down lathes, shears, furnaces, and presses, walking through a scrum of once-omnipotent white hard hats blocking the exit. Even workers typically cowed by management joined the celebratory mood, like conquering heroes as they exited the now silent plant.

Members of Local 1569—all 625 of us—had shut down PST for the first time in a decade. The furnaces went cold, and the steam presses ceased hissing. In the mere blink of an eye, the power equation flipped. Without workers, with production at a dead standstill, PST was powerless. We had shut the mother down!

After the grueling regimen of punching in every afternoon at 3:30 p.m. and hustling for eight hours to make rate, the first few days on strike felt like the early days of summer when school lets out. Strikers spent a few hours walking the line in the June sun and three times as many hours cooling off in front of an air conditioner, drinking beers at Jim & Nancy's or Mr. Mort's.

Despite the shared intoxication of our new life of leisure, I insisted that the caucus formulate strike strategy. Each of us committed to walking the line every day. We collectively decided to start printing "Unity Bulletins."

Unity Bulletin #1 outlined available government benefits: 1) food stamps; 2) AFDC (Aid to Families with Dependent Children); and 3) Title 19 medical benefits. And we printed the phone number and address of each office providing benefits. As the official Local 1569 leaders had done nothing to communicate with the membership, *Unity Bulletin* filled a much-needed informational vacuum.

Our second week out, PST sent a letter to strikers' homes, threatening to cut off health insurance. The company assumed that since the workforce was all male, wives could be scared into pressuring husbands to return to work. In *Bulletin* #2, a high-seniority, well-respected striker, Ray Haynes, wrote: "Our wives want a good contract as much as we do. Don't think that by writing a letter to our homes you can begin to turn them against the strike. We're sticking together."

The class collaborationist Steelworkers international initiated back-to-work pressure by threatening to cancel strike benefits to *some* members, citing a restriction that benefits be paid only on an "as-needed" basis.

In retrospect, I'm flabbergasted that we had to wage a full-scale assault on the international to secure a mere $21 a week (equal to $100 today). We agreed that the international's "need" criteria would divide younger, single strikers, with less obvious need, from older workers with families. A *Unity Bulletin* responded that our monthly union dues entitled *all* to benefits; we hatched plans to picket the local Steelworkers offices. Fearing adverse publicity, the international caved in and released support benefits for all.

PST assembled a motley crew of supervisors and sales reps to staff the high-pressure tank line. While the scab crew turned out minimum production, the few new tanks being produced hurt morale. We met to develop a strategy to halt scab tanks leaving the plant.

Our next *Unity Bulletin* read, "Stop the Trucks. Stop Production!" With no approval from the AWOL Local 1569 leaders, we decided to up the ante by blocking trucks from crossing the line. When we heard a truck approaching, we piled out of Jim & Nancy's and raced for the picket line. The company called the police, and within minutes a half dozen squad cars arrived, lights flashing. The police pushed us back onto the sidewalk to force an opening for the truck.

Our caucus, which we had dubbed Unity, agreed to confront Teamsters Local 200. We piled into Eyebolt's car and drove to Gateway Trucking to hand out to Teamster drivers leaflets asking them to steer clear of our picket line.

The Gateway dispatcher, a Teamster 200 member, offered to distribute leaflets to his drivers. The Local 200 steward committed, "If you guys are union, that's good enough for me. I'm telling my guys to steer clear."

Local 200 put out the official word to its members that our strike was sanctioned, instructing drivers to honor our line.

Despite Local 200's endorsement, the "hot load loophole"—trucks driven by PST managers, not Teamsters—remained a problem. While the quantity of tanks that supervisors were producing could barely fill a truck, we didn't want any tanks leaving the plant.

We decided to put a stop to hot loads. One of our guys welded together nails into the shape of jacks (used in the kids' game). He filed off the heads of the nails so that a sharp point always stood upright. One team distracted the West Allis cops while another team crowded the picket line and surreptitiously dropped jacks onto the driveway. I forewarned co-saboteurs to drop all their jacks so that, if arrested, no one would be in possession of incriminating evidence.

We were stoked and ready when word spread that a supervisor was driving a truck toward the gate. We rushed the picket line, with a few clustering in front of the squad car. When the cop ordered us to move back to allow the truck to enter, we slowly complied.

By the time the supervisors had loaded a few pickle baskets of tanks into the truck, all four tires were flat as a pancake. An uproarious cheer went up as the driver realized he couldn't move. The police had seen nothing and couldn't pin blame on any individual. After a few more guerrilla attacks on hot loads, nothing moved out of the plant.

In the seventh week, a new and potentially damaging threat arose when a few strikers' families were threatened with eviction. In *Unity Bulletin* #6, we reiterated the government programs available and proposed to physically block any eviction. Knowing a potentially violent confrontation was brewing, and under pressure from strikers, the union ponied up with emergency rent and mortgage payments.

Then, on a fateful Friday morning, Unity and the strike suffered a demoralizing blow: Eyebolt's Trans Am fell victim to repossession by General Motors Acceptance Corporation (GMAC). Eyebolt (whose real name was Curt) had fallen behind on payments—no surprise with strike benefits of $21 a week. When GMAC first contacted Curt and he explained his situation, GMAC agreed to let him pay just the interest, but they reneged.

We convened an emergency meeting. I opened, "We can't allow this repossession to stand." But what I heard back expressed the fatalism of the disempowered. A judge had signed off on the repossession. The only time most of this crew had dealt with the law or a judge had been on their way to juvenile detention or fighting a DUI. From their perspective, the law amounted to an endless series of recriminations directed against them, whether in school or on the street.

A lot rode on my response. "We're gonna organize a picket line in front of GMAC in Brookfield. After we raise hell out front, some of us will push into the office and refuse to leave without Eyebolt's keys."

Big Carl begrudgingly chimed in. "Okay, brother, but you better be right."

The night before the picket at GMAC, I thought a lot about the importance of us getting Eyebolt's car back. We had gone tit for tat: blocking scab trucks, helping members secure government benefits, making sure everyone received strike benefits, forcing the union to cover house and apartment payments in arrears. The outcome of the repossession fight would have a major impact on morale.

About fifty people assembled—some unemployed from UWOC, a few supporters from other unions, and the rest PST strikers.

Brookfield Square epitomized the vanilla minimalls dotting suburbia. On the second floor, behind a wall of glass, sat GMAC's offices. As we formed our picket line, office workers peered at us with expressions of incredulity.

A few squad cars of Brookfield police pulled up, lights flashing, like some kind of major crime was going down. Meanwhile, the picket line continued with persistent chants of, "GMAC, give back Curt's keys!" Four of us, including Curt, headed in.

We were politely escorted to an executive office, as if we were there to buy a car. The general manager opened the dialogue. "I understand that you gentlemen are here because your colleague experienced a repossession of his vehicle. I sympathize with your colleague, I really do."

"Listen," I said. "No chit-chat. We're here for one simple, nonnegotiable reason—to get Curt's car. GMAC reneged on a promise to allow him to simply pay the interest. We honor our word; we expect GMAC to do so as well. We've been on strike for eight weeks, and we're damn pissed you took a striker's car. We've got a lot of guys outside who aren't leaving until you return the keys. In a few moments, they'll be joining us up here to find out for themselves what's going down. Your move."

The general manager turned toward us, "We'll give Curt his car back. The reason is there was an unfortunate misunderstanding, and we'll take his word."

When we dangled Eyebolt's keys in front of the picketers, everyone wildly cheered and chanted "The workers united will never be defeated!" and "Victory to the pressed steel strikers!"

We headed back to the line with a newfound sense of power and determination. Curt was back in the driver's seat of his tricked-out Trans Am. We had beaten the largest vehicle finance company in the country. We hoped PST would be next.

Before we had time to catch our breath, PST put another offer on the table. Our picketers were beginning to show signs of fatigue. Fewer members were showing up for picket duty; many had taken other jobs. The collective weariness constituted our greatest vulnerability.

Unity met to formulate our response to the latest proposal, which no member had yet seen. As strikers headed into the meeting to vote, we handed out a leaflet titled "If the Offer's Not Right—We'll Keep Up the Fight!" On the backside, we printed a two-column scorecard, with "Union Proposal" heading one column and "Company Offer" the other. The first column outlined union demands on wages, pensions, and insurance. The other column we left blank so members could rate the company's offer.

Based on the terms the union leadership ran down, the majority voted for ratification, not sure that more could be won. We certainly gained more than we would have without striking, plus solidarity had been the name of the game for eight weeks.

Once we were back on the job, the company resorted to petty harassment, retaliating for contract gains. What the strike had forced out of PST, management sought to take back. In a microcosm, PST stood for and followed the rules of industrial capitalism. Whatever meager concessions the working class extracts from the owning class are merely a temporary gain subject to being eroded in capitalists' relentless drive to recapture and maximize profits.

And then something unexpected occurred. In my mailbox one day was an official-looking letter with the American Motors logo on the envelope. To my shock, the letter offered reinstatement at AMC with full back pay. The NLRB had appealed AMC's refusal to rehire me, and a federal appellate court upheld the board's reinstatement order. It had taken almost two and a half years, but I had kicked AMC's ass!

I had been through a lot with my buddies at Pressed Steel and felt bad cutting out on them. I had started at PST as an outsider, not realizing that the white working-class suburb of West Allis constituted its own world. I had worked hard to overcome initial distrust of who I was and what I was up to. We had evolved from a Thursday-night bowling team into a militant rank-and-file caucus.

With no defections, Unity helped spark and sustain the first strike at PST in over a decade. In a partial victory, we secured contract gains, despite the union. Along the way, we fiercely struggled over deep-seated racism that pervaded many of the white guys' thinking and sometimes their actions. We had butted heads frequently, but both they and I had learned a lot from each other.

It was difficult to say goodbye as I had enjoyed our camaraderie. In my daydreams, though, I had already planned my victory lap at AMC.

CHAPTER 11

Back on the Trim Line— 1,008 Days Later

O ver a thousand days after Al and I were discharged, the Seventh Circuit Court of Appeals had definitively ordered AMC to reinstate us, with full back pay at 6 percent interest. Through dogged willpower, I had outlasted the AMC-FBI cabal. Their final option for keeping me out of the plant: the US Supreme Court. Fat chance!

A memo from the plant's director of industrial relations circulated to the "supervisory group in charge of [my work] area": "Messrs. Melrod and Guzman should be treated the same as any regular employee . . . the results of the NLRB case should not have any effect on the day to day relationship between their supervisors and them."

In preparation for my first day back, January 5, 1976, I photocopied and magnified an image of my back-pay check. After 1,008 days, I had every intention of grinding it in AMC's face. Expressionless security guards, rather than hauling me out of the plant, now escorted me up four floors to trim.

I displayed the copy of my back-pay check above my head, like a boxer displaying a title belt. Cheers greeted me as I slow-walked down the aisle. Even those who hadn't previously supported me couldn't help but enjoy that David had, at long last, whipped Goliath. Everybody loves an underdog winner's story.

As higher powers would have it, I was assigned to the section of Will Luv, the same supervisor who had unceremoniously kicked me out of his section during the struggle against speedup. Luv copped an attitude right off the bat, resentful that I had clawed my way back. Here I was again, smirking at him like a mischievous child poised to commit a repeat offense—I harbored every intent to be a stone-cold recidivist.

Assigning me to Luv was a setup. Being the sole Black boss in trim, in fact, one of the very few Blacks on supervision, from jump street Luv acted all hard-ass, a real Mr. Tough Guy.

Barely a month after reinstatement, plant security singled me out. Heading in on February 19, I flashed my ID.

"Hey, you—Melrod! Over here."

Under my arm I carried a stack of papers headed "'76 Auto Contract—A Time to Fight!"

"You're not permitted to take those papers into the plant. Leave them with me, or I'll call the captain."

It was round one. Rather than punch in late, I dropped the papers in my car.

Before the first car passed on the line, I demanded that Luv get my steward so I could formally protest the guard's interference. When the steward hadn't arrived within a half hour, I walked off, as bodies ran by my workstation, work undone. Either Luv or I was going to establish the upper hand, and I preferred that it be me.

Meeting with me and my steward, Seefeldt, Luv speed-dialed Labor Relations, who upheld the guard. This resulted in a first grievance from me in what would soon develop into constant conflict with Luv, who physically towered over me, particularly when he wore his platform shoes.

I had reconnected with former members of Fight Back. The guard busting me did not stop less visible caucus members from smuggling in hundreds of the newspaper-style '76 Auto Contract—A Time to Fight! handbills (published by Auto Workers United to Fight in '76, which included other political cadre in auto, plus activists in a few Detroit plants).

FELLOW AMC WORKERS: The '76 contracts are coming up at a time of crisis throughout the economy and auto industry, at a time when auto giants have launched a whole new wave of attacks....

For us [at AMC] to budge a single inch would be a setback for all autoworkers, by the same token, we can set a fighting example for everyone defending and extending what we have.

OUR DEMANDS [an excerpt]

* FULL SUB BENEFITS—NO CUT OFFS! [SUPPLEMENTAL UNEMPLOYMENT COMPENSATION DURING LAYOFFS]

* STOP THE VICIOUS SPEED UP

* IMPROVED COLA [COST OF LIVING ALLOWANCE] & ACROSS THE BOARD WAGE INCREASE

* DEFEND VOLUNTARY OVERTIME

* DEFEND THE RIGHT TO STRIKE—NO BINDING ARBITRATION

* NO ATTACKS ON THE STEWARD RATIO

Unusually, AMC's contract was set to expire congruently with those of the Big Three. As our agreement included vastly superior contractual provisions, we faced perilous bargaining. As the smallest automaker, AMC would surely demand "parity," which for us spelled concessions.

Flipping the paradigm, Fight Back called on Big Three workers to fight for a contract like ours. We urged the AMC rank and file to hold the line, the way Local 75 (Milwaukee) and Local 72 (Kenosha) had held strong in the past.

In April, we were notified of a slowdown in production, with three employees slated to be cut from each section, almost one-third of each section's workforce. The work of those redundant employees was to be distributed to those of us remaining.

Bill Wolfgram worked on the other side of each car body. To compensate for the layoffs, we were issued new job assignments, allocating additional work. Despite explicit contract provision providing each employee three days to learn a new job, Luv jumped the gun and issued us verbal warnings for poor workmanship and failure to perform work assigned.

In our next car, Bill turned. "Hey, Melrod. How'd I get to be the lucky guy to draw you as a partner? No one gets a verbal on the second day of a new job assignment. I feel like you're the target and I'm fucked by default."

"Sorry, Wolfgram. Not much I can do. You're stuck with me, so we better do this right. I'm already on my second verbal since I got back. If you agree we got too much work, we best be on the same page, particularly if we're gonna ride the line."

"Let's do it."

As each of us exited the car, we let out simultaneous yells: "I want my steward!" And, with that, the rumpus commenced.

Luv covered us both with utility workers, as we sat in the lunchroom to wait for our steward; Seefeldt came strolling down the aisle.

"What's up, boys?"

"We need to file a standards grievance. There's way too much work on our jobs, and fucking Luv wrote us up on day two. We need our three days, and you gotta get the write-ups pulled."

"Let me try to work this out informally before you guys reduce it to writing."

"Okay, cool. But make sure you got my back. I just been on the street over a thousand days and feel like I'm being railroaded. You gotta put the brakes on this shit."

Luv stationed himself feet from my work area. Working at a normal pace, after fifteen or twenty minutes Wolfgram and I drifted past our workstation. Then we'd let work go to get back to our spot on the line.

Luv began keeping a log on me, as he just stood, silently scratching away on a pad. To add to the pressure, gaggles of supervisors clustered near our workstation. I felt like klieg lights were focused on our every move.

"Fuck, Wolfgram. It's tough holding this pace all day." I was truly exhausted since riding the line required total concentration to establish a normal pace and then not break the slowed rhythm.

After days of playing scribe, Luv took me off the line.

"Melrod, look at this list. You're fucking me. This is what you've missed over two days. Damn if you and Wolfgram aren't gaming me. I ain't gonna let you two make a fool of me!"

"Look, Luv, your little list is bullshit. Just ask Glen if I've missed all that work. [Glen was the next guy down the line.] If you guys don't cut this harassment, I'm headed pronto to the NLRB as you're violating the posting that instructs the company to refrain from interfering with me under the Labor Act. I'm calling your verbal warning and your log bullshit harassment."

"Get back on your job, Melrod. You're a pain in the damn ass."

I complained again to Seefeldt. "Look, Seefeldt, Wolfgram and I are doing the exact same job. They haven't been riding his ass. That's cool, but I'm getting set up. Luv's on my case big time."

Seefeldt, acknowledging he was out of his league, brought head steward Kojak into the dispute, and together they committed to taking the dispute to Luv's boss, Berger. Either Kojak took a strong stand, or my threat to run to the NLRB backed Luv off. On May 5 we were issued notice removing our verbal warnings, accompanied by new, more reasonable job assignments.

"Never a dull moment with you. Good job, Melrod."

"Thanks, Wolfgram."

The slogan "Get AMC Off Our Backs" tied our contract organizing to a contemporaneous political campaign. Before Nixon embroiled the country in the Watergate scandal, before being exposed as a conniving crook, he proclaimed 1976 the "Bicentennial Era," even dubbing Air Force One the "Spirit of '76."

For many across the country, July 4, 1976, offered a stark contrast with Nixon's jingoistic message. Official unemployment hovered above 8 percent, with real numbers reaching double digits. Many veterans, recently back from Vietnam, were suffering chronic unemployment. Many experienced the devastating health effects of exposure to Agent Orange (not yet recognized by the government as a legitimate medical issue), while others suffered from chronic PTSD. At the same time, people of color were up against racial injustice and ingrained institutional racism, extreme poverty, inferior schools, the so-called war on drugs, and neighborhoods cursed with crime.

In opposition to the hoopla and hyperbole of the official bicentennial, political activists countrywide planned to descend on Philadelphia to march in opposition. One such effort was initiated by the July 4 Coalition, which included Vietnam Veterans Against the War, Unemployed Workers Organizing Committee, Revolutionary Student Brigade, Revolutionary Communist Party, and other allied groups.

Fighting Times signed on to the July 4 Coalition and hit the AMC gates with a flyer:

We've Carried the Rich for 200 Years
Let's Get Them Off Our Backs!

These are crucial times for us at AMC. At this rate the SUB Fund [supplemental unemployment] will run bone dry by August or Sept. We are not responsible for the bosses' so-called hard times, and we refuse to pay for them. We demand—NO CUTOFFS IN SUB PAY!
1976—Millions walking the streets looking for jobs and still more shoved out the door while plants close down. Those still at work, worked to death, chained to the bosses' machinery. Our cities falling apart. Our schools, hospitals and firehouses shut down.... and the drums of another war beating louder. All this amidst lies of recovery and the fireworks celebration.

The caucus embraced the call to protest the bicentennial, wearing and selling T-shirts and buttons by the hundreds with the slogan "We've Carried the Rich for Two Hundred Years—Let's Get Them off Our Backs." It became cool to wear a T-shirt or button—establishing the wearer's identity as rebellious and antisystem.

I visited Bill Roby, still working in trim, to deliver a T-shirt. I glanced at his bookshelf and noticed *Das Kapital* by Karl Marx.

"Hey, Roby. What's up with *Das Kapital*?"

"When I got stateside from 'Nam, some brothers on the base had a political-type study group. We read part of *Das Kapital*, but I gotta be honest, bro, Marx is a hard dude to take in. I wish he'd been a little more to the point. But he's cool."

"Yeah, I've read a lot of Marxist writings, and you're right—it can be tough stuff. But what Marx writes about socialism makes a lot of sense when you compare it to capitalism."

Roby thought for a bit and then added, "Yeah, that's the political shit brothers on the base were talkin' 'bout. What's so good about a fucking system that treats Black people like shit and sends us to fight their fucked-up war? Our fight is right damn here! You hear me?"

"I hear ya, bro. I get fucking tired of the company running out their boogeyman shit about communism, trying to turn people against me."

Judging by the success of T-shirt and button sales, we generated a lot of support for the July 4 campaign. As only a few could make the trip to Philly, we brought the message home with a rally in front of the plant and a flyer, tying national issues to those we faced every day.

On the day of the rally, T-shirts and buttons dotted the lines. Hundreds of mostly young workers met in front of Valent's bar. Through the bullhorn, I called everyone together, chanting: "We've carried the rich for two hundred years! Let's get them off our backs!" Workers milling around during lunch wandered over.

I covered the basic injustices and inequalities plaguing American society as well as the upcoming contract:

> We at AMC will soon be confronted with a difficult choice: to make drastic contract concessions or face the company and international's threat of losing our jobs.
>
> Remember—when AMC paints the halls red, white, and blue, that is patriotism for their class of bosses, not for our class of workers. We cannot betray the founders of our union and allow the company to drive us down to the level of the Big Three.
>
> We head to Philly on July Fourth to take a stand with workers from all over the country who similarly are fighting to move forward and not allow the bosses to push us backward. It won't just be us in Philly but veterans from the Vietnam Veterans Against the War (VVAW) proclaiming "We Won't Fight Another Rich Man's War!" and

the Unemployed Workers Organizing Committee (UWOC) demanding "Jobs or Income Now."

Our flyer promised an open mic. A few guys jumped up to throw out words of complaint against AMC and the system. As twelve thirty approached, we all scurried toward the plant. After lunch, rally talk was widespread. Some agreed, others disagreed, but, regardless, anti-bicentennial talk was the trend.

I joined members of Local 75 on summer break, the time of model changeover. While workers were on vacation, AMC dropped a bomb, announcing one thousand layoffs.

Fighting Back pulled together a plan to fight the layoffs, refusing to passively accept AMC transferring production of the Gremlin model to the Kenosha plant.

Local 75 leadership fell deafeningly silent. We decided to take our struggle to the leaders' doorstep. About fifty rank-and-filers convened a picket line to protest the layoffs in front of the AMC employment offices, and from there we marched to the nearby Local 75 office to demand the convening of an emergency membership meeting.

No big surprise: we found empty offices, the board having decamped to UAW headquarters in Detroit. Days later, we again crashed the office, demanding a meeting with Local president Harold Templin. Sitting across from us, Templin refused to convene a membership meeting. "This executive board will not call a meeting because you few, who don't represent Local 75, want one."

I shot back, "While you hide in your air-conditioned offices, members are in an uproar about the transfer of the Gremlin. Just stop and look at what happens when the union cowers. First the sewing department got shipped out, next soft trim left, most recently the carpet department ran away to nonunion JP Stevens, and despite an overwhelming strike vote you didn't lift a finger to resist. Ten years ago, ten thousand Local 75 members worked here, five thousand worked four years ago, now we're down to twenty-four hundred while you sit and twiddle your thumbs. The damn plant is running away! Soon you'll see a vacant building." (It's now a Walmart.)

Templin, in a cowering state of compliance with AMC and the international, whimpered, "There's nothing for us to tell people at a membership meeting."

We knew our chances of blocking the move were minimal, but silent complicity was unacceptable.

We urged members to stand up:

Rally 12 Noon—We Demand Jobs from AMC

On July 3 while most of us were heading out on vacation, AMC snapped their fingers and tried to make 1000 jobs disappear....

[We say] to hell with the 1000 layoffs. We've got to organize to fight for our jobs and our survival.

In Sunday's newspaper it was announced that 393 of us will be eligible to transfer to Kenosha.... It's like swallowing poison in a sugar cube.... And we don't want to go bumping brothers in Kenosha out on the streets. We demand jobs from AMC for all of us.

Today at 12:00 noon on Richards St. we will be holding a rally to demand our jobs from AMC. We are calling on everyone to attend the union meeting at Serb Hall this afternoon to demand that Local 75 take up the fight against the layoffs.

Fighting Times and the United Workers Organization copublished the leaflet. A few rank-and-file caucuses at Milwaukee factories, such as A.O. Smith, Briggs and Stratton, Inland Steel, Master Lock, and Rexnord, had recently banded together in the citywide United Workers Organization (UWO). The UWO agreed to support us autoworkers, as the cutting of one thousand jobs at AMC epitomized the devastating loss of factory jobs all across Milwaukee.

The transfer of the Gremlin to Kenosha raised sharp divisions, pitting Milwaukee against Kenosha. While we advocated union solidarity, some Local 75 members adopted the attitude of "fuck Kenosha," and some in Kenosha Local 72 adopted the attitude of "fuck Milwaukee." The UAW should have striven to forge a bond in fighting for jobs for both locals, but the local leadership and the international handed the keys to the company, greenlighting AMC's divisiveness.

On Thursday, July 22, forty-seven adults and four children picketed the AMC employment office. The precise number comes from an internal AMC memo drafted by James Madden, supervisor in Labor Relations. (The memo was produced during an NLRB hearing.)

We picketed in a circle, effectively blocking the driveway into the employment office. "Stop the Layoffs" and "Stop the Runaway of 1,000 Jobs," our signs read. Unbeknown to us, AMC had hired a squad of Pinkerton security guards—antilabor goons with union-busting origins in the 1850s.

Per his memo, Madden had accompanied the Pinkertons as they filmed our picket line. The memo identified four picketers as AMC employees, all active with Fighting Times: two African American members, Willie Williams and Louina Allenn; one white guy with a thick Appalachian drawl, Phil Haney; and me.

Our press release succeeded in drawing a gaggle of reporters. All four local TV channels conducted interviews, allowing me to speak about our anger at having one thousand jobs ripped from under us.

In each interview I asked the same rhetorical question: "On this so-called bicentennial, what kind of rich man's system is it that considers workers disposable, to be discarded like so much used machinery? I'll answer: a class system under which the working class suffers at the hands of a class of wealthy bosses. We won't passively accept that inequity. We're here picketing today to put the system on notice: we're here to fight to save our livelihoods."

That night, many homes in Milwaukee tuned in to TV news devoting a significant segment to AMC's job dislocation. Our picket line may have been small, but our message reached tens of thousands.

Madden ordered me to disperse the "illegal" picket line, which I rudely declined to do. We crossed the street for a rally. Willie Williams and Phil Haney took the bullhorn to condemn the loss of jobs. James, a Black brother from the railroad union, delivered a message of solidarity.

The following Thursday, upon returning to work, we were officially notified that we had been laid off due to a "change in job location" and were instructed to report to Kenosha.

On the same day, the four of us who had been identified at the employment office were issued two-week disciplinary suspensions for "illegal picketing and interference with production."

We filed grievances to protest the suspensions. After reaching the fourth step, the local dropped our grievances, washing their hands of the matter and the thousand jobs.

But the suspensions directly contravened the NLRB's order on the terms of my reinstatement. Months later, under the headline "NLRB Rules against AM on Protest," the March 9, 1978, *Milwaukee Journal* reported: "The American Motors Corp. committed an unfair labor practice when it disciplined four workers in July 1976 for picketing in protest of the loss of 1000 jobs at the Milwaukee plant, a National Labor Relations Board law judge has ruled."

When AMC refused to implement the judge's order to withdraw the discipline and clear our records, the full NLRB reaffirmed the order.

Along with some 350 others, I followed the Gremlin to Kenosha.

CHAPTER 12

Hey, Kenosha, Here Comes Tribe Milwaukee

Transferring to Kenosha felt uncomfortably akin to the first day at a new school—new kids, new pecking order, new rules—you get the idea. Main Plant, where I was assigned, sprawled over 108 acres, surrounded by parking lots and bars, plenty of bars.

With a nagging knot in my stomach, I climbed the stairs to my new home department: 838—trim. There I found Kenosha workers huddled in clusters staring at Milwaukee people, while those from Milwaukee gathered and groused about the long drive, the rumored lousiness of the union (Local 72), and myriad complaints, real and imagined. I flinched at hearing divisive comments that we (Milwaukee) were surrounded by a bunch of "country bumpkins" and "hillbillies": Tribe Kenosha vs. Tribe Milwaukee. The place reeked of toxic divisiveness.

Local 72 played a memorable role in the creation of the United Auto Workers. The extract below is lifted from the draft thesis of a departed working-class comrade, Mike Braun from Appleton, Wisconsin. (Much of the information following that is based on Erik Gunn's *Born Fighting: 75 Years of Unionism: The History of United Auto Workers Local 72, 1935–2010.*)

> In 2008, [before the Kenosha plant closed], UAW Local 72 had been in existence seventy-five years, making it the oldest local in the UAW. On Nov. 9, 1933, workers in the Final Assembly Department at Nash Motors in Kenosha sat down on the job, refusing to work, refusing to leave the plant during their shift. The Nash workers were protesting the new piecework-based pay scheme averaging only thirty-five cents an hour and less than three dollars a day. The union had existed on paper for months, but the sit-down was the baptism by fire that eventually forced the company to recognize their bargaining rights. The significance of this event in Kenosha becomes clearer when you remember that the Great Flint Sit-Down against General Motors, which most historians

acknowledge as the turning point of the 1930's CIO organizing drive, occurred four years *after* the Kenosha sit-down. [Emphasis added]

Following the nation's first convention of autoworkers in … 1935[,] called by the AFL, the Kenosha union was rechartered as AFL-UAW Local 72. Local 72 was one of only sixty-five locals to send delegates to the founding of the UAW. Radicals played significant roles in the early years. The "Nash Worker," a clandestine shop paper put out by Communist Party members working in the Nash plant, first appeared in January 1932. Felix Olkives and other members of the Socialist Party from the Kenosha Trades and Labor Council are credited with getting the first Nash workers to sign up with the union.

In 1937 a new personnel director, Harry Beutlich, arrived at Nash, determined to curb the clout of the union and nullify "past practices." There was no written contract, and past practices established the rules by which management and the union coexisted, with many enhancing the local's shop-floor power while tying management's hands.

Beutlich instructed supervisors that chief stewards would no longer be permitted to leave their jobs on union business. When Paul Russo, a militant left-wing unionist and final assembly chief steward, left his workstation to take up a collection for a union member whose house had burned down, he was discharged.

The assembly department sat down to demand Russo's reinstatement. When word spread of the firing, the shop walked out. Soon sister locals in Racine and Milwaukee joined in solidarity. As Russo, who I had the opportunity to meet, recalled, "For three days not a wheel turned in the Milwaukee, Racine, and Kenosha plants." Powerless to resume production, the company relented, reinstating Russo and restoring the right of stewards to leave their jobs to represent union members.

Management again set out to terminate the strictures of past practices later that year. As reported in the *Kenosha Labor* newspaper, Beutlich wagged his finger at the Local 72 executive board, "We're going to take back the property of Nash-Kelvinator. You fellas have run it long enough." Beutlich issued instructions to block board members and stewards from leaving their jobs to handle grievances. He also unilaterally slashed wages.

Faced with entrenched company obstinance, accompanied by threats to move production, the local decided to negotiate a written agreement. When negotiations stalled, Local 72 struck.

NASH WORKER

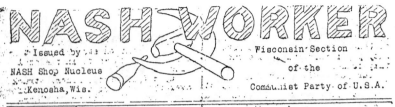

Issued by
NASH Shop Nucleus
Kenosha, Wis.

Wisconsin Section
of the
Communist Party of U.S.A.

Volume #1.   January 1.1932   Price 1¢.

THE NASH "XMAS PRESENT"

Christmas has just gone by and the Nash workers can now check up on what they have to be overjoyed about. Before the holidays the bosses,thru all their press,promised the return of prosperity and a happy time for all. WHAT DID WE GET? After working like slaves for Nash under the whip of wage-cuts and speed-up,to make $4,000,000 for the Co. in the first 9 months of 1931, we have been forced to take a wage-cut of 25 to 35% off from our starvation wages.

In former years Nash gave the workers an "Xmas present" of $10 to stop the kicking about low wages & other rotten conditions. But this year when 200 workers came to the office expecting to get a check,as usual,they were told to get out.The cost of the lousy basket of groceries that was given out amounts to $2.67 on the retail market. This is supposed to make up for the 4 wage-cuts we have received in the last 2 years;for the killing speed-up and the ill-treatment we have gotten. This is considered enough for the workers,by Nash who pockets nearly 6 millions of dollars himself,this year,made out of our sweat and blood.

Nash-Master Slave-driver.

Nash talks about poor business when the workers protest against low wages,but HE IS A LIAR! His methods of driving the workers and getting more profits are copied by other bosses of the U.S.,who recognize Nash as an artist at this game.

Gov't is a tool of Nash.

Those of us who voted for politicians,Republican,"Progressive" or "Socialist",can now see how badly we were fooled when we thought that

(over)

by voting for politicians we could change conditions. Today we see Nash,who cuts our wages,serving on La Follette's "Unemployment Committee" and in reality giving La-Follette orders on how to defend the profits of the rich and force the unemployed to starve.

Only struggle will help the workers who are starving. The workers will never better their conditions by trusting to politicians. Only by building up GRIEVANCE COMMITTEES in every dep't of the plant and fighting every attack that the boss makes upon us will we be able to resist starvation.

The workers of Nash must organize and fight in the Auto Workers Union,one of the unions of the revolutionary Trade Union Unity League. A union controlled by the rank and file of the workers,instead of bosses unions of the A.F. of L.

WORKERS OF NASH PLANT!
ORGANIZE GRIEVANCE COMMITTEES!
BUILD A LOCAL OF THE AUTO WORKERS
(UNION!
JOIN THE COMMUNIST PARTY!

The *Nash Worker*, a clandestine shop paper put out by Communist Party members in the Nash plant, first appeared in January 1932. The paper issued the call to "Build a Local of the Auto Workers Union" (precursor to the UAW).

Three thousand pickets covered plant gates for three weeks. Nash collapsed, signing the local's first written contract, described by Paul Russo as "one of the best ever signed in the automobile industry."

The new contract recognized Local 72 as the exclusive bargaining agent. The agreement established a grievance procedure and strengthened seniority rights for layoff and recall—a key provision since supervisors had previously relied on favoritism to determine layoffs. The agreement further provided that if workers were called in to work they would be paid a minimum of one and a half hours' pay for the day, as on many days workers sat idle, leaving work with zero compensation.

Fast forward. Again, from Mike Braun:

> The wildcats of the 1960's are evidence of Local 72's go-it-alone approach.... The wildcats [were] in defiance of [Walter] Reuther [international UAW president] because he opposed any strike activity between contracts in the UAW. In June 1965, there were two wildcat strikes within a week of each other, protesting American Motors management conducting numerous time-studies on jobs.... The week of Oct. 7–14, 1969, saw thirteen wildcats in Milwaukee and Kenosha. William Lundberg, the president of AMC, made a public plea to Walter Reuther to stop the wildcat strike[s]. Reuther was not very successful, and the New York Times concluded that the workers in Milwaukee and Kenosha "[had] been in not-so-quiet rebellion against the international union.

Because AMC production was so heavily concentrated in the Kenosha facility, Local 72 had the inordinate power to paralyze all manufacturing.

The Kenosha plant produced all engines and most metal body parts for AMC products, plus the bulk of auto assembly. While the concentration of production in a single facility allowed for high efficiency, it left AMC vulnerable to the union's militant exercise of its power.

My Department 838 job assignment, as in Milwaukee, was installing taillights, but now I used a large, heavy rivet gun. In my area there were few Milwaukee transplants, which suited me fine since I intended to integrate myself into the life of 838, disregarding where one lived, be it Kenosha or Milwaukee or somewhere else nearby.

Initially my life in trim bordered on schizophrenia. At break I'd hang with Milwaukee buddies, at lunch I'd head outside to eat at Madory's bar, where Kenosha workers hung out, and I thus went back and forth like a Ping-Pong ball. At first Milwaukee people felt betrayed, and they continued to rigidly self-segregate. But ever so slowly the dynamic shifted.

Determined to bridge the divide, I sought out longtime 838 chief steward Russ Gillette. Gillette had a reputation among Kenosha folks for being militant, but, as far as I could tell, that was ancient history. I figured, however, that if I got to know Gillette, it might open the door to meet the 838 stewards, arch advocates of Tribe Kenosha.

"Hey, Russ—been hearing a lot about ya."

"Good or bad?"

"Oh, good, for sure [a bit of a white lie]. My name is Jon Melrod. Wanted to introduce myself to you and your stewards."

"I know that name. You're the one who got fired for raisin' hell. Supervisors been talking 'bout you comin. They say you're gonna take over our union. They got their eyes on you. That's why they put you in Garrity's section. He's a ball-buster!"

"I ain't planning on taking over no union [*not right away*, I thought]. We're all part of Local 72. What's up with Garrity?"

"He's one bad-ass boss—100 percent company. He'll jump in and do our work whenever he's short on people, but I don't advise you write him up. He won't take kindly to it. My advice: watch yourself."

A tangential benefit of breaking the ice with Gillette: his stewards, fiercely loyal to him, began acknowledging me. Baby steps for sure, but steps nevertheless.

My other route to integrating myself required hanging out at the taverns across Fifty-Second Street: Freddie's and Madory's. Madory's was more welcoming and patronized by young and Black workers, who transformed the bar's neglected backyard into an outdoor dice parlor and social club. Black guys and a few Latinos hung out behind Madory's drinking pints out of paper bags. I became tight with the Madory's crew—Sloane, Jessie, Ernesto, Pedro, William, and Brown, all from Racine or Kenosha, and others, obliterating any vestige of a Kenosha versus Milwaukee vibe.

To fully acclimate, I needed to eliminate the geographic divide by moving closer to the plant. I relocated to a one-bedroom apartment in Racine, just twenty minutes from Main Plant.

Never far behind, my nemesis, the FBI, issued a tracking memo: "Jon Melrod . . . moved to Racine, WI. He is employed with American Motors in Kenosha, Wisconsin."

An earlier memo noted:

On October 6, 1976, the below-named individuals were observed in Kenosha, Wisconsin, where they distributed copies of "The Worker" newspaper and also distributed leaflets concerning the strike of the Ford Motor Co. in Detroit, Michigan, and auto workers' attempts to win themselves a decent auto contract during 1976:
[name redacted]
Jon Melrod
[name redacted]

John Drew had already laid a solid organizing foundation at the Kenosha plant. In 1975 John and a half dozen young workers from final assembly had launched the *Fighting Times* newsletter. The workers who planned, published, and distributed the newsletter also identified themselves as a caucus by the same name.

Another plant activist, Tod Ohnstad, published his own modest newsletter, *On the Line*. Tod, from Altoona, Wisconsin, had been an antiwar activist.

On the immediate horizon that summer was the 1976 auto contract. In preparation for the showdown, Fighting Times collaborated with the newly formed Auto Workers United to Fight in 76 (AWUF), a loose-knit alliance of auto worker caucuses, including members of several leftist groups, to forge a united rank-and-file strategy. (According to Mike Braun's research, around thirty or more leftist or left-leaning caucuses functioned in US auto plants during this period, both revolutionary and reform caucuses.)

We issued our first precontract flyer:

76 CONTRACT—TO HELL WITH AMC'S PROFITS/ORGANIZE TO FIGHT
In little over a month and a half the national auto contracts will be expiring for 700,000 UAW members....

It's no coincidence that the juggling of 1000 jobs from the Milwaukee Body plant [came] down right around contract time. AMC would like nothing better than to see Kenosha and Milwaukee autoworkers battling it out against each other for a few measly crumbs. This divide and conquer strategy is a perfect cover for them to move in and strip us of voluntary overtime, the right to strike, and our steward ratio of 1–35....

Auto Workers United to Fight in 76

The international designated Ford for the first round of talks and called a strike, largely over economic issues. The UAW's 163,000 workers shut down Ford's 102 plants in twenty-two states. Years earlier, the international had usurped bargaining from local control, conducting negotiations behind closed doors, relying on international staff and an army of lawyers. Commonly strikers didn't even know what the contract entailed until after the strike was settled.

At AMC, Local 72's executive board retained full power to negotiate, with the international relegated to a backseat, allowing the local much greater maneuvering room.

Like with "FIGHT SPEED UP" T-shirts, the company imposed a skirmish line around the wearing of "NO SELLOUT IN '76" shirts. Every time the company criticized the wearing of the shirts, more people donned them as a statement of rebellion.

Each of the three provisions AMC sought to take away in the 1976 negotiations had a long and storied tradition. The three fulcrum issues had become deeply etched in the DNA of AMC workers. The first was voluntary overtime. In 1969 AMC had brought to the bargaining table demands to take away hard-won historic gains. Rejecting takeaways, Local 72 struck. By the end of a twenty-six-day walkout—only the 1939 strike was longer—the union beat back concessions and *won key gains*, such as voluntary overtime.

The second issue was the 1:35 ratio of stewards to workers. Walter Reuther, UAW president from 1946 to 1970, eliminated the steward system at GM, Ford, and Chrysler, replacing it with a "committee person grievance procedure" that allowed for just one full-time committee person for every three hundred workers. Local 72 successfully defended one steward for every thirty-five workers, a chief steward in each department, and an assistant chief on second and third shifts. The chief and assistant chiefs were full-time (and company-paid), while stewards spent much of their workday engaged in union activity (company-paid) and otherwise on their regular jobs.

In 1976 the steward body consisted of close to three hundred foot soldiers, many quite tenacious in policing the contract, providing the local with powerful eyes and ears on the shop floor.

The third power the company sought to take away was the right to strike over grievances. Local 72 was vested with tremendous leverage due to the strike option as the final step of the grievance procedure. Reuther eliminated strikes over local grievances at GM, Ford, and Chrysler in the early 1950s, drastically diluting the rank and file's shop-floor power.

Over the protracted period of the 1976 negotiations, the international clamped a gag order on all information. While an educated membership makes for a strong, participatory, democratic union, denial of information allows union bureaucrats to control a quiescent, perpetually dissatisfied rank and file.

In the lead-up to AMC's contract expiration, Fighting Times caucus meetings functioned as a center for exchange of information on developments in the Big Three and the likely impact on our negotiations. Our relationship with AWUF provided us with a national information network.

Once Ford settled, despite widespread opposition, *Fighting Times* summed up relevant lessons: "The Ford strikers were on the bricks for 4 weeks and the International managed by hook and by crook to railroad a sell-out settlement down their throats. Some of the losses included: more forced overtime, a SUB pay cut of $5 a week, a loss of $109 in our COLA [cost of living allowance, and]... less benefits for employees with under 1 year seniority."

The only way the international managed to sell the contract was to keep the details secret and rig the vote in many places. Nevertheless, the highest number of production workers in history, 40 percent, voted for rejection.

The Ford pattern raised an alarm. It didn't portend well for AMC.

In one of our larger caucus meetings, we discussed how battle lines were being drawn. Auto companies, claiming hard economic times, had set out to shift financial burden onto their workforce, with the international green-lighting extensive concessions.

Our Contract Bulletin rang the alarm:

WAGE FREEZE NO WAY!

In the first week of January, AMC made its contract offer to its over 10,000 workers in Milw., Kenosha, and Brampton Ontario. The offer was a total freeze on wages and benefits for one full year....

We've already given AMC a 97% strike authorization vote. We can not and will not accept any wage freeze.

At a critical time when the local union board should have been educating about upcoming contract issues and organizing resistance to the proposed wage freeze, their presence was scarce. Fighting Times, still a small core of activists, wielded a megaphone at the gates with our Contract Bulletins.

Mass distribution of flyers evolved into an effective organizing tool. With well over a dozen gates, and many departments running two shifts, the handing out of forty-five hundred to five thousand newsletters or flyers required group participation. As I had primary responsibility for two high-traffic gates through which workers in paint (837), trim (838), and metal (836) departments entered the plant, I pulled together a fluid team of fifteen to twenty workers to assist.

While our team skewed young, it well represented the gender and ethnic makeup of the workforce. I say "fluid" since individuals varied: some helped for fifteen or twenty minutes, others merely stopped to chat (rendering distribution a social event), while still others shouldered the responsibility as a serious commitment, ensuring that *everyone* going in or coming out received a flyer.

Few openly criticized us at the gates. At contract time, virtually everyone hungered for information, and the caucus did our best to satiate that hunger.

One common denominator linked those active in distribution: a shared consciousness of being activists in a rank-and-file movement, standing in opposition to the international and local leadership's coziness with management. We were rebels.

The caucus itself was amorphous, as was the commitment level of participants. Funds came from contributions, raffles in the shop, beer busts, and pool tournaments at local bars. Summer picnics were popular social gatherings, with Blacks cooking raccoon and Latinos cooking barbacoa (slow-cooked baby goat). Picnics, house parties, and other social events provided the social glue that created a strong solidarity among caucus members and other activists.

Being part of Fighting Times acquired a broad definition, which extended the caucus beyond core activists. Even meetings were fluid, often informal assemblies in a tavern, while at other times a sit-down session at a member's apartment to plan content for a newsletter.

The most formal meetings included distribution of an agenda and might include a political theme, such as "celebrating the role of women in the labor movement." We sometimes showed a film, like *Finally Got the News* (about the League of Revolutionary Black Workers in Detroit).

The caucus cultivated a balanced membership, with the percentage of Black, Latino, and women activists—about 35 percent Blacks, about 15 percent Latinos, and about 20–25 percent women—a bit higher than each group's composition in the plant.

To bridge racial divides and create class solidarity, Fighting Times sponsored numerous social events to bring disparate Local 72 members together. From left to right: John Neil, John Drew, and Jessie Sewell (all caucus members) clowning at a party at the author's house.

Aware that AMC's bargaining position was strengthened by a surplus of cars at dealers, we advocated limiting overtime.

CONTRACT ISSUE NO. 2
NO OVERTIME DURING LAYOFFS

In many departments people are being asked to [work overtime]. AMC is trying to turn out the greatest number of cars at contract time....

According to our contract... employees have the right... to decline overtime. For sure AMC wants to take this away in our '76 contract. They would love to be able to come down the lines and dictate to us how many hours we have to work. But there is no way that we will give an inch on the issue of voluntary overtime.

By joining together to use our rights now we can strengthen ourselves for the upcoming contract showdown. This is exactly what happened a couple of weeks ago in 836, 837, and 838... when they asked for Saturday overtime. All during the week 2nd shift in 838 had been refusing two hours over, and on Thursday so many people turned down Saturday that the company had to go around cancelling.

Not until December did AMC locals convene a third negotiating session. Acting on rank-and-file apprehension at being kept ignorant of proceedings, our caucus organized a car caravan to the site of negotiations in Milwaukee.

Conscious of being branded dual unionists (functioning as our own union), we decided to beat the UAW propaganda machine to the punch by inviting the Local 72 board and regional director Ray Majerus to attend our rally to "update us on progress."

The oafish Majerus took the bait, telling the press we did "not represent the majority view among union members." Reading it another way, Majerus might have said, "The UWO *does represent a minority* of the union members," a characterization acceptable to us. The key: recognition as an opposition within Local 72.

The *Kenosha News* reported, "About 10 carloads of Kenosha workers joined a caravan Saturday afternoon from the Allis Chalmers plant to the UAW headquarters.... [Organizer] John Melrod ... [said that] a representative of the UAW bargaining unit did not accept his invitation to attend the rally.... "We are fed up with speed-ups in production coming at the same time as layoffs.... [S]ettlements with Ford and other companies were unsatisfactory." Melrod acknowledged a claim by union officials that the rally was aimed at "spreading discontent" among workers, but said "our people are already discontented."

A headline in the next *Fighting Times* read: "76 Contract—Wage Freeze & Takeaways Stopped—BUT!" Though cryptic, the headline capsulized the outcome of the 1976 contract battle. Here's how we analyzed the 1976 agreement, in part:

> Although the final settlement stopped the threatened takeaways and wage freeze, the money we received added up to pocket change. The only ones happy about the situation were AMC and UAW Regional Director Ray Majerus who went on tv to say "I think it's a contract I can live with."...
>
> As bargaining reached the wire neither the union leaders nor the company dared to bring the freeze or the takeaways before the membership. [Nevertheless] we lost hundreds of dollars in retroactive pay, pension, and SUB payments....

Local 72 President [Ralph] Daum even came up with the lame rap for the membership, "We bargained like a responsible union that sacrifices for AMC." …

10,000 of us sacrificed a total of $3.2 million in retroactive pay, the top 37 AMC directors increased their salaries by a total of $2.5 million—a 26% increase. The company just about paid for the increase for 37 fat cats' salaries with our sweat and blood.

But the very fact that we did stop the freeze and the takeaways is a victory for the rank and file at AMC.

While the primary front in our 1976 contract had been beating back the wage freeze and other takeaways, we achieved a breakthrough: that open jobs *be posted* and be *awarded by seniority*.

At membership and steward meetings, anger over racial discrimination and cronyism over job assignments had been a consistent point of contention. The bubbling up of anger from the shop floor had forced the issue into negotiations.

The new posting system constituted a solid victory over the use of race and favoritism. The victory was particularly significant since *no such system* existed in the Big Three.

Dissatisfaction with the 1976 contract provided a receptive audience for a *Fighting Times* broadside on our spineless local president. *Fighting Times* juxtaposed his words urging members to sacrifice with his actions racking up overtime hours.

RALPH "UNCLE TOM" DAUM CALLS FOR *SACRIFICE*

In an attempt to persuade us to accept the '76 rip-off contract, Ralph Daum, President of Local 72, called for sacrifice to "help bail AMC out of hard times." [Daum] tightened his belt so tight last year that between June 29, 1975, and Dec. 18, 1976, he pocketed 1400 hours in overtime just on Saturday, Sundays and holidays alone!!! His $9000 in overtime came to thousands more than many of our laid-off brothers and sisters made during the entire year.

CHAPTER 13

The Slow Climb to Union Leadership

Notice went up announcing the yearly steward elections in October. I signed up to run in a field of twenty.

I spent every day circulating, introducing myself to anyone with an outstretched hand to shake or an ear to bend. Many Kenoshans, I learned, knew who I was from the rumor mill that had churned before and after Milwaukeeans' arrival. Many were skeptical of voting for a guy from Milwaukee; distrust still ran deep.

On election day, I drove three Kenosha guys to union headquarters, calculating that at least I had four votes.

After the vote count, I peered over the crowd, straining to find my name on the list. My eyes fixed on the black X's next to the names of seven newly elected stewards. I spotted my name at the very bottom with a mere *three* votes! What the fuck?—one of the guys I had driven to the polls hadn't even voted for me! I had rarely felt so ostracized.

During assembly-line monotony, I had an abundance of time to ruminate and analyze. True, all of the winning candidates were Kenoshans, folks in Gillette's orbit. Still, I thought, over the past months I had been a constant fixture at the gates handing out flyers and selling the *Worker*.

Handing out literature disparaging living and working conditions under the capitalist profit-driven system pegged me as a political radical but not necessarily as a union militant. Criticizing capitalism and corrupt union leaders was easy but didn't sufficiently earn people's trust to represent them in daily confrontations with management.

By shift's end, I had come to terms with my embarrassing loss. I promised myself I'd dig in to demonstrate that I had the guts to stand up to management and the capabilities to represent 838 members in the day-to-day disputes that define life on the line.

Of course, I knew that my political views were a negative for some of my coworkers. When Mao Tse-Tung died, the *Worker* ran an article discussing socialism in the People's Republic of China (as socialism still existed in China at that time). As I had every month, I hawked the paper at the two gates to Building 40, selling around fifty copies.

After work, I stopped at Madore's. Suddenly I felt something hard jutting into my side. I looked down to see the barrel of a .38 revolver. A voice pierced my shock, "I'm Deadeye DiMarino, motherfucker. I'm a member of the National Socialist White People's Party, and I'd like to blow away your fucking ass—you commie Jew."

"Hey, Deadeye—hold up. Let me buy you a shot before bad shit goes down. Hey, Madore! Yo, Jim. Two shots of VO."

Deadeye remained frozen, his pistol remaining steady, as we perched on our bar stools. I kept thinking, *How the fuck do I get out of this shitty-ass situation? It's doubtful he's gonna shoot me right here, so I gotta convince him we've got shit in common. But—he's a goddamn Nazi!"*

Jim slid shots of VO across the worn wooden bar. Nobody seemed to notice that I had a gun sticking in my stomach.

"Hey, Deadeye, what department you in?"

"842."

"You guys got union issues going down?"

"Yeah."

"Hey, drink up. The next one's on me. Yo, Madore! Double shots and two PBR drafts."

"Look, Deadeye," I continued. "I'm not sure what you heard about me, but I'm all about the union and Local 72. We got that in common, right?"

"Yeah, guess so, but ain't you a fuckin' commie?"

"Look, bro. We all got different ways of looking at shit politically. But we got a lot more in common. I know the company's been cutting jobs in 842—ain't that right? *Fighting Times* been writing 'bout shit going down in 842. You been reading it?"

"Yeah. My beef ain't with *Fighting Times* or shit you do in the union. I told you, I'm in the National Socialist White People's Party, and I hear bad talk about your politics."

"Hey, Madore, how about two more shots and PBRs to chase 'em. I got 'em covered."

By now, both of us were slurring our words, barely balancing on our bar stools.

"Look, Deadeye—a lot of people talk about me. They talk shit about you. I heard your name before, and that's cool. We each bust ass across the street, and we both depend on the Motors for our jobs. I'm all about keeping those jobs here in Kenosha and sticking up for my union brothers and sisters. You with me on that?"

"Yeah, Melrod—I hear that. Maybe you ain't so fucking bad. We're both down with the union, so maybe that makes us okay. Damn—I'm getting hammered."

A couple of shots later, a shit-faced Deadeye was telling me he loved me as a union brother. Finally, we both slid off our stools and wobbled out the back door.

In late 1977 sentiment had been steadily percolating in opposition to Ralph Daum. Daum had been elected the local president in 1967 as a "hard-nosed" negotiator and firm upholder of the grievance procedure. He had ridden that reputation while steadily creeping into the company's bed and also becoming beholden to the international.

To give expression to shop-floor sentiment, we solicited letters about Daum's arrogance, autocratic style, and corruption. One such letter, printed in *Fighting Times*, reported on Daum's attendance record at important meetings:

> Ralph Daum's attendance record of emergency grievance meetings from Feb. 2, 1977, through May 25, 1977, [during which] there were 46 emergency grievances. Daum attended 5 and missed 41!
>
> Regular meetings with management January 3, 1977, through June 3, 1977, [during which] there were 43. Daum attended 8 and missed 35!
>
> Regular board meetings February 17, 1977, through June 7, 1977, totaled 20. Daum attended 7 and missed 13!
>
> Meetings with the company on our local working agreement in September of 1977—Daum never attended one!

Meanwhile, management launched an assault on the union stronghold in the Motor Division. The shop grapevine blew up with news that 817 piston department chief steward Charlie Underwood had been discharged for sabotage.

For as long as anyone could recall, 817 chief stewards and stewards had dominated the shop floor. The union controlled the pace of work and the scheduling of overtime, and it exercised strict contract enforcement. During Charlie's eighteen consecutive years as chief, he had *never permitted* a discharge to stick.

For the caucus, the Motor Division constituted foreign turf, populated by high-seniority workers with skilled machining jobs. Rallying behind Charlie offered the opportunity to extend the reach of Fighting Times as well as to crusade for militant union principles.

AMC laid off the third shift in 817 and cut four jobs. Workers pushed back, refusing overtime. Underwood's firing, based on him declining to repair a machine, was clearly retribution.

Fighting Times issued a plant-wide flyer.

Stop AMC'S Speedup
Rehire Underwood/ Fight for Every Job

On April 7th AMC fired Dept. 817 Chief Steward Charlie Underwood on a b.s. charge of sabotage. Charles Underwood was fired because the men in his department were standing up to the company's policy of throwing a whole third shift out the door, plus four jobs on first and second, and then trying to force first and second to work over-time. 7 IE [industrial engineers] were crawling through 817 at one time. When 49 out of 50 in 817 turned down 10 hours on Sat. and Sun., sticking up for their union brothers' jobs, AMC retaliated by firing [Charlie]....

At 5:20 [on April 2] machine #11651 broke down and Underwood was told to fix it. [S]eeing that it was more than a 10-minute job and he was going home at 5:30—Underwood punched out.

For decades, wildcatting had been 817's remedy of choice, rather than waiting on the cumbersome grievance procedure. This time, however, one of Local 72's most militant and trusted members, Rudy Kuzel, counseled against a wildcat, fearing that repercussions would outweigh the efficacy of a noncontractual job action. Kuzel feared that under the feckless, if not traitorous, leadership of Daum, those participating in a work stoppage would be hung out to dry.

Only Rudy—a nineteen-year veteran of the Engine Plant and 817, a steward, a ten-year veteran of the executive board, and a long-term union militant feared by the company, the local leaders, and the international—possessed the prestige and respect to hold 817 back from shutting down. Rudy's reputation was such that Engine Plant workers knew he would *never* allow Charlie's discharge to stick.

Caucus members hit every gate:

STOP THE ATTACK ON THE UNION
REHIRE CHARLES UNDERWOOD!

At this Saturday's union meeting *we demand that brother Underwood be brought back into the shop immediately!!*

The membership meeting turned into a standing-room-only event. Speaker after speaker lined up to blast Daum's ineffective efforts to win Charlie's reinstatement.

When Rudy rose to speak, a hush fell over the packed hall. Wearing his standard blue nylon UAW Local 72 jacket and sporting a buzz cut, Rudy began speaking, his voice a booming, gravelly baritone affected by years of chain-smoking unfiltered cigarettes:

> Brothers and sisters—the part that Charlie supposedly sabotaged cost $9.37 and takes just a few minutes to replace. The company doesn't even claim to have any actual proof, only their opinion, for what that's worth, that Brother Underwood is guilty of alleged sabotage. I don't believe it, and you don't believe it.
>
> Brother Underwood must be brought back with full pay, no disciplinary conditions, or we demand whatever action necessary to win reinstatement. This local has always protected our own! Brother Underwood is willing to submit to a lie-detector test that will settle this matter in Charlie's favor.

No one had anticipated Rudy's offer for Charlie to undergo a lie detector. Rudy played three-dimensional chess with outstanding success. (Charlie's defense marked Rudy's return to activism after a decade's hiatus. His "hibernation," he later told researcher Mike Braun, was based on his disdain for Daum's "dictatorial" treatment of the membership and coziness with management.)

Following Rudy's address, the hall burst into wild cheers, affirming willingness to sacrifice paychecks to save a union brother's job.

The minute Daum gaveled the meeting to a close, John Drew, Tod Ohnstad, and I weaved through the crowded hall to approach Rudy.

"Rudy, we're the guys from Fighting Times, and we want you to know that we support you and Charlie 100 percent. What can we do?"

There was silence, and we waited a bit nervously. Rudy was a novel breed of unionist: an unimposing, middle-aged white guy who single-handedly wielded the power to shut the plant and had repeatedly demonstrated the guts to make it happen.

"Charlie and I appreciate you boys' support. Why not come by my house, and we'll talk."

Not long afterward, John Drew and I headed to Racine to meet Rudy. Years later, when Mike Braun interviewed him, Rudy recounted what he remembered saying to us: "You guys are doing a good job, but you need to drop your outsider posture and jump headlong into Local 72 activity and run for union office, convention delegate, and appointed union committee positions. Take yourselves seriously."

Rudy told Braun: "The guys from Fighting Times were smart, energetic, and honest.... Too many people in unions are motivated by personal gain, like getting an easy job. But not these guys.... They came into Local 72 like a fresh wind. *They helped save it.*"

When the membership convened for a strike vote, the hall overflowed and cracked with defiance. Ten grievances were on the floor, and the most important demanded reinstatement of Charlie.

Ninety-seven percent voted to strike—a powerful demonstration of solidarity and an overwhelming rebuff of Daum's class-collaborationist leadership and AMC's assault on the union. Not long thereafter, Charlie was reinstated. The lie detector test turned up clean, and allegations of sabotage dissipated.

Like in much of industrial America, a chasm existed between the maintenance department and production workers, maintenance being populated mostly by "privileged" white skilled and semiskilled workers. A priority of the caucus was to bridge that divide.

When I heard about a dustup in maintenance between a boss and a steward, with the steward being discharged, I found a source in maintenance to give me a rundown. I then reported in *Fighting Times*:

Maintenance Wins
AMC bit off more than they could chew when they tried to fire a maintenance steward. [A boss] named Zapparoni told an 861 [maintenance department] steward to get out of his area.... When the steward continued to carry on his union business Zapparoni accused him of pushing and fired him.... But... 12 witnesses said the steward had not touched the boss.

The next day from 9:30 am through second shift till 12:30 [the next morning] maintenance sat tight.

[Management was] running around the plant like chickens without heads trying to keep production running.... Some production workers in 836, 837, and 838 [assembly departments] showed solidarity with maintenance when they filed lists of grievances.... Not only did the company agree to drop any penalty on the steward but [it is also] studying whether to discipline Zapparoni.

After the article ran, I noticed maintenance workers reading the *Fighting Times* and nodding at me as they walked by.

A foundational premise of the caucus's commitment to fighting for fairness and equity was to squarely take on racism in *whatever form* it manifested itself. There was certainly no shortage of discriminatory acts to bring to members' attention as well as issue a call to action whenever possible.

In late 1977, for instance, *Fighting Times* recapped a story in which a Black worker asked for a pass to go home due to illness. His boss refused, spouting degrading racial slurs. *Fighting Times* reported, under the headline "No Boys Work Here":

The [supervisor]... had to show off his ignorance and prejudices... by getting in the Black brother's face and calling him a boy....

Trying to divide us doesn't do any of us any good and only gives the company an opening to deny all us workers our rights. We don't have to take these kinds of insults from anyone, no matter how white [their] shirt is.

Caucus members' discussions frequently revolved around the broader implications of racism, including workplace racism but going well beyond that. Fighting Times positioned itself to struggle against racial intolerance and white privilege both inside and outside the shop.

In 1978, Fighting Times signed on to support the freedom struggle led by the United League of Mississippi and its leader Skip Robinson. Billy Drew, editor of the *Worker*, traveled to Tupelo to scope things out. Billy reported that the United League had come into existence during a resurgence of the KKK. Through the league's leadership, Black communities of northern Mississippi had initiated struggles to protest police beatings, organized citywide boycotts to demand more Black employment, prevented land grabs of Black-owned property, promoted armed self-defense, and sought to elect Black people to political office.

In Tupelo, the league had initiated a boycott of white-owned businesses that refused to hire Blacks and targeted the brutality of local police and their KKK allies. On a Labor Day weekend, caucus members John Drew, Kenny Williamson, Wincy Roman, Earline Henderson, Sam Hanna, and I boarded a packed bus heading to Tupelo.

It is noteworthy that Kenny, Wincy, and Sam were all Vietnam vets of color. Kenny had grown up not far from Tupelo, and I remember him telling me how he'd had to move aside when whites approached on the sidewalk. Earlean, also from the South, recounted similar incidents of overt racism while growing up.

Kenny, Wincy and Sam all returned from Vietnam believing that the system had used them as cannon fodder. All were pro-union, pro–Fighting Times, and militant in the shop and in broader political struggles against white supremacy and for justice.

When rundown shacks, rusting cars on cinder blocks, and streets without sidewalks appeared along the road, I was transfixed by obvious regional distinctions, most indicating widespread poverty and lack of basic infrastructure. Finally our bus came to a stop in Tupelo, and my eyes fixed on a disturbing sight: a line of fully decked-out Klan members.

Twelve Klansmen were lined up in front of the Tupelo Police Department headquarters, from which they had just exited. Cops were the KKK, and the KKK comprised the cops.

All wore perfectly starched white robes with pointed hoods. While robes and hoods intimidated, the heavy-duty axe handles they displayed looked dangerous.

I worried and wondered. *How the hell are we gonna protect ourselves if the Klan and cops whip out their pistols or start whaling on us with their shiny new axe handles? It's not like we can dial 911! "Hello operator, can you send help? The Klan is kicking our northern asses. Oh, and by the way, we're the contingent from Wisconsin with Blacks and Puerto Ricans with big Afros, brownish Latinos, and, yes, I'm white and Jewish. I just talk kinda funny."*

Our march of hundreds fell in behind a beat-up pickup. In its bed lay an arsenal of shotguns and semi-automatic long guns. Many of the intrepid young brothers leading the march were vets and not intimidated by armed white racists. If the Klan were to start shooting, I felt confident that United League marshals were well equipped for self-defense.

Formation of bedecked Klansmen carrying axe handles marched out of the *Tupelo Police Department*. The police *were* the KKK and the KKK *were* the police.

Lining the route were clusters of angry whites waving Confederate flags, faces contorted with rage, voices spewing hate. But, as we marched, I felt the enthusiasm and energy of our multiracial, multi-ethnic crowd surge. We had solidarity, a bond of shared purpose and righteous struggle.

When we boarded the bus for the long ride home, we all breathed a sigh of relief. *Fighting Times* reported:

From Miss. to Wis.—Fight Discrimination

On Labor Day weekend a few of us from Local 72 joined a freedom march of 100's in Tupelo, Miss. Black people there have been standing up, marching and demanding to be treated like human beings.

The struggle has grown into a full blown movement against discrimination, focusing around the fight for jobs. A 90% effective Black boycott has been organized for 4 months against city businesses.

The unemployment rate of Blacks is twice that of Whites, and income is only $4365 a year, almost half the lousy $7706 income for Whites. It is these divisions and poverty conditions that [help] keep the South a racist, nonunion, low-wage runaway haven for big businesses.

Practically everyone in the shop knew the degree to which we prioritized the struggle against racism and how far we were willing to travel to take a stand, even to square off with the infamous white-robed KKK.

The caucus tried to demonstrate AMC workers' commonality with other workers through two more events that year: May Day and food delivery to striking coal miners in southern Illinois.

Calls in *Fighting Times* to join the May Day march in Milwaukee opened the door to seriously engaging political discussions. We sought to explain what the day stood for in 1970s America, which was *not* tanks and missiles in Red Square.

We explained that the holiday originated in the United States in the 1890s over the fight for the eight-hour workday. More recently, the US capitalist class had sought to demonize the holiday, but it was still celebrated worldwide as International Workers Day.

In *Fighting Times*, we linked May Day to local struggles:

Why We March on May Day

The American Dream isn't what it used to be. The Brass workers [a local Kenosha plant] had to walk the picket lines for 6 months to win a few cents. If you have 5 years or 25 years, working at Lakefront or on the Big Line [in the Main Plant] is like holding a part time job, where you just barely qualify for vacation pay [as a result of the shortened work schedule due to lack of orders].

May Day is the day working people take a stand against these abuses.

To put May Day in perspective.... We found clippings from 1936 about a May Day rally...in Kenosha. 600 workers came out to march on the 50th anniversary of the fight for the 8-hour day and to hear a

Annual May Day march through the streets of Milwaukee (author on left with clenched fist raised). Behind the author to the right in glasses is comrade Billy Drew, who departed this world early after a valiant battle against pancreatic cancer. Holding the banner to the author's left is comrade Mike Braun, who died suddenly and prematurely from a heart attack.

socialist speaker talk about the workers struggles of that time. The Kenosha Trades and Labor Council sponsored that event.

In the same newsletter, we advocated working-class solidarity with a strike in the coalfields:

A few weeks ago a group of 10 Local 72 members travelled to southern Illinois to bring our solidarity and a trailer load of food to striking coal miners. The miners set us straight on what the main issues were. It wasn't so much wages they were fighting for, but the right to strike, improved pensions and guaranteed insurance.

For all of us meeting—Black, white and Chicano autoworkers from Wisconsin and coal miners from Southern Illinois—it was a hell of an experience.... We got the feeling that there was nothing that could stop workers when they are united.

Support for the 1977–78 coal miners' 110-day strike garnered widespread support at frequent political demonstrations in Milwaukee.

The miners wanted to let every Local 72 member who bought a [support] button or gave a donation know that they appreciated our solidarity.

The 1977–78 national coal strike lasted 110 days, so hauling food to southern Illinois aided day-to-day survival for strikers. Prior to our solidarity mission, caucus members sold hundreds of buttons supporting the strike to raise funds for the food.

May Day marches and trips to Tupelo and southern Illinois were important to convey that the caucus was fighting a broader political battle than Local 72 versus AMC. We sought to elevate the consciousness of caucus members and to get them to consider themselves not only union militants but also class-conscious radicals, part of a broader struggle beyond Kenosha.

CHAPTER 14

Contract of 1978 Draws Battle Lines

After the 1976 contract ratification, dissatisfaction with Ralph Daum's local presidency boiled over. His reputation for cutting the mic at meetings to silence dissent, his threats to remove committee members if they didn't vote his way, a scandal over the purchase of candy for a holiday event, and his deplorable attendance at grievance meetings all were seen as trampling on union democracy and transparency.

Everyone in the caucus wanted Daum out. How could we be confident, however, that another "leader" who promised reform wouldn't tomorrow morph into a new Daum?

Fighting Times introduced a contender for Daum's position, Gene Sylvester, who had served as recording secretary. As far as I could tell, he had done little to distinguish himself. Rudy, however, had positioned himself squarely in Sylvester's camp, being the brains behind Sylvester's "reform" campaign.

Our article introducing Sylvester sought to balance competing interests: empowering the rank and file while electing a local president who would respect the will of the membership.

Sylvester Challenges Daum

A couple hundred people who want change showed up to hear what Sylvester had to say [when he launched his campaign to unseat Daum].

A lot of people in the shop want to vote against Daum. What is needed is real change not just a different face.

The program that Sylvester put out began to touch on some of the things we need. Like—maintaining the steward ratio, improvements in pension... and more democracy in the union. Above all we need a united and fighting union, not a begging one.

Sylvester's campaign presented an opportunity. With the contract set to expire in months, we were well positioned to force Sylvester into a militant posture and explicit commitments.

John Drew, Tod Ohnstad, and I met with Rudy in the run-up to the election. Rudy encouraged our support as well as making clear that a Sylvester administration would include militants, regardless of politics.

Despite Daum's efforts to enforce discipline on his network of patronage positions, the tide of history swept over him. Sylvester's promises to wage a militant contract struggle, as well as to restore transparency and democracy, delivered Daum a lopsided defeat.

Daum's defeat set the stage for a drastic realignment of power, providing an opening for John, Tod, and me to become part of the local's structure without compromising our politics or principles or our independence to publish *Fighting Times*.

The 1978 contract expiration on September 16 rapidly approached. The opening skirmish had jumped off in May in response to an announcement that the line speed would be jacked up by eleven cars a shift, an additional one and a half bodies an hour. An increase in production signaled the stockpiling of cars to strengthen the company's hand in bargaining.

We stood at the gates and handed out flyers promoting resistance to the speedup.

11 CARS A SHIFT—MORE $$$ FOR AMC

The line speed is increasing by 11 cars a shift.... We heard a lot of b.s. last week about 75 people being called back. But the fact is that most of them are covering sick leaves and the jobs of 28 people who retired in April.

We printed a list of actions to build resistance:

1. See your steward—demand [that they] check your [job] assignment.
2. Work at a normal pace—file a production standard grievance.
3. Stick together. Back each other up.

And we made our points clear in advocating for a good contract:

Improve working conditions:
- I.E. [industrial engineers] off our back
- Stop contract violations
- Equality with the big 3

FIGHTING TIMES

PUBLISHED BY THE UNITED
WORKERS ORGANIZATION

RACINE - 632-6689
KENOSHA - 652-3759

LABOR DONATED

P.O. BOX 1571 RACINE

GOOD CONTRACT OR NO CONTRACT SEPT. 16

DO WE HAVE TO GIVE UP TO CATCH UP?

Over the last 2 years we've slid far behind the Big 3 in wages and benefits. At the same time, inflation and food prices have skyrocketed and our pockets are feeling the pinch.

Now with AMC in the black, many people are saying the '78 contract should be PAYBACK TIME! But some others are asking, if we catch up on the money, don't we have to give up on the working conditions—right to strike, steward ratio and voluntary overtime?

This isn't the first time we've been caught in this bind. In 1967 the union bought AMC's hard times pitch and gave up $1.25 an hour in wages and benefits. In 1969 it took the longest strike in Local 72 history to catch up to the Big 3!

In good times or bad times AMC calls on us to sacrifice our rights and benefits to keep the "little 4th competitive". Over the years AMC pleaded poverty and then turned around and

CONT. PAGE 3

Four to five thousand copies of *Fighting Times* were distributed by caucus members to two shifts at some fourteen gates. The caucus established the principle of not working without a contract—12:00 a.m., Sept. 16. Local 72 President Sylvester adopted the principle and during the 1980 wildcat pronounced, "Although the International has not sanctioned our strike, we hope the membership will follow our tradition of no contract—no work."

We urged that there be no contract extension past September 16 and noted:

> At the opening negotiating session in Detroit, [American Motors] once again pleaded poverty.
>
> Working conditions have deteriorated to the point that the company is trying to run like a nonunion shop[,] turning the contract into a book of blank pages. Getting an emergency break, time off, seeing a steward in a half hour, bidding on a good job, getting a fan, or winning a grievance—all too often are pipe dreams.
>
> In this year's contract we have no need for statements from company men like UAW Int'l rep Greathouse who said on tv that "AMC once again deserves a break."
>
> The very fact that the company is scheduling overtime like crazy shows that they want to build a big stockpile for Sept. 16.

John Drew, Tod, and I set out to revive a defunct Local 72 organization, the Stewards Club. Through discussions with veteran unionists, we learned of the prior existence of the Stewards Club, which had brought together militant stewards to develop bottom-up strategy.

With Charlie having returned as 817 chief and now a firm confederate, we set out to pitch him our idea of reviving the Stewards Club, hoping to parlay his support into issuing a call to reconstitute the club. Through our relationships with Charlie and Rudy we had bridged our youthful militancy with the more senior, veteran trade unionists in the Motor Division.

Charlie lived in Zion, Illinois, a small town south of Kenosha that had been a magnet for southern whites. Zion had a reputation as being culturally conservative and populated with a large community of devout white Christians as well as remnants of the KKK.

Jim Bashem, 837 chief and another southerner, also lived in Zion, as did my good friend and 837 steward Rich Hughes, who later replaced Bashem as chief. Rich and I regularly debated his Klan sympathies, and I would harshly condemn the KKK as white bigots responsible for the murder and lynching of Black people throughout US history.

Rich typically responded, "Melrod, you don't understand. The Klan are really a bunch of good ol' boys, kinda like the Dukes of Hazzard. Back home, the Klan is part of our heritage."

Years later, Rich and I collaborated as chief stewards of adjoining departments. We never settled our KKK disagreements; Rich took his beliefs to the grave. When he died, he lay in an open coffin in his best Sunday suit. On one lapel was a Local 72 union pin; on the other was Klan paraphernalia.

John Drew and I headed to Charlie's trailer park. Charlie opened the door with a big, toothy smile, his hair styled in an Elvis pompadour, with an oversized belt buckle holding up his jeans. "Come on in, boys. Glad you made it down my way."

Charlie signed on as the first chief steward. Armed with this commitment, we reached out to other active rank and filers, stewards, and chief stewards.

I approached 837 chief Bashem, up the line from 838. Bashem cut quite the distinctive figure, always sporting a three-day stubble (before it was hip), hair cut military short, seriously overweight, and disheveled. He spoke in a thick southern drawl and was always ornery. A hard-core, veteran militant, he had little time for young acolytes such as me who had yet to win a steward election. Persistence prevailed, however, and Bashem warmed.

I soon relished lunchtime chats with Bashem about his World War II exploits as well as his history in Local 72. Bashem had been imprisoned in a German POW camp. Always the intrepid leader, he had been delegated by other imprisoned GIs to orchestrate a nightly crawl under the barbed wire to go haggle with local farmers for a few potatoes. Bashem's nighttime runs provided vital supplements to near-starvation rations.

After dodging Nazi prison guards, taking on the paint department superintendent was easy. One lunch, Bashem recounted his toughest bargaining session with superintendent Eugene Caputo. Grievances had backed up. Caputo dug in his heels and refused to budge.

Bashem issued an ultimatum demanding a bargaining session. Otherwise, he threatened, "Not a minute more overtime gets scheduled. Fuck your production! My people are on my ass and won't stand for this crap."

A day later, Bashem walked up the metal stairs to the suspended glass office where grievance meetings were held. There he found Caputo, feet on his desk. Bashem opened his briefcase and took out two hefty stacks of grievances. He then reached into his briefcase and took out a handgun, setting it down on the table.

Caputo looked across the table and said, "I hope the fucking safety's on, Jim."

"Listen, Caputo, ain't neither of us leaving this room till every one of these grievances is settled or moved up to the board step. My people are chomping at the bit to shut the department down." Hours later, Bashem descended the steps with only a few unresolved grievances.

At lunch with Bashem, I pressed my luck. "Here, Jim, read this letter we wrote with Charlie Underwood. We want to pull the Stewards Club back together. We need an organization to organize folks and to push the board. What ya think?" Bashem signed on.

We wrote an open letter to the membership of Local 72:

Fellow AMC Workers:
A few years ago the Stewards Club helped get people united. For this September's contract we need a similar rank and file action caucus in order to circulate contract literature around the plant, keep people informed... and get communications going between... departments.

Twenty-two activist rank and filers, stewards, and chief stewards signed on.

Local 72 had a solid bench of Black union leaders, some of whom stepped forward to support the Stewards Club. Black leadership stemmed from the 1940s and '50s, when African Americans migrated from the South into the industrial heartland, places like North Chicago, Waukegan, and Racine.

Almost every Black hired by AMC worked in the company's segregated foundry, which turned into a fertile breeding ground for militant Black trade unionists. In the late 1950s, when the foundry was shuttered, Blacks bumped into other departments, bringing their militancy and leadership skills, often being elected as stewards and chief stewards.

Black trade unionists influenced Local 72's early participation in the national civil rights struggle. Local 72 spoke out for integration of public schools in the late 1950s. The local's Fair Employment Practices Committee sent a delegation to meet with the manager of the Kenosha Woolworth's to voice disapproval of the chain's segregated southern stores. That history on civil rights was part of the reason Local 72 won a Martin Luther King Jr. holiday before other unions.

Two of these notable Black unionists signed our open letter: Otis Wilson and Robert Fletcher. I vividly remember arriving at the Stewards Club meeting and seeing a distinguished, tam-wearing, dapperly dressed, quite emaciated, elderly Black brother resting on a walking cane. Meeting Robert "Fletch" Fletcher turned out to be a seminal life event for which I am forever grateful.

By the time I met Fletch, he suffered from advanced multiple sclerosis. His legs could barely support his upper body. I soon touched base with Fletch on an almost daily basis, either by phone or dropping by his house in Racine, to query him on how to better represent people. Fletch possessed enormous wisdom and welcomed the opportunity to thrash out complicated union issues, advising me on how militant I could and could not be—counseling me to push right up to the precipice but avoid getting fired.

Attending the meeting about reviving the Stewards Club were a respectable number of Local 72 activists comprising a rainbow of ethnicities and ages. I don't recall many details, but extending our reach beyond core Fighting Times activists constituted an organizational step forward and raised issues soon to become key to the 1978 contract.

The Stewards Club, however, did not take off. I learned that organizations and entities are born and evolve at specific times, propelled by historical and political conditions. Those conditions can't be replicated by wishful thinking. Regardless, the meeting linked us with new activists, stewards, and chief stewards, and overall we accomplished part of what we had hoped for.

The local board scheduled a strike vote. Based on input from the Stewards Club meeting and from sounding out sentiment in the shop, Fighting Times members gathered to stamp out hundreds of buttons: "GET I.E. OFF OUR BACKS—GOOD CONTRACT IN '78." These buttons would proliferate widely as focus turned to September 16.

We committed to do everything in our power to prevent a contract extension. The caucus printed hundreds of blue T-shirts emblazoned "NO CONTRACT—NO WORK." And we also produced another button: "ORGANIZE TO FIGHT—NO TAKEAWAYS OR EXTENSIONS." The caucus network sold shirts and buttons in far corners of the plant, and these were not identified as being from Fighting Times. The unifying message and absence of caucus branding achieved the intended result: the message was embraced by more than just caucus activists.

Suddenly, like a thunderbolt hurled by Zeus, a surprise player appeared. Word circulated that the nationalized French auto giant Renault might have interest in a collaborative venture with AMC.

Although we had just heard about Renault, the script was old.

As we wrote in *Fighting Times*:

French Blackmail?

Knowing that job security is about the number one concern for most AMC workers—Renault is trying a little old-fashioned blackmail.... According to rumors, conditions for a partnership include giving up such rights as voluntary overtime, right to strike (including at contract time), steward ratio, number of retirees, etc.... But the day when 10,000 of us [workers employed at multiple AMC facilities] will crawl on our knees is a long way off. If rumors of Renault's takeaways are for real—they better find another place to build their cars.

You may already have wondered: How did these Fighting Times people print tens of thousands of pages on a basement mimeo machine, hand-fold tens of thousands of eight- and twelve-page newsletters, and distribute them at some fourteen gates? How did they stamp thousands of buttons and silkscreen hundreds of T-shirts? How did they successfully solicit articles from so many departments in a plant running three shifts? I look back and ask myself those same questions.

At the inner core were three very committed, motivated, comradely activists with a high degree of dedication: John Drew, Tod Ohnstad, and me. Each of us held individual political views, but we shared a common vision of what needed to be accomplished in Local 72. Add we agreed that capitalism, the daily exploitation of the working class, needed to be replaced with something more equitable. Speaking for myself, that was socialism.

Around us were many concentric rings of folks with differing degrees of commitment. Some stamped buttons, others silk-screened T-shirts, folded flyers, handed out *Fighting Times* at the gates, raised money, put on parties, attended caucus meetings, organized picnics, attended union meetings, and solicited letters. Others struggled through writing letters and articles.

The caucus became increasingly organized. Jimmy Mithke, a Vietnam vet and a skilled electrician and carpenter, donated time to build light tables, facilitating layout of the newsletter and flyers. Dave Mattson, who worked two stations from me, turned out to be a prolific and witty cartoonist, capturing the everyday ironies and humor of factory life. To characterize Fighting Times as a rebel crusade would not be misleading.

By means of flyers, T-shirts, and buttons, we agitated for the precontract membership meeting to pass a motion restricting any contract extension. Our intent was that the plant would shut down at 12:01 a.m. without a ratified agreement. And the rank and file agreed. Our broadsheet reported: "With *only 1 vote against*[,] the rank and file passed a motion at [the] membership meeting ordering the executive board not to extend the contract past Sept. 16!"

Gratified by the vote, I walked through 838 after we handed out the "NO CONTRACT NO WORK" broadsheet. It looked like church: bowed heads intensely reading our summation of the union meeting. The floors were devoid of discarded paper.

As the clock ticked toward expiration, negotiations were shrouded by a veil of secrecy. Regardless, we were unrelenting in asserting the 12:01 a.m. deadline.

FRIDAY MIDNIGHT
No Contract—No Work!

With contract expiration only days away most of us have been kept in the dark as to what's actually happening.... We know that on Sept. 5 AMC rejected 60 out of 60 union proposals.... And we know AMC is serious about [its proposed] takeaways:

1. No right to strike over grievances

2. Mandatory overtime

3. Reduction in ratio of stewards to workers: one union rep... for each 250 people

4. No relief [workers]: By [stopping] the line at breaktime [rather than keeping it running with relief workers] the company could cut hundreds of relief [workers] off the workforce. [As doing relief work relieved the boredom of being on the same job every day, it was a coveted position, and this takeaway was quite unpopular.]

[The] fact is that we, the thousands of rank-and-file members of Local 72—not 15 board members <u>or</u> the International, decide what contract is acceptable.... <u>We are the ones who have the final vote on any proposed contract.</u>

NO EXTENSIONS

Friday midnight is it! Every minute past 12:01 only lets the company build up a stockpile. 8000 OF US UNITED AND STICKING TOGETHER IS WHAT AMC FEARS AND SEPT. 16 IS THE TIME TO PUT SOME FEAR INTO THEM!!

We had thrown down the gauntlet. Having focused a lot of my organizing in Building 40 (departments 836, 837, and 838), I felt confident that Fighting Times had chalked up enough credibility to trigger a midnight walkout.

Regardless, a walkout, particularly if unauthorized by union officials, is a precarious proposition. Supervisors would, without doubt, walk the lines threatening to fire those who left before the shift's end at 12:30. The key was to create enough disruption and chaos that management lost control and people felt empowered to walk off moving lines. Leaving the line a half hour before the end of the shift, in the face of a direct order to continue working, constituted a dischargeable offense.

On Friday, the last day of the old contract, electricity filled the air. When the buzzer rang for lunch, I rushed outside to meet John Drew and Tod, who both worked second shift. Caucus activists unfurled a large banner in front of the plant gate—"NO CONTRACT NO WORK 12:01"—as hundreds roared approval. On the bullhorn, I launched into chants of "12:01! 12:01! No contract, no work!"

I had persuaded Rich Hughes, 837 steward, to say a few words. He didn't say much, but he got the message across: "We gotta stop any takeaways. Both my parents been in this shop for years, and we've fought for everything we ever got. If we got nuttin' by 12:01—we shut it down!" Clenched fists shot up like geysers, hundreds in unison.

As the afternoon crawled by, all attention focused on midnight. The dam was cracking, and a midnight walkout appeared inevitable.

As we came out at our shift's end at 3:30 p.m., we greeted second shift: "Catch you at midnight." "Don't take no shit—shut it down." Our energy was contagious, with most second-shift workers responding enthusiastically, revved up themselves.

At 10:30 or 11:00 p.m., a large group gathered on Fifty-Second Street, and the crowd grew increasingly animated. At around 11:30 p.m., we unfurled the banner from the lunchtime rally and opened up on the bullhorn. Chants of "No contract, no work!" and "12:01! 12:01!" grew in volume, intended for those inside to hear. Just moments before midnight, our volume increased still more, as if our chants would pull folks out like a giant magnet if we were loud enough.

When the clock hit midnight, a momentary silence descended. I wondered whether second shift would have the temerity to shut the plant. Momentary gloom swept over me. Had we miscalculated?

Suddenly a few workers trickled out. Then the trickle turned into a steady flow, and we outside greeted second shift with cheers.

With workers having just disobeyed management, who had threatened discipline, the mood was defiant and at the same time festive. For at least that one night we had broken the chains that bound us to the assembly lines that ruled our daily lives.

Charged with energy (and fueled somewhat with alcohol), the crowd moved into Fifty-Second Street, blocking traffic. As the *Kenosha News* reported in the morning:

> Some trouble arose at the Kenosha plant, when the midnight dead-line passed and there was no word of a settlement.... About 200 AMC workers [a low estimate], who said they would not work without a contract, gathered right after midnight outside Gate 15....
>
> Police said the group had been drinking and became belliger-ent, throwing bottles and attempting to overturn an automobile. Police were forced to block off 52nd street... for about two hours to restore order. Police said that the crowd of AMC workers swelled to 350 [another lowball estimate] and refused to let cars pass, and that some had loudspeakers directing the others in the crowd [that was true]. About eight squad cars were called before it was over.

The *Kenosha News* also reported: "Tentative agreement on a two year contract [has been reached].... The new national contract is for two years, rather than the one-year length of the old contract. It is believed that the company sought the longer contract to enhance negotiations with Renault."

Local union leaders issued no statement regarding negotiations. Stepping in to fill the void, Local 72 rank-and-file members, stewards, and chief stewards made picket signs and coordinated assignments to ensure that there were pickets at all gates. Leaders were those who showed initi-ative, and there proved to be no scarcity of them.

The international withheld information about negotiations, as if knowledge and information were somehow dangerous. To fill the void, the caucus sought to provide as much news as we could garner. (While I no longer remember, it is a safe bet that Rudy fed us accurate information.)

Down in my hot, windowless basement, we hastily churned out a half-page flyer:

STRIKE BULLETIN 6:00 pm Saturday
We *are* out on strike! At 12:01 second shift showed AMC what NO CONTRACT—NO WORK means. As of 4:30 pm Sat. the report from negotiations was:

1. The Board has a tentative economic agreement that we have *not* yet voted on.
2. 60 grievances are still unresolved.
3. 22 working agreement proposals have *not* been settled.
4. [Management] working pay to the union member has not been settled.
5. IN ADDITION the company still wants a modified form of *mandatory overtime*.

Despite the news media and International rep Ray Majerus trying to pretend that we're not on strike—we are! We can't let the International dictate to us what a "sanctioned" strike is.

Caucus members and other activists drove to picket lines to disseminate the flyer, the only source of information. Picket lines held strong until 11:00 a.m. on Sunday, when word passed down that the board had ordered pickets to pull back. Still handicapped by a total lockdown of information, there ensued widespread grumbling about returning to work Monday without having voted.

Once again, we retired to my basement to produce a flyer, this one for Monday morning:

Good Friday / Blue Monday

At 12:01 Friday night second shift walked out and shut AMC down tight. Until 11:00 am Sunday pickets covered every gate.... Being ordered back to work without the membership first voting on a contract is bad unionism.

A ratification vote should *force* the company and their partners in the International to agree to a good contract *before* we go back in. Friday the membership, stewards, and chief stewards took it upon themselves to organize a walkout and set up picketing for the weekend, despite the blackout on negotiations by the Board.

We provided a summary of the tentative agreement—as many details on the economics as we had ferreted out—importantly including the company's withdrawal of demands on voluntary overtime, the right to strike, and reduction of the ratio of stewards to workers. Plus we learned that AMC had agreed that the punitive hour's pay for a supervisor caught performing union work would go to the person writing the grievance.

When ratification votes were tabulated, most agreed we had again beaten back takeaways, maintaining our contract superiority to the Big Three. We hadn't been bulldozed by Renault's threat of not entering a collaborative venture without major concessions. The agreement passed, though voted against by the usual 20 percent whose anger and disdain for the company trumped *any* agreement.

In a post-contract *Fighting Times*, we summed up:

> The '78 contract was an improvement over the last 2. If you don't believe that the people got the power[,] check out the settlements that were reached Sat. and Sun. after the walkout: all open jobs will be posted with no restrictions by the company, copy of [job] assignments with timing to the chief stewards, [supervisors] working paid to the employee [who writes the grievance], all jobs opened due to retirements, quits, discharges... will be posted, letters [signed] on leaving in the heat, the right to take vacation time off work, and limiting multiple codes.

While we attributed the gains to "people power" and said that "the fact that the membership had voted in some board members willing to stand up for the people was a plus."

We concluded: "Now that the balance of power in the shop is starting to shift in the people's direction, it's time for the membership and the board to force AMC to treat us like human beings. The people got the power—not a few white shirts and ties! PS: DON'T FORGET THAT BOUNTY HUNTING IS LEGAL AGAIN!" Bounty hunting, so called by radicals, provided that the individual who wrote a grievance demanding pay for a manager working would now receive the hours of pay on their weekly check—a "fuck you" gain that felt good to have secured.

CHAPTER 15

"Melrod Wears a Training Bra"

Our yearly May Day observance a few months earlier had been particularly relevant for AMC workers since it followed an April 12 announcement that all production would cease at the Milwaukee Body Plant. Workers with twenty, twenty-five, and twenty-eight years invested in AMC were to be cut loose.

The UWO scheduled our May Day march to kick off at the AMC employment office, with plans to carry a black-draped coffin with the words "AMC Body Plant." Although the company sent us a letter saying our use of their parking lot was not authorized and would "constitute trespassing," we declined to move the rally.

A couple hundred workers, unemployed folks, vets, and students gathered at AMC and held a defiant rally in the company's parking lot. In a dramatic gesture, we lined up behind the draped coffin and marched into the street chanting "Jobs or income now!" and "AMC says cutback, we say fight back!" in tribute to the generations who had passed through the doors of the plant.

Annual departmental elections were scheduled for mid-October in 1978. I felt confident and well-positioned for the steward elections. Importantly, I wasn't running alone. I had been active with several young workers, handing out *Fighting Times* at the gates to Building 40, circulating petitions, and strategizing how to motivate folks to become involved.

Four of us decided to run as an informal slate and assist each other in campaigning. Jimmy Graham, who had come to my defense in 1972 for selling the *Worker* back in Milwaukee, John Griffin, and Louie Volpentesta teamed up with me to challenge Russ Gillette and his cronies.

Never had Gillette faced an election challenge from a coordinated multiracial opposition. Steward elections in 838 rated low on most people's priority list, and the same uninspiring clique had run things the same way for years. Less than one-quarter of the department typically voted.

Adding two African American candidates, Jimmy and John, constituted the first challenge to the all-white Gillette steward body that had systematically ignored complaints of racism.

I hustled to visit everyone to solicit votes, around three hundred people. As I campaigned, moving from workstation to workstation, I explained how I thought the union should function at the departmental level—with more transparency, more militantly, and more inclusively—as well as taking up the vital issues of race and sex discrimination.

Seventy-three cast their ballot for me (out of one hundred who voted); I placed sixth, becoming a line steward. I had progressed from a mere three votes to just thirteen votes fewer than Gillette. Louie, John Griffin, and Graham lost but received twenty-seven, thirty, and thirty-five votes respectively, a decent showing for their first election.

Griffin's and Graham's vote totals in the thirties indicated that a block of Black workers had voted for the first time, upping the number of total voters casting ballots to one-third of the department. The 1978 vote turned out to be a harbinger of more transformative changes.

When Gillette presented my blue steward button, I felt deeply honored. I was stepping into the shoes of thousands of front-line stewards who had preceded me back to the 1930s, when our fledgling local had gone to the mat to secure the right to represent members. I intended to honor their memories and militant, take-no-shit tradition.

Honored or not, when I went to the bathroom soon after the election I experienced a taste of what I was in for. I sat down. Staring at me on the stall door in black grease pen someone had scribbled: "Melrod wears a training bra." At least that slur was creative. *I'd like to meet the author*, I thought. I'm sure I did, but no one dared cop to it.

One day I noticed Department 842 forklift truck drivers abandoning trucks, clogging aisles, and refusing to work. As line workers, we envied 842 as a world unto itself, as the jobs were off the perpetually moving assembly line that had most of us trapped all day, every day.

Mystery shrouded the process by which one got into 842. Rumor had it that 842 was controlled by the Italian clique in management, in collaboration with the Italian clique in the union. Bottom line—you had to be connected to break into the department; people of color and women rarely scored a job in it.

Prior to the stoppage, I had minimal contact with 842 drivers. At the gates, they often refused flyers. My impression was that 842 stewards had instructed their members to steer clear of us.

The stoppage offered a golden opportunity to learn more about the dynamics of 842 and maybe penetrate their insular bubble. I sought out drivers and their stewards to figure out what had gone down, then reported in *Fighting Times*:

842 Overheats

AMC lost another round with 842.... Union brothers in 842, along with their stewards ... let the company know that the people's safety is more important than AMC's profits.

One particular truck was known to be overheating 6 to 8 times a day. The driver had pulled over to put cold water in the hot radiator. As he loosened the cap his hands got burned by the steam. He dropped the cap and couldn't find it.

The foreman ordered him to lower the seat back over the radiator and drive with no cap on it. Sort of like sitting on Old Faithful.

This particular brother told the boss where to get off, as did the next man who was ordered to drive the truck. They were both suspended on the spot, as was the steward who backed them up....

The word started passing—"Either the company brings the 3 back ... or 842 walks. We've parked our trucks before and we'll do it again."

In a few minutes the 2 drivers were back on the job. The next morning the steward punched in and was back to filing grievances. In addition a truck had a gasket replaced in the record time of one night!

The article worked wonders for my relationship with Department 842 drivers and their stewards. More than a few drivers blew their horns in solidarity as they cruised by.

One of the most biting complaints about stewards was that many never followed up, often not pursuing complaints to resolution. With the right to get off the job at any time, there was no excuse for poor representation except laziness, being intimidated by management, or having been co-opted by the lure of time off the job and extra overtime.

I determined that none of those characterizations would ever apply to my representation. It became my practice to learn everyone's name and visit everyone in my section once a day, if not twice, to check up on any concerns or problems and to follow up on every complaint and grievance, no matter how trivial.

My boss Garrity notified me that another supervisor, Pillar, needed me in his section. Pillar maintained a modicum of humanity, despite having switched sides by donning a white shirt.

"Listen, Jon," Pillar said. "I got a problem with Abdul. He's still probationary. I don't want to fire him, but he's falling behind and sending scrap down the line. I've given him three days to learn his job, but he's not progressing. I can't cover for him much longer."

I met Abdul in the lunchroom. In broken English, Abdul complained that he had too much work on his job and couldn't keep up. I dialed back the conversation and asked him where he was from.

"I'm Palestinian. My family immigrated to Detroit. I never worked in factory. Not used to the speed to keep up."

"Okay, Abdul. I'm here to make sure you don't get fired. Try to finish each car. You're on probation, so technically you got no union rights. No matter to me as I'm here to protect you. I'll get Pillar to give you more time."

Next day, Pillar said to me, "Jon, Abdul just ain't catching on. You know I don't want to can his ass, but there's only so much I can do."

Abdul and I walked to the lunchroom.

"Steward," he said, as if an epiphany had dawned on him, "I figured out problem. Pillar is a Jew, and he don't like me cuz I'm Arab."

I paused. "Wow, Abdul. I gotta tell you: Pillar ain't a Jew, but I am."

A look of panic crossed Abdul's face as my words sank in. The only thing preventing him from being fired his Jewish steward.

"Look, Abdul—we're cool. I don't care if you're Arab or Jewish. I'm your steward. But Pillar's given you four days to learn the job, and I can only hold him back from firing you for so long. You gotta give the job your best shot."

Neither Abdul nor Pillar ever asked for me again regarding Abdul's job. I figured the "Jew" comment shook up Abdul and that he had decided to make sure he worked on every car. I laugh about the incident to this day. What are the odds that in a plant of seven thousand workers in Kenosha, Wisconsin, six thousand miles from Palestine, Abdul ended up with the sole Jewish steward in a plant where only three Jews worked?

Whenever we got word of racist incidents, particularly if perpetrated by management, we sought out the story, either to write about or, if called for, act on it. One such egregious incident occurred in the Motor Division. As we reported:

AMC Supports Discrimination
823 Conditions Lead to Firing

Motor Division Superintendent Massey must think that every engine produced is another dollar in his own pocket. The way he keeps people in 823 running like horses on a track is unbelievable....

It's bad enough for seniority people but the way [he] treated probationaries dated back to the days before the slaves were freed....

One of the roughest jobs in 823 is taking engines off the end of the line. The hoist is hard to operate without the engines swinging back and forth.

This is supposed to be a one [person] job, but that week the company had 2 probationaries doing it. In fact, it's more dangerous with 2 doing the job and getting in each other's way. Neither of them had proper break in. The man operating the hoist periodically bumped the engines into the other man's back....

In this type of situation hassle and tension are bound to occur. In this case the man operating the hoist was White and the man helping was Black. After the engine struck the man accidently a number of times an argument developed and turned into a racial hassle. What occurred next is not perfectly clear, but the Black man was fired for alleged physical violence. The other man was talked to by the company.

This type of discrimination only does the company good. AMC creates the lousy working conditions that lead up to this type of hassle.... This situation that the company created led directly up to the racial hassle that resulted in the firing of the Black brother.

While at AMC, and at other factory jobs during my discharge, I understood the fight against racism and white supremacy to be more than a personal, moral issue. In Madison, while majoring in labor history, I studied how white supremacy had so divisively and detrimentally impacted the labor movement by the existence of jarring racial inequalities in the working class. History is replete with examples of how the owning class has employed the second-class status of Black labor to destroy unionizing drives, break strikes, force down wages, and fundamentally weaken the unity of workers by perpetuating and exploiting two tiers divided along racial lines.

Once *Fighting Times* became known as a voice against racism, we no longer needed to root out articles or incidents of discrimination. Stories found us.

2836 Petition Against Racism

On October 9, 17 people in 2836 [Lakefront metal] filed a mass grievance against the racist graffiti written on the walls of all the bathrooms....

There are slurs on just about every racial group with about 95%... anti-Black. The people who signed the petition were 8 Blacks, 8 Whites and 1 Mexican. The grievance called for the company to repaint the wall and for the union to stand against this type of racism.

One of the slogans on the wall says, "All men should be free, let nigger slaves do the work." The fact is, as we all work side by side busting our Black, White and Brown asses, we are <u>all</u> slaves to the white shirt. Anything that divides us like this graffiti weakens our unity in the union.

So far some Board members have toured the area and there has been a promise to repaint the bathrooms.

The Kenosha plant was predominantly white. On a personal level, some whites harbored deeply racist attitudes. One such example hit uncomfortably close to home. I was dating a young white woman from Department 838 named Sandy. I invited Sandy to a department party.

Earlene Henderson was a young, single Black mother who moved to Racine when we got her hired at AMC. Through Rudy, we scored a special application with a stamp on the top pushing the applicant to the top of the hiring list. Earlene had been politically active in Milwaukee and supported *Fighting Times*. She frequently assisted in distribution after hiring on at AMC in Kenosha.

Sandy had gone to the restroom. Earlene came over to sit on my lap in a flirtatious manner, even though there was nothing intimate between us. When Sandy returned, I watched her face contort. Earlene, unaware of any issue, went off to dance with her date.

"What's that nigger doing sitting on your lap? I don't want to see that bitch here again or I'm gonna kick her nigger ass!" (Sandy wasn't kidding; she slept with a .22 caliber pistol.)

"Wow, Sandy. What kinda fucked up talk is that? I don't ever want to hear you use that word again. It's hurtful. That's KKK b.s."

"I don't even know what KKK is."

"Ku Klux Klan. Didn't you learn about the KKK in school?" Sandy had graduated from high school in Kenosha a few years earlier.

"No—no idea."

Man, I thought. *What a lousy educational system. How can someone graduate from high school and not know of the KKK?* I wondered if Sandy even knew the history of slavery. Without knowing the history of slavery, how can anyone be expected to understand the legacy that slavery left behind?

"The Klan are a bunch of white racists who run around like fools in white sheets with their faces covered and terrorize Black people. In the South, the Klan lynched, beat up, and bullied Black people to stop them from voting. The whole point of what I'm doing in the union is to stop that kind of bullshit." Oh, well. I figured our relationship was destined for a short life.

CHAPTER 16

Revitalizing Department Meetings

A fter winning the steward's position, my plan for transforming the union in Department 838 required me to navigate new territory. My day-to-day interactions as steward basically limited me to representing the thirty-five people in my section. For my next strategic step, I focused on winning the department chair position, predicated on a plan to revitalize monthly meetings as a venue for raising issues. Meetings were sporadic, unplanned, and attended by only a few, mostly the Gillette clique attending to drink unlimited beer for a dollar.

My two election challenges for chair pitted me against George Massey, a high-seniority repair worker. Repair was a privileged job to which one was assigned by management without an open bidding process. Repair jobs also included the lucrative perk of overtime. Massey was a long-term Gillette sycophant, and challenging him meant running against the Gillette crew.

After I announced my intent to run, Gillette toadies launched a red-baiting campaign, with the refrain of "he's an outsider." Unfortunately, I hadn't yet garnered enough department-wide support to win the election.

On my second challenge, however, I resoundingly beat Massey. At the time, there were 425 people working first shift. Among the 425 were enough new hires and young people to undermine Gillette's prior stranglehold.

Before the vote, I caucused with other activists to formulate specific plans for transforming departmental meetings into open democratic forums. We agreed that I should commit to printing monthly agendas to announce topics to be discussed.

I also intended to use the agenda to obligate Gillette to deliver a monthly report on resolution of grievances. While that might sound tame, public accountability constituted a radical threat to Gillette's reign. Individuals who usually groused only to those around them would be able to publicly demand information on their backlogged grievances.

Lastly, I proposed scheduling outside speakers. Since many complained that their jobs were overloaded, I initiated plans to bring in union time-study reps to educate people on their contractual right to work at a normal pace and to file a "standards grievance." Other issues were to include health and safety training and discussions of how to use the Working Agreement as both a shield and a sword.

Once elected, I forced a begrudging commitment from Gillette that he would attend meetings where he could be held accountable.

For the first meeting, held directly after first shift, I limited the agenda to safe topics like this one:

> Over the past months dozens of 838 members have suffered time off the job injuries. Many of these injuries are industrially related, in particular tendonitis or carpal tunnel syndrome.
>
> We have invited 2 specialists to speak and answer questions in order to brief us on the proper procedure in the event of industrial injury... such as tendonitis.

As carpal tunnel syndrome plagued so many Department 838 workers due to the repetitive nature of line work, two specialists on the topic led to a surprising turnout of almost eighty.

In the spring of 1979, gas prices shot up. Mechanical pumps at gas stations were unable to register prices above ninety-nine cents per gallon, and station owners posted handmade signs for prices over that amount. Gas shortages also led to long lines at the pumps.

Protests over access to gasoline followed the February 1979 revolution that installed an Islamic republic in Iran, forcing the US-bankrolled dictatorship of the shah into exile. The mainstream press and Washington politicians sought to divert blame for the "oil crisis" to the anti-US government of Ayatollah Khomeini. The fact was, however, that Iran supplied such a negligible portion of the oil the US imported that this disruption could not have been the sole reason for the crisis. Yet the unceasing propaganda tagging Iran as the culprit sparked xenophobic verbal attacks on Iran, as people ignored facts. A faction of workers in the plant had begun wearing "NUKE IRAN" T-shirts, and we felt a need to address the lies about the issue that the mainstream media were promoting.

The UAW came under pressure to take a stand. From the front page of the July *Fighting Times*:

UAW Calls Nationwide Sit Down
Fight the Gas Rip-Off!!!

On August 22nd UAW members across the country will stop work to protest the biggest ripoff of the decade: soaring energy prices, make believe shortages and huge oil company profits. "We will ask the nearly 1.5 million men and women in the UAW across the country to put down their tools and pick up their pens to write postcards to Washington. The time has come to put the oil companies and their political allies on notice that the American people *have had it.*"

—Douglas Fraser, UAW President

Soon after Fraser made the announcement, AMC management decided to shut the line for six minutes right before the noon lunch break. Rather than risk an unruly incident if we had been left to their own devices, management sought to place a control valve on the shutdown.

The absence of background facts outlining the real roots and causes of the crisis prompted me to write in *Fighting Times*:

Facts Behind the "Oil Crisis"

FACT
- The press and politicians blame Iran for the present shortage. Iranian oil is only 2½ % of the total U.S. supply....

FACT
- The press and politicians claim that the Arabs and OPEC are making out like bandits. From Jan. '77 to June '79 prices at the pump rose 33 cents. *30 cents of the increase went to U.S. multinational oil monopolies!*

FACT
- As far back as 1974 Rockefeller's Standard Oil profits were $3.1 billion. According to Federal investigators, "In 1979 the 20 major U.S. oil companies over charged the public $336 million for oil transfers from their foreign affiliates."

We surely didn't convince everyone to stop falling for the "blame Iran game." Regardless, *Fighting Times* presented a logical, well-reasoned argument and opened a few minds.

One of the democratic traditions that survived the Daum era were the local's monthly stewards' meetings at which reports were delivered informing stewards of grievance settlements. The meetings were also a forum to discuss pressing collateral issues.

Despite my being a new steward, the meeting offered the opportunity for me to bring up the oil crisis. With some trepidation at facing more than a hundred first-shift stewards, I knew what I had to do.

> It is up to us stewards to make this short work stoppage and protest a success. We can't sit back and rely on the International. The large oil monopolies, in cahoots with Washington politicians, have orchestrated the current crunch at gas pumps in their almighty drive for profits at the expense of working people.
>
> I make a motion that Local 72 prepare a leaflet based on the July issue of *Solidarity* [UAW international magazine, the staff of which was more progressive than the international] to be distributed at every gate... to ensure that all our members are educated to the stoppage and postcard campaign.

To my surprise, the motion passed by unanimous consent.

Holding the position of department chair I had the opportunity to put the oil crisis on the August agenda. Reflecting growing interest in the monthly meetings, close to one hundred attended, many showing first-time interest. More people attended the meeting than had attended the prior two Local 72 membership meetings. The shared sentiment was that "workers are being ripped off BUT six minutes [for a shutdown to write postcards] isn't enough." Members wanted more.

A bit before the August 22, members of Fighting Times met and agreed that there was enough support to pull off a more militant action. We reached consensus that US president Jimmy Carter's criticizing the American people for "lack of confidence in the government" dodged the real roots of the oil crisis and that he deserved to be hung in effigy at a mass street rally.

The influx of young people in the plant had radically altered the landscape. Most were rebellious and disdainful of the company as well as most authority. While their pot smoking, heavy drinking, and partying was apolitical, their awareness of being ripped off created the opportunity to channel their rebellious spirit.

We announced a protest rally to the media, which translated into newspaper headlines reading "UAW to Hang Carter." Local radio broadcast news of the hanging during the drive to work. As people arrived the morning of August 22, we were at the gates with flyers:

HAVE YOU EVER WANTED TO SEE THIS MAN HANG?

IF SO—RALLY 12 NOON BY GATE 15

STOP THE GAS RIPOFF

In Department 838, events rolled out exactly per Local 72's official plan. At 9:30 a.m. all stewards got off their jobs on "union business" to distribute postcards, pens, and "STOP THE OIL RIPOFF" buttons. By eleven, virtually every worker in the department had pinned on a button.

As the line halted at six minutes to noon, young people, unprompted, started chanting "Stop the rip-offs! Stop the rip-offs!" Three TV cameras were there, and radio and print reporters also gathered in a scrum at the gate. Members of the Milwaukee UWO held up a noose and a dummy of Carter.

Excitement swelled as folks exited the plant with large shopping bags of peanuts to throw at the Carter effigy. A couple of shop militants, including me, delivered short speeches. At twelve thirty, Kenosha radio reported that two hundred radicals had gathered on Fifty-Second Street, and scenes of Carter's mock hanging were broadcast on three Milwaukee TV stations.

The *Milwaukee Worker*, having known in advance of our plans for the day, put out an issue offering a deeper political perspective, going beyond Jimmy Carter and gas prices. We sold more than one hundred papers at the rally.

Had AMC not planned for the six minutes to be directly followed by lunch break, there is no telling whether any limitations would have been observed by angry Local 72 members.

With quite a few Vietnam veterans in the plant, and with a number active in the UWO, we made a special effort to reach them. Support for these vets and the fight against racial discrimination frequently went hand in hand.

Sam Hanna, a Black UWO activist who had marched against the Klan, had been hired in 1970. Sam had worked sixty-one days before he was drafted, then spent nine months in Vietnam. Upon returning home in 1973, Sam reported to the AMC employment office, only to be told he no longer held a job.

Undeterred, Sam pled his case in federal court, which ordered AMC to rehire him in 1977 with full restoration of seniority. Stung by the court's decision, management targeted Sam.

Sam's job in Department 828 required him to make up license plate holders. Word reached me on a Friday that Sam had been fired for alleged misconduct. Over the weekend, we met with Sam to ascertain what had gone down and develop a strategy for winning reinstatement.

By Monday, we were ready with a flyer:

Defend a Union Brother

Friday morning Sam received his check and found it 30 hours short. [His supervisor Garry Burrow] told Sam that he hadn't punched in for 3 days. [While Burrows would have noticed a three-day absence, he instead chose to fuck with Sam over the pay shortage.]

Brother Hanna then requested to see his steward.... When the steward did not come after 30 minutes Sam started putting tags on some of the operations. [Burrow then suspended Sam and began to harass him.]

Sam left his job after being suspended.... Sam was talking to the chief steward and steward when Burrow again approached Sam and asked him who was on his job.... At this point Burrow claimed Sam spit on him although no one else present saw this. At 2:30 that afternoon Sam was fired for misconduct.

After we distributed the flyer, I headed to Department 828 where I knew Don Grisham, the chief steward. Don had filed an emergency grievance, explaining that both he and the line steward had sworn that Sam never engaged in the conduct alleged by Burrow. We jointly agreed that a petition needed to be circulated to support the grievance.

On the front page of the April 1979 *Fighting Times*, forty-five hundred copies of which went out at the gates, we wrote:

AMC had it in for Sam since he walked back into 828 in November '77. The company did not like the idea of losing to a Black assembly line worker. Sam got write-ups and time off for his attendance which was not worse than many others in the plant....

In the past it was established practice that a union man could not be fired on the word of a company man alone. Now that the company is trying to weaken and break the power of the union it is no coincidence that they are coming down on minority people.

In breaking news, we also reported in the April issue: "At last Saturday's union meeting authorization to set up a strike vote was passed unanimously.... There are 65 unresolved grievances including Sam Hanna's discharge at the review step. A date for a strike vote will be set if the grievances aren't resolved."

Concurrent with Sam's discharge, management terminated a Black steward on the hood line, Reuben. Management rarely fired a steward. In Reuben's case, not only was he Black, the chief and the board member were also Black. The superintendent had the reputation of being a venomous racist.

821 Victory over Discrimination
Reuben Collier Rehired

After 2 weeks on the streets for a racist, phony firing Steward Reuben Collier is back on the job... with full back pay.

On the hood line in 821 [industrial engineers] tried to raise the rate from 150 an hour to 200.... People in the department united to resist this speedup and a grievance was filed.

Brother Reuben Collier stood up for people and demanded that the contract be enforced. The Chief Steward and Board Member in 821 are also Black and the strong stand taken by the union was too much for a racist Superintendent named Brian Phillips. Phillips has shown a total unwillingness to bargain with Blacks and is reported by witnesses to have said, "I am tired of 'niggers' in the union telling me what to do."

[His supervisor and another manager started shouting in Reuben's face about him not wearing safety glasses while at the chief steward's desk, away from the welding area. Collier put his arm up for some breathing room.] For this he was charged with being abusive to a supervisor and insubordination. Two days later he was fired on this total frameup charge.

Rueben Collier is back in the shop now; but in fact he should never have been out on the street.

AS WE WENT TO PRESS WE LEARNED THAT SUPERINTENDENT PHILLIPS HAS BEEN TAKEN OUT OF 821.

A couple of factors were of particular importance as we addressed Sam's and Rueben's discharges. First, we pulled no punches in going toe to toe with upper management. A factory is governed as an autocracy, with a rigid chain of command that depends on unchallenged power to maintain discipline.

As with Sam Hanna, we were on the case the Friday of Reuben's discharge and were ready on Monday with a flyer and petition. Over time, our actions were rewarded. At election time we knew we could rely on many workers of color and women who viewed us as their stalwart advocates and defenders.

While a steward like Rueben rarely stayed fired for long, such matters were handled typically as a company-versus-worker issue. Not in the pages of *Fighting Times*, however. If superintendent Brian Phillips said anything foul about Blacks, we didn't hold back from branding him a despicable racist.

CHAPTER 17

Department Meeting Confronts Racist Chief Steward

T he ups and downs in auto, based largely on consumers' preference for this or that model, meant assembly plants went through cycles of layoffs and expanded employment. As noted, the Kenosha plant saw a mass hiring of young workers who were rebellious and not cowed by the company or the union. And dissatisfaction with Department 838 chief steward Russ Gillette reached a tipping point.

Gillette's name did not even appear on the vote tally for the 1979 stewards' election. I can no longer recall if Gillette went on sick leave or chose not to run, but he'd had enough. Gillette's departure fractured his clique's standing.

When election results were posted, I had placed second with 132 votes, topped only by Peggy Applegate, the only woman steward.

For the election, I organized a team of fresh, young activists, loosely affiliated with the UWO, to run for stewards' positions.

Of the twelve positions (twelve reflecting the growth of the department), four of our candidates won in addition to me: Jimmy Graham, JoAnne Haley, John Leyendecker, and Cathy Meirs. The most significant victory accrued to Graham as the first steward of color in 838, having been voted for by both Blacks and whites with a total vote over one hundred.

The vote totals presented a conundrum. Kojak, my former Milwaukee head steward, was elected and announced his intent to run for chief. Gathings, who had placed behind me with 127 votes, also announced he was running for chief. Gathings hailed from the 838 old school, having been a charter member of the Gillette clique.

Gathings was a pickup-driving, tobacco-chewing, self-proclaimed cowboy with an inflated belly hanging over a large turquoise belt buckle. Like quite a few in the plant, Gathings's other job was tending his farm, and he also held a semiskilled repair job.

Joanne Tank and Jimmy Graham, both Fighting Times activists, were elected as stewards in the 1979 trim department elections that dislodged the conservative "all-white" Gillette clique.

Rather than run for chief, I opted to let Kojak challenge Gathings, planning to devote the year to teaching UWO-affiliated candidates how to become effective union reps. I could be patient, as I was down for the long haul.

Gathings, still able to rally Gillette's base, beat Kojak, who had appealed primarily to former Milwaukee guys.

By virtue of being chief, Gathings gained entitlement to overtime if *any worker* in 838 on his shift was scheduled to work overtime. Gathings sucked up every minute of overtime, providing a fat paycheck but also inextricably tying him to management, as a piglet latched to its mother's teat.

While daily interaction between Gathings and me remained superficially cordial, underlying tension tinged our every conversation. Our clashing outlooks surfaced with venom one Monday morning. Heading for nine thirty break, I ran into an animated scrum of young department members. "Melrod, did you hear? Gathings told Cathy (the steward) she shouldn't be kissin' on a nigger. It's way fucked up."

A group of Department 838 folks had been partying behind Madore's bar after work the preceding Friday. Cathy and Jessie Sewell, a Black worker, exchanged a kiss. A kiss between a Black guy and a white woman—nothing more.

Nevertheless, the incident was stoking a brushfire, and I needed to get the facts down.

Jessie worked one station up the line. I had spent hours hanging with Jessie, and other regulars, behind Madore's, drinking pints. Jessie was also a solid Fighting Times ally.

As soon as I could get a utility worker to relieve me, I checked in with Cathy. She was a new steward, and I had been mentoring her to adopt a more confrontational stance with management.

"Hey, Cathy—heard some bullshit's going down with Gathings. He's been running his mouth spouting racist shit about Jessie and you. What's up?"

"Jon, I'm afraid for this to turn into a big public incident. I don't want Gathings coming down on me."

"I hear you, Cathy, and I get it, but Gathings got no right to talk about you. Just because he's chief doesn't mean he's got any business getting in your face about who you want to party with or who you kiss! That's sexist, racist b.s. Plus you're a steward now, and you need to set an example of good unionism. Gathings, and I don't care if he's chief, can't go around mouthing racist bullshit. He's gotta treat you like a grown woman, with respect. Gathings is way out of line."

"Jon, please let me think about it."

"Cathy, it's not you causing trouble—it's Gathings. But if you feel like it's over and want to drop it, I'm cool."

By lunch, the whole department buzzed. Blacks were outraged. Many grabbed me, wanting to know what could be done. In the past, a racist incident might have sparked an angry reaction and then fade; *not this time*, I thought.

As department chair, I put the incident on the agenda. I met with the other stewards who had run with me, and we discussed our obligation to address racism at the department meeting. Graham took a strong position, as he had previously complained about Gathings's shit attitude toward Blacks.

With increasing intensity, word spread of a confrontation going down. Black people, many of whom had never thought of attending a meeting, beat the drum to call out Gathings. Similarly, many younger whites took offense at Gathings's old-school behavior.

I needed to get Jessie onboard. "Hey, bro. Que pasa? What's up with this Gathings bullshit? He's been mouthing some nasty name calling 'bout you."

A pained look crossed Jessie's face, a stark contrast to his usual clowning demeanor. He looked hurt and embarrassed. Even though he was free and equal to Gathings, he felt stuck taking shit from a self-proclaimed cowboy whose primary reason for being chief was greed.

"Melrod, what I'm gonna do? Ain't nobody care. Gathings is chief."

"Fuck that, bro! We got our guys—Ernie, your main man—and Pedro got the Mexicans. We got the Blacks who are tired of racist shit. We got the young people and the Fighting Times people. We don't gotta let this slide. We gotta jack Gathings up. It's on the agenda for the department meeting. Ya with me?"

Tension on the floor ratcheted up. I noticed Gathings huddling with his white repair buddies (there being only one Black 838 repair worker).

It might have been the largest department meeting in 838's history. I looked out, and many of our people had shown up, particularly Blacks. I also noticed a gaggle of repair workers and a smattering of old-school, conservative types who I assumed had attended at Gathings's urging.

I called the meeting to order. Old business first.

"Hey, Melrod, we ain't here for no old business. We're here 'bout what Gathings said about Jessie."

"All right then, new business."

I called an audible, turning toward Gathings sitting next to me, a rather uncomfortable seating plan.

"Jim, I believe folks want to hear about the incident with Jessie and Cathy that involves you."

"Yeah, yeah. I wasn't serious. I was just joking 'bout what I said. It ain't that big a deal."

I'd been watching Jessie; his face tightened. He sat for a few uncomfortable seconds. I waited for the slightest movement of his hand and immediately called on him before he put it back down.

"I been hearing Gathings has been talking about me. He got no business talkin' about me being Black or any color."

Gathings, in a voice barely audible, said, "Yeah, I shouldn'ta said nottin'."

This can't be the end of it, I thought. *This is too important.*

I saw Graham's hand. "Jimmy."

"That ain't an acceptable apology. If Gathings is chief, he can't be talkin' racist shit about no one. The union is about us all. The union's strong only if we are together. I never want to hear no one using language calling a brother or sister that fucked-up word! You hear me, Gathings?"

"I didn't mean no harm."

"Gathings—ain't the point. Your talk is harmful. You got no right talkin' about Jessie or Cathy. Ain't your business."

For the first time, Blacks in the department stood their ground and made their voices heard, not just about the incident with Jessie and Cathy but also how they felt ignored and disregarded by the union. Gathings had been the catalyst, but the discussion was cathartic for airing long-held grievances about discriminatory treatment and favoritism—from both management and union.

Somebody tapped a keg, and I noticed people filling big red cups with beer. Beer on an empty stomach, particularly as tempers flared, didn't portend well.

"I think we covered the agenda, but I have a few comments. First off, I want to thank the huge turnout. Anyone who's got something to say can say it here. Having said that—the bottom line is there's no place for racism in our union, no way, no how! Adjourned."

Steward John Leyendecker and I chatted in the beer line. Beers in hand, we talked. In the drift of the crowd, we ended up across from Gathings and Massey. You could cut the tension.

Gathings stared at me with palpable scorn. We couldn't have come from two more different worlds. I had left the East Coast for college in Madison. He had stayed on the farm and gone to work young at AMC. He chewed tobacco. I smoked pot. His proudest moment was when his daughter placed first at 4-H for her cow, and I had come from Milwaukee and uprooted his world, in his eyes.

"Hey, Melrod. I don't like what you been saying about me."

"Only talkin' truth, Gathings. You had a chance to call me out but didn't. I don't like hearing how you dissed my partner Jessie. I can't change your thinking, but we all got to act right in the union."

"Fuck you, Melrod. I'll say what the fuck I want."

The space between us shrank. I braced for incoming, but then Leyendecker inserted himself between us. Leyendecker, at least according to him, had been a Navy SEAL. I admit, he threw down like a guy who knew how to fight.

"Go ahead, you redneck, bring it."

Massey jumped in. "Let's all cool it. Meeting's over."

"Yeah," I said as Leyendecker and I turned to leave.

In a testament to the power of grassroots union democracy, the

Chief steward Jim Gathings (right) provoked an uproar in the trim department when he disrespected a white woman steward and Fighting Times activist for kissing a Black man (Jessie Sewell), leading to an angry confrontation at a department meeting where racism in union ranks became a hotly debated, contentious issue.

department meeting had taken up the key issue of racism, previously ignored or swept under the carpet.

I fought an ongoing battle over bringing copies of *Fighting Times* into the plant.

For the September issue, Jessie and I were set to hand out about 350 newsletters. A larger-than-usual crowd approached all at once, forcing me to physically back into the plant to hand everyone a copy. Two managers approached in a golf cart and instructed the guard, "Get him [me] the fuck off company property."

"Who the hell was that rude motherfucker?" I asked the guard.

"Boss Hog from Motor Division. He busted my chops for letting you hand out papers on company property."

It was time to put an end to the incessant interference with my handing out of *Fighting Times*. On October 16, I headed through Gate 15 after lunch. The guard on duty happened to be Doug Claude, whom I recognized.

"Hey, Claude: a heads-up. Next time I hand out *Fighting Times*, you're on notice: I'm gonna be on company property!"

"Look, Melrod, the plant manager instructed all guards to prevent you from distributing literature on company property."

I headed to the chief's desk to dial plant security.

"This is Melrod, steward in 838. I need the spelling of the guard's name at Gate 15 for a complaint I'm filing that you guys are interfering with my protected rights under the National Labor Relations Act."

Pause. "It's C-L-A-U-D-E, but it don't matter as you can't hand out stuff in the plant."

On October 23, Paul Bosanac, field attorney for the National Labor Relations Board, filed my fourth or fifth complaint. My winning streak continued as the board ordered AMC to cease and desist from interfering with the distribution of protected materials, even in the plant, unless I interfered with production.

CHAPTER 18

Into the Street to Save Our Jobs

I n January 1980, the year was ushered in like every other: cold, gray, and icy, always icy.

With contract expiration eight months out, shop-floor skirmishes intensified as both Local 72 and AMC management tested and probed how far each was willing to push or be pushed. Pressure ratcheted up, as if Renault was in the wings scrutinizing management's daily interactions to assess the future of its venture with AMC.

As discussed, a bedrock principle of our Working Agreement required that any modification of a job assignment (the tasks to be performed at each position on the line, detailed down to the second) could be implemented *only* after the impacted employee received twenty-four-hour advance notification by a supervisor and a steward. The employee was obligated to begin performing the new operation only after contractually proper notification.

On Friday, January 11, supervision notified all Body Shop workers in 836, 837, and 838—without a steward present—that the company intended to institute job changes on Monday morning. At lunch, in bars, and in canteen areas, heated, boisterous, and defiant conversations erupted over management's improper notifications.

Caucus members and allies from the affected departments passed word that, come Monday, all should strictly abide by contract and perform jobs exactly as they existed on Friday.

Existing practice was that chief stewards determined the implementation of job changes based on seniority. Local 72 won the seniority system to replace the practice of management moving employees as they wished, often based on favoritism, racism, sexism, or simple bribery.

In the affected departments, there might be hundreds of reassignments, many or most requiring retraining. All those reassignments were to be written out by the chief steward and given to management for notification of employees.

From management's perspective, the tangled and intricate web of moves that required the retraining of hundreds was highly inefficient and costly, but we lived by our rules.

Friday's effort to circumvent past practice unleashed a groundswell of rebellion, which turned into a seismic eruption. Line workers in the hundreds demanded to see their stewards.

Stewards sought guidance from chief stewards. Chief stewards put board members on notice that "no way, no how" would Building 40 cooperate come Monday morning.

Over the weekend, caucus members met to draft a call to resist:

ATTENTION—836, 837, 838
DON'T LET AMC STEAL YOUR CONTRACT RIGHT

Time and time again AMC tries to ignore and violate our rights when it inconveniences their precious production schedule....

As soon as your supervisor tries to make you implement an illegal job change or elimination *or* resorts to any harassment, call for your steward immediately. Together we can make the company respect our contractual rights and rights as human beings.

Monday morning at 6:00 a.m., we jammed each of the two gates with our people handing out the flyer in a defiant show of strength.

Workers in 836, 837, and 838 whom the company had notified to switch shifts ignored the notifications and reported to the shift on which they had worked on Friday. Total and complete chaos ensued.

Stewards walked the lines ensuring that no weak links buckled. There is unbridled strength in collective resistance. Even those who might normally have complied with the company were swept along.

Red-faced supervisors and frustrated general supervisors made angry threats, issued "direct orders," and even resorted to personal pleas, but workers stuck together, not giving an inch. Management retaliated by issuing disciplinary action, docking the pay of some.

Half-built cars ran down the line with repair workers in tow, frantically trying to slap on parts that had been thrown into passing bodies. Lines stopped and started. When supervisors ordered workers to perform work not on their job as of last Friday, the ubiquitous retort was "Get my steward!"

With few completed bodies, more than two thousand employees in departments fed by 836, 837, and 838 were sent home early on Monday and

Tuesday. Supervisors gathered people to read aloud a letter from corporate management blaming short hours on an "unauthorized work action" caused by "union misleadership."

As we wrote in *Fighting Times*, "The company promised *in the future* to give proper notice. No way, was the answer of stewards and the people. At 11AM on Tuesday the company backed down and agreed to give 24-hour notice to take effect at 11AM on Wednesday."

Management had badly miscalculated. If Renault was watching, they saw Local 72's power and willingness to protect hard-won gains.

The Renault-AMC partnership had little direct impact until rumors circulated in March 1980 that AMC intended to transfer 480 jobs from Kenosha to its plant in Canada. The announcement did not go down well. On March 11, 1980, *Fighting Times* issued an alert:

Fight to Save Our Jobs
Can We Let AMC Lay-Off 1000 People in Kenosha[?]

Right now . . . nearly 2700 Local 72 members are laid off, yet at the same time the AMC plant in Brampton, Ontario is working *overtime*. By the middle of May, American Motors plans to move daily production of 120 Concords/Eagle wagons and 4 doors from here to Canada. With this additional layoff of 800–1000 people it may well take upwards of 10 years seniority to stay working in Kenosha.

Fighting Times printed a detailed analysis of how international capitalists moved auto production around the world like a checkerboard, without concern for seniority or families of generations of workers. We concluded: "We must take action now before it is too late. . . . The Local 72 Executive Board has filed an emergency grievance questioning AMC's . . . plans to move our jobs out of town. This is merely the first step and has to be followed up by an all out campaign and offensive."

A campaign ensued, during which an unfortunate jingoistic undercurrent blamed Canadian workers for "stealing" US jobs. *Fighting Times* aggressively placed blame squarely on Renault: "This was not a question of Canadian workers trying to steal our jobs. The whole mess started when AMC Renault [stepped into the picture]."

After the *Fighting Times* lambast, the local's leadership circulated a "Save Our Jobs" petition. Caucus members, line stewards, and shop floor activists solicited over six thousand signatures. While signatures alone wouldn't scuttle company plans, the petition put the issue directly in front of each of the six thousand members who signed.

Like a game of high-stakes poker, the caucus and the board took turns raising the bets. First the caucus published an alert about the pending move of jobs. Next, the board filed an emergency grievance. Then the caucus went to the gates with a second, more-detailed flyer pinning blame on Renault for double-dipping by first demanding concessions and then punishing Kenosha workers with the loss of jobs. Next, the local passed a petition and, under pressure to take more militant action, called for a mass rally on Fifty-Second Street under the rallying cry "Save Our Jobs." On March 26, thousands blocked the street from sidewalk to sidewalk. Hundreds held aloft handmade signs, and raucous chants filled the air. The press extensively reported on the rally, filling homes in the Milwaukee area with images of angry AMC workers in the street fighting to stop the loss of jobs.

Local 72 leadership distributed a flyer implicitly threatening a work stoppage. Despite work stoppages being expressly prohibited, the board was pressured to draw a line in the sand.

On April 2 the board met with the company and afterward reported some progress. The work stoppage was held in abeyance, but the threat remained real. While conventional thinking in the US union movement posits that little can be done about a corporation's plans to manufacture wherever it choses, that held little sway with workers determined to fight for their livelihoods.

At the April 11 membership meeting, a motion calling for a strike vote passed *without opposition*, arming Local 72 with an official strike vote.

On April 28 the company retreated, issuing an announcement that *no jobs* would be moved. On May 4, recall notices were sent to 250 previously laid-off Local 72 members in an all-out victory.

Fighting Times summed up, explaining just how far along Renault's scheme had progressed: "The company [AMC Canada] even went so far as to give pre-employment physicals to 1000 people and set a 2nd shift start up date . . . for the Brampton plant."

While the runaway jobs initially appeared a fait accompli, the rank and file mobilized once the caucus spread word of the pending catastrophe. The joint power of the rank and file and the board in Kenosha culminated in a reversal of a corporate decision concocted in France.

Before turning undivided attention to our September 16 contract expiration, the caucus engaged in several significant political struggles. Rudy

March 11, 1980, Fighting Times issued a plant-wide alert that AMC planned to move 480 jobs to its factory in Brampton, Canada, resulting in the loss of 800–1,000 jobs in Kenosha. A petition signed by 6,000 members, a strike vote without opposition, and a March 26 mass rally of thousands on Fifty-Second Street raised hell, blocking the transfer of work.

Kuzel had committed in the lead-up to Sylvester's election that Local 72 standing committees would no longer operate as a patronage system.

As pledged, Sylvester appointed three of us: John Drew to the Fair Employment Practices Committee (FEPC), me to the Education Committee, and Tod to the Legislative Committee. (There is a prescient aptness to Tod's appointment to the Legislative Committee as he would go on to serve two terms on the Kenosha City Council and as I write is serving a fifth term in the Wisconsin State Legislature.)

John's appointment to the FEPC meant the opportunity to breathe new life into the committee and its activities, both in the shop and regarding outside struggles for equality. As Fighting Times reported on the thirteenth anniversary of Martin Luther King Jr.'s assassination, the FEPC, in conjunction with UAW Region 10, chartered a bus to transport a large contingent of Local 72 members to an April 4 civil rights march in Milwaukee led by a union coalition.

John also proposed that Local 72 celebrate Dr. King's birthday. On January 16, 1981, three hundred predominantly African American members turned out for the FEPC's first in what evolved into a yearly commemoration of King's contribution to the struggle for justice and equality. Some of the

On the thirteenth anniversary of Dr. King's assassination, the Local 72 Fair Employment Practices Committee, with John Drew as a newly appointed member, charted a bus to transport a contingent of Local 72 members to an April civil rights march in Milwaukee led by a broad union coalition to demand a national holiday honoring King's fight for justice and against exploitation.

Black Local 72 members in attendance had participated in the 1968 walkout that had shut the plant following King's assassination.

Black labor leaders from the area spoke at the event about existing racism in local factories and the close links between the labor movement and the Black freedom movement.

The highlight of the Dr. King celebration was recognition that Local 72 had negotiated a paid day off in April to honor King on the anniversary of his assassination. Local 72 proudly became the first in the UAW in this regard, a precursor to the 1983 passage of a federal holiday.

The annual MLK program at Local 72 headquarters grew in size and importance year by year. In 1984, before I left, close to a one thousand Local 72 members and friends attended our memorial.

CHAPTER 19

Contract of 1980: Renault Looms

The prelude to the 1980 contract originated a year earlier, with the first overtures to American Motors by Renault—then the seventh-largest world automaker.

Before Renault acquired an interest, American Motors and Local 72 had survived their decades-long history cloistered together, to some degree, in a cocoon. While the overall economy took its toll on car production at Nash and later AMC, management and union weathered the ups and downs, while the company maintained its ranking as the "Little Fourth." AMC workers' economic benefits trailed a bit behind the Big Three, but Local 72 hung on to its vastly superior Working Agreement, besting the Big Three in areas like the right to strike, steward-to-worker ratio, and voluntary overtime.

Commencing in 1978, however, inflation swept the country, reaching double digits in 1979. The auto industry took a nosedive, with tanking sales accompanied by massive layoffs. AMC sought a lifeline. In 1979 Renault, the French state–owned automaker, acquired a 22.5 percent interest for $150 million. Renault badly needed AMC's network of twelve hundred dealers to sell its Le Car, which had caused a buzz in the United States.

Meanwhile, AMC limped along at its inefficient, antiquated Kenosha facility—the oldest continuously operating auto plant in the world, where unfinished bodies still needed to be trucked across the city for final assembly.

AMC, in need of new products for a changing marketplace, sought a cash infusion, while also bargaining for Renault's most advanced front wheel–drive technology in the world. Renault offered a $90 million loan and increased its ownership to 46 percent. Then it asserted total control in 1983 when it gained a 49 percent ownership stake.

With Renault in the background and contract expiration approaching, *Fighting Times* said:

Prepare Now for the 1980 Contract!

Bargaining with the world's 7th largest multi-national auto company puts Local 72 in a new ball park. . . .

Based on Renault's profit charts they [AMC] can't plead poverty [as Chrysler and VW recently had done]. . . . But, without even hearing Renault plead their case you can pretty well predict their bargaining stance for September. In order to stay competitive with GM and Ford they will tell us at AMC that we will have to give up contract concessions in order to insure the successful launch of the Renault car in 1982.

Dave Mattson illustrated with a drawing depicting an angry octopus, wearing a French beret, labeled "Renault Empire," standing astride France, Sweden, Spain, Latin America, and Wisconsin. With Renault in the game, the rules were to forever change. No longer would Local 72 leaders travel three hundred miles to Detroit to meet with unsophisticated US auto industry managers. Shots would now be dictated from across the ocean in Paris.

Fighting Times set out to develop the understanding that we were now only one cog in a worldwide empire. Kenoshans, whose lives revolved around "the Motors," many with families who had worked at the plant for multiple generations, faced a new reality. AMC was but one spoke in a gigantic worldwide wheel.

Local 72 leaders and the international now had to look across the ocean. No longer were names like Gerald Meyers and Roy Chapin Jr. slipping off management tongues. Rather, it was names like Jose Dedeurwaerder and Jean-Marc Lepeu.

The caucus focused on Renault and how it fit into the looming contract battle. The rank and file needed to prepare for what promised to be a new set of adversarial relations—little Local 72 versus the Renault behemoth.

How willing would our members be to battle our French overlord? The caucus again issued a call to walk out on 12:01 a.m. the day our contract expired. Borrowing from past campaigns, we mass-produced stickers, buttons, and T-shirts, tagging September 16 as a deadline: after that, "NO CONTRACT/NO WORK." My basement turned into a beehive of activity, printing three-inch-square stickers by the thousands, stamping buttons, and silk-screening T-shirts, one run after the other as we continually sold out. Our network now extended plant-wide, as did demand for our contract paraphernalia.

A few months earlier we had reached a considered decision to transform the United Workers Organization into the United Workers Caucus of Local 72 (UWC). John Drew had led a discussion of the UWO's negatives and positives. The prevailing sentiment was that we should rebrand as a caucus within Local 72 with a primary focus on AMC, while not excluding participation in outside political struggles.

The discourse constituted a reality check. I hadn't grasped, prior to the meeting, that in some caucus members' minds we had drifted toward being "too political," too focused on "outside issues." The UWC made perfect sense; it followed the UAW's history of caucuses within the membership.

While I embraced the adjustment, I felt a personal imperative to find the right formula for injecting political discussions and actions to facilitate a deeper, radical, class-conscious understanding of events outside of AMC. For years, selling the *Worker* had been a tool for promoting political discussions, but the *Worker* had ceased publication.

Tod Ohnstad, a member of the first UWC steering committee, helped craft a statement of purpose: "As an independent rank and file caucus within Local 72 we are united in our commitment to a fighting, democratic union. We strongly oppose any attempts by the International to dictate to UAW Locals, either at convention time or contract time. We are not another union outside of local 72. We are a fully democratic caucus and our group is open to local 72 members of various political persuasions."

Having learned from the contract struggle in 1978, when we unsuccessfully attempted to resurrect the Stewards Club, we strategized with a veteran Local 72 militant Jim Robeson.

Robeson had been a powerful left-leaning leader, having held numerous elected positions, including the local's executive board. With a flair for the dramatic, Robeson collaborated with Rudy Kuzel and Willie Foxie, another Black board member, to wear black berets in the 1969 contract negotiations, raising the specter of Black militant influence. This flummoxed both AMC and the international and led to press coverage of the militant Panther-like attire, even sparking comparisons to Black-led DRUM—the Dodge Revolutionary Union Movement, which shook the UAW and the industry in the late sixties.

We enlisted Robeson to chair a "meeting to get organized" to convene shop activists to mobilize the rank and file, applying pressure on the board to fight for a contract with economic parity with the Big Three, without concessions.

The body settled on three essential demands, later adopted almost verbatim by the board: no extension past 12:01 a.m. on the day of contract expiration, equity with GM and Ford on economics, and no takeaways.

The 1980 negotiations opened in Milwaukee on July 16. Representatives from Local 75 (Milwaukee), Local 12 (Toledo Jeep), and Local 384 (Brampton, Ontario) joined the Local 72 board on the bargaining team. Negotiations were headed by international rep Ray Majerus, recently appointed the UAW's AMC Department director.

Mainstream media propounded propaganda claiming that the company had lost $84 million in the fourth quarter. To counter the media narrative, the UWC launched a fact-based education campaign, distributing a detailed broadside:

The *Facts* behind AMC's $84 Million Loss

The fact is that even though sales may be down from last year, the company continues to make money whenever they sell cars. [W]hile AMC claims profits are down, *total revenues in the first half of '80 climbed to $1,579 million[,] up 6% from $1,488 million in '79*. No one in the union wants to have to walk a picket line, but if we're forced to, a strike would certainly make AMC bargain.

Renault + AMC = $23 Billion

The future of AMC... isn't so rough. They are in a partnership with Renault. Renault has <u>committed</u> $200 million to AMC in exchange for 22% of the stock. Renault is a $20 billion multi-national corporation owned by the French government, and Renault is the 7th largest auto maker in the world!!!

The backside of the broadsheet presented figures from 1967 to 1980 for AMC's profits and losses and for Local 72's contract losses and GM's contract gains. The facts and figures posited that Local 72 members were entitled to and could win economic parity.

While we sought to educate members about the economic realities of AMC/Renault's position in the industry, our most important activity was day-to-day organizing to prepare for the countdown to 12:01 a.m., September 16. "NO CONTRACT/NO WORK" buttons, T-shirts, and stickers proliferated widely, not just among UWC members and existing activists but also among new people throughout the plant.

As the deadline approached, we devised detailed plans to ensure a walkout at 12:01 a.m. I met with Poor John, a biker in the all-Black King Cobras. Cobras on their Harleys had dramatically led an earlier May Day march from the AMC Body Shop in Milwaukee.

"Poor John, we gotta shut Building 40 at 12:01. You done more years at the Motors than me, and you know folks won't walk off the line unless we rev them up and give 'em courage. Bosses will be policing the lines. I'm gonna buy a dozen whistles. Are you hip to lining up your guys to blow the shit out of the whistles at midnight? I got other people lined up to chant 'No contract, no work!' and 'On strike, shut it down!' With whistles blowing, no way the company can keep people on the line."

"Melrod, you know I'm with you, brother. I been with you since them Milwaukee days when they had your ass fired. You'll see us on the street at midnight when we shut this motherfucker down."

The caucus went to the gates with a final flyer, quoting local president Gene Sylvester:

NEGOTIATIONS NEAR 12:01 DEADLINE
UNION CALLS FOR NO EXTENSIONS

OUR BASIC REQUEST IS THAT WE FOLLOW THE PATTERN AT GM AND FORD. . . . *THERE SHOULD NOT BE ANY EXTENSION OF THE AGREEMENT, THE COMPANY HAS HAD MORE THAN ENOUGH TIME.* . . . —Gene Sylvester

LOCAL WORKING AGREEMENT: On July 31 the company presented 32 contract takeaways. The Executive Board presented 80 proposals to improve. . . .

ECONOMIC AGREEMENT: proposals call . . . for economic equity with GM and Ford.

On Monday, September 15, we were apprehensive, fearing the board or international might order us to remain on the job while negotiations continued. Eight hours on first shift lasted an eternity.

When the end-of-shift buzzer rang, I headed to find Wolfgram, my partner from Milwaukee. Wolfgram had prepared a large "12:01" banner to hang out the second-floor window at 11:30 p.m. to signal that the sentiment in favor of a midnight walkout held on the lines.

Not knowing what to do with myself, I headed home.

I pulled back up to Madore's minutes before 9:00 p.m., finding a rowdy contingent of first shifters who had never made it home. By 11:00 p.m. the crowd had swelled further, like metal shavings drawn to a giant magnet.

Quite a few Milwaukee guys arrived. I grabbed a bullhorn, feeling like I held a starting gun.

The crowd had grown to hundreds, and it was time to pull people together. Caucus members passed the bullhorn, leading chants of "No contract, no work!" and "12:01! 12:01! 12:01!"

"Let's move to the other side of the street so they can hear us!" I yelled. As one, a couple hundred people crossed Fifty-Second Street, crowding Gate 15. We chanted as loud as we could and hoped those inside knew we were counting on them to walk at midnight. If nothing else, this was the best show in town, and with we all anticipated what was yet to unfold.

At 11:30 p.m. someone shouted: "Look! Look up at the second floor!" Wolfgram had come through. A five-foot banner—roughly emblazoned "12:01"—fluttered from second-floor windows. A roar rose from the crowd— and chants: "Walk! Walk! Walk!"—loud enough for those inside to be aware that hundreds were waiting for them.

The 1978 walkout had commenced with a trickle, but at midnight on September 16, 1980, a tsunami crashed out of the plant. Fearing a loss of control, management had feigned calling the shots and notified 836 and 837 that the lines would shut down early due to sudden "part shortages."

Management tried to keep the other lines running till 12:30 a.m. As Poor John recounted:

> I was checking the wall clock every few seconds. [Supervisors] and big bosses were stationed up and down the line peering at us like pissed-off cops, but I had my boys ready. When the clock hit twelve, I started blowing like a motherfucker. My guys joined like we planned. The first few people who walked off got chased back to their jobs by supervisors, but we kept blowing and people were yelling "walk, walk, walk." Then, man—the whole place went crazy and *everyone* headed for the exits pushing supervisors out of the fucking way. It was some kinda heavy shit. We did it. We had da power!

Hundreds streamed out, breaking free from the assembly line, grins on their faces and fists thrust in the air. We were one! People hugged and greeted each other elatedly. Resistance was exhilarating and liberating.

Wild cheering erupted as word spread that Lakefront second shift had wildcatted.

In the exuberance of our newfound power, we blocked Fifty-Second Street, just because we could—prompting the arrival of squad cars that

September 1980, workers in the trim department started blowing whistles and chanting "12:01, 12:01," leading to a mass walkout despite management futilely trying to keep the lines running. Author with arms raised, calling on wildcat strikers to take over Fifty-Second Street.

kept their distance. Back and forth we marched, chanting: "No contract, no work!" "On strike, shut it down!" A couple of caucus members had painted a bedsheet "No Chrysler Contract," referring to the recent concession contract. The banner was tied to the fencing at the gate.

We used the bullhorn to assemble people in front of Freddie's. Then one speaker after another grabbed the bullhorn and called for a contract that provided equity with GM and Ford. Others spoke about rejecting Chrysler givebacks, particularly since the 1980 concession contract. Chrysler had shut three plants indefinitely, with two other plants retooled for K cars using robots to perform 98 percent of the spot welding. The crowd responded with chants: "Chrysler contract—no way! Chrysler contract—no way!"

Not till two or three in the morning did the crowd thin. I was in no shape to drive but knew I had to be on the picket line at dawn, and I slowly maneuvered back to Racine.

Awaking to a pounding headache, I headed, on an empty stomach, back to the plant for picket duty as the sun rose. Department 838 chief Gathings shot me a look of disgust, pissed at losing wages. Overnight, picket lines had been organized by members taking the initiative to ensure that every gate was covered. Radio trucks and coffee patrols soon followed. Initial

Exuberant strikers flood the street, blocking one of many police cars, in a celebratory show of defiance to the daily oppression of being chained to the mind-deadening assembly line.

disorder transformed into an orderly wildcat thanks to the initiative of stewards, chief stewards, and committee members.

Once I had covered Gate 15 for a couple of hours, I headed to check other gates. Everyone with whom I spoke expressed anger and disgust at Majerus. Majerus had already appeared in the media calling the strike unauthorized and issuing instructions to return to work—spitting into the wind.

Tuesday afternoon, with unity spirits running high, a press release from local president Sylvester circulated: "Although the International has not sanctioned our strike, we hope the membership will follow our tradition of NO CONTRACT, NO WORK, [maintain] the picket lines and support the executive board. We feel the AMC bargaining team is dragging their feet."

The "tradition" of "no contract, no work," as far as I knew, had been established in 1978 when the ranks had chosen to walk out at our caucus's urging.

On Wednesday's evening news, Majerus announced a tentative settlement that *did not include a working agreement.* While Majerus might have thought he had a settlement and could order our membership back to work, 40–50 percent of workers refused to return on Thursday. Those who had reported were sent home by management after a few hours.

Despite the information blackout, and during confusion sowed by Majerus, the caucus put together a flyer to hand to any who straggled in to work and to those still walking picket lines.

NO CONTRACT, NO WORK!

So far the International has refused sanction. But as the TV news said last night the strike is sanctioned by the thousands of Local 72 members who are picketing and staying off the job....

The rank-and-file members of Local 72 should have the time to examine any proposed contract and vote on it before production resumes....

STRIKE INFORMATION:

- The Executive Board bargained until 5 a.m. Wednesday morning on the Local working agreement. They will go back into meetings on the economic agreement on Wednesday afternoon.
- Picketing is being set up on a voluntary basis at the union hall.

Majerus's betrayal took its toll by sowing uncertainty, splitting the more militant from those who felt compelled to follow the path of least controversy. But upwards of half of workers in Building 40, a strong bastion of the UWC's influence, refused to report on Thursday morning.

All through the day, the news media pumped out propaganda promulgated by the international that the strike had ended. I hung out most of the day at Madore's, hooting and booing, along with the rest of the clientele, at news reports on TV that AMC workers had returned to work.

Second shift in Building 40 was scheduled to report at 4:00 p.m. At 3:00 p.m. more than two hundred second-shift workers gathered at Gate 15, along with many in the caucus. The UWC had built a committed, loyal base who now looked for guidance: Go back to work or stay out on an unsanctioned wildcat? The very word *wildcat* carried an emotional charge—a feeling of defiance and rebellion.

A lively impromptu discussion on the street ensued about the international's sabotage of the strike, fueled by anger that we hadn't yet voted on a tentative agreement. Basically, we were being told to trust Majerus and return to work before learning the terms of a new agreement. A vote was called right there on the street, and the consensus was to shut down second shift.

Many of us headed to Freddie's and Madore's. As the news came on the bar TVs, Majerus's puffy face filled the screen as he claimed that the

AMC strike had concluded and that employees had returned to work. His self-serving statement flew in the face of reality.

At some point in the early evening, Jim Madore motioned for me to take a phone call. *Shit,* I thought, *this can't be good. Who even knows I'm here?*

"Melrod, this is Rudy." Who else could it have been with that low, gravelly voice?

"Hey, Rudy. What's up?"

"Jon, you gotta go back. I can't force you, but I'm strongly suggesting that we can't protect your job if the plant stays down. The company ain't gonna put up with another day of the strike, and Majerus is with them."

"But Rudy, we haven't even seen a tentative agreement, let alone voted."

Damn. One minute I was riding high, and now I felt like I had been doused with ice water.

"Jon, I understand. I've always been straight with you. We've gone as far as we can this time around. Don't get fired. I don't want to tell you what to do, but I hope you're at work tomorrow."

My first instinct was to tell Rudy "Fuck the company and fuck the international!" I realized, however, that consequences for both me and those who chose to stay out might be disastrous. Better to go back in, consolidate gains, and build on the advances we had achieved.

"Okay, Rudy. I hear ya."

In the months before expiration, we had done our work well in preparing the membership to resist concessions. The Sylvester board had taken the same stance. Majerus, however, threw a wrinkle into the equation. Majerus had developed a fetish to be on the AMC/Renault board of directors. If Doug Fraser held a seat on the Chrysler board, Majerus sought the same prestige. The stepping-stone to Renault's board required Majerus to corral the Local 72 membership.

The *Fighting Times* commented,

You might ask—was Ray [Majerus] suffering from a conflict of interests? Was he more worried about gaining a position on the AMC board than in representing the rank and file of Local 72?

The International in their printed highlights of the recent [Local 72] agreement claim that . . . "he (Fraser) is now in a position to influence the board (Chrysler) on all decisions that . . . affect . . . jobs." [Yeah, right!]

196

Rather than bargaining for a seat on the board the UAW should begin taking action on an industry wide basis to protect the jobs of UAW members.

Majerus and the international no longer think like the rank and file. Majerus came into negotiations and told our board *he* was going for... added prestige for himself.

In summing up the 1980 contract for his thesis, Mike Braun wrote: "The UWC had been at the center of the wildcat, alongside the steward structure of Local 72. They [UWC] gained valuable experience and a vastly improved reputation for their role. The wildcat strike gave the bargaining committee what Gene Sylvester called 'the maximum bargaining pressure.'"

In fact, the company didn't really bargain until *after* 12:01 a.m. When details of the contract were finally released, we held our own. The company failed to claw back any significant takeaways.

Significantly, we won a paid holiday in memory of Dr. King, the first such provision in the auto industry. John Drew's efforts to revitalize the FEPC and push the committee to take a more active role in the civil rights movement had paid off with a historic victory.

CHAPTER 20

Scab of the Month: "What's a Wohlgemuth?"

By spring 1979, people almost universally accepted *Fighting Times* as part of the shop's natural landscape. A rough barometer to judge readership was to look around after we distributed an issue. If only a few of the forty-five hundred to five thousand had been discarded, we considered the newsletter successful. As time progressed, fewer and fewer copies landed on the floors or in garbage cans.

Almost by happenstance, we started a column we dubbed "Scab of the Month," not referring to strikebreakers but borrowing from a definition by author Jack London: "A scab is a two-legged animal with a corkscrew soul, a water brain, a combination backbone of jelly and glue. Where others have hearts, he carries a tumor of rotten principles."

Anyone who's ever worked in a factory, or any workplace, has experienced a particularly nasty, mean-spirited boss. With folks regularly besieging us with complaints, *Fighting Times* opened its pages to any aggrieved employee with a story to tell about this kind of scab—a management scab.

Success of "Scab of the Month" depended on protecting the anonymity of the aggrieved person. If someone submitted a story or told us a story about a racist, sexist, or just plain nasty boss, we were game to print it. Eventually *Fighting Times* weaponized Scab of the Month so that it carried real consequences.

One of the early columns spotlighted favoritism practiced by a particularly slimy superintendent:

828—What's a Wohlgemuth?

Dear Fighting Times:

Question: Why is it that in 828 a woman on the line with 5½ years got the Thursday and Friday of the week before Thanksgiving off when higher seniority people were denied the same days off?

Question: Why is it that this same woman had already received permission to take off Thanksgiving week before the company announced we would be down that week?

Question: Why is it that when this woman was sick on the job extra help was thrown in so she could stand around for the day?

Answer: She is the girlfriend of 828 Superintendent Wohlgemuth who had planned to [spend] Thanksgiving week in Florida. When confronted by the union with the fact that seniority is supposed to prevail for time off, the Superintendent answered, "*I'll decide who's off.*"

The letter, just three questions, raised an outsized ruckus. Before the influx of young workers in the mid-seventies, management lived by "old school," good ol' boy rules. A boss could, without a stir, bestow favoritism on an in-plant girlfriend or a woman with whom he chose to flirt.

Fighting Times set out to smash such old norms, and when we exposed Frank Wohlgemuth by name, we skewered a previously acceptable pattern of in-plant sexism and favoritism.

In calling out Wohlgemuth, we hit a soft spot in the company's armor. Management's power is rooted in the fiction that its authority is set in stone. But management, consisting of only a small fraction of the workforce, is able to maintain industrial discipline only as long as they keep rigid control over the more numerous but subordinate workforce. If the workforce rebels, withholds its labor, or disrupts production, management's authority diminishes.

A story about another Wohlgemuth would follow:

828 SON OF A WOHLGEMUTH

A Wohlgemuth is a type of creature that gives special privileges to his friends and relatives because of his position.

Son of Wohlgemuth is now on the gravy train. After being at AMC for only a year he was "qualified" to work in 834 repair on the 30 day program, along with a whole group of bosses' kids and others who know people at the top. In that time he got 185 hours of overtime.

Department 834 shone like a golden spoon. Work in 834 was slow-paced and allowed for plentiful overtime. The company had instituted a program that permitted employees to work in 834 regardless of seniority. Of four hundred applicants, only fifty hit the jackpot.

In 834 overtime flowed for Leonard Wohlgemuth (son of Frank), adding up to fat paychecks, up to $1,000 per week. So it went for low-seniority bosses' kids and others with friends in high places.

Now this kid has made relief [another job awarded without regard to seniority] with absolutely no experience or qualifications.

Relief should be posted and bidded on just like any other job. Take favoritism out of the hands of bosses.

Son of Wohlgemuth took our critique personally, later joining a group of supervisors who sought to muzzle *Fighting Times* through a company-financed lawsuit.

The October/November 1979 issue spotlighted sexual harassment:

SCABS OF THE MONTH

(Please excuse the language in this article, they are all direct quotes from management.)

1st prize 838

"I WISH ALL OF MY PEOPLE WERE PROBIES [probationary employees]—I'D TAKE CARE OF THEM."

Without a close second this supervisor on nights in 838 [Stevie Freeman] has earned the title of "scab of the month." Not long ago every time he walked by a certain woman he would intentionally brush against her rear. She asked him not to do it and his reply was, "I can brush against your 80 year old ass anytime I want—all I have to do is excuse myself." When hauled into the office he claimed he had accidentally brushed her. In that case the division head told him to walk on the other side of the car . . .

In another case a woman innocently asked him if she could have a stick of gum. His answer, "If I can have a bite of your tits."

Or how about this—After the fire in Building 40 on October 12, the smoke was thick in 838. A couple of women whose eyes were watering badly asked Stevie for a nurse's pass. In front of 3 stewards he told them, "You're nothing but a bunch of pussies." That remark earned him his 3rd trip to the office. This guy is the original "Male chauvinist pig."

His favorite anti-union trick is to completely ignore a steward and walk the other way when approached. A couple of stewards fixed him good one night when 7 . . . trailed him wherever he went.

Remember[,] Stevie—SCABS GET OLD AND FALL OFF!

I stayed late one night to investigate Freeman. I had heard about his antics from Joanne Haley, whose boyfriend Rich was second-shift assistant chief. The panoply of stories about Freeman's behavior seemed so preposterous that I remained a bit skeptical until I personally checked out his record.

As a courtesy, I stopped by the chief's desk to let Rich know I had stayed late to investigate Freeman for *Fighting Times*. Grateful for assistance in holding Freeman accountable, Rich walked me over to Frenchie, whom Freeman had been harassing.

Frenchie seemed embarrassed to recount events. After I let her know that we were planning to write about Freeman as Scab of the Month, her eyes welled up with tears of shame and anger.

"Frenchie, trust me," I said. "It's just a matter of time before we knock Freeman on his ass. He can't be allowed to treat you like a dog—he's the damn dog!"

Next I headed for the woman who had asked Freeman for a stick of gum. She turned out to be a shy Latina and still a probationary, meaning she couldn't even file a grievance to defend herself.

After gentle cajoling, it became obvious she had suffered utter humiliation from Freeman's verbal abuse. She had a new baby and feared losing her job if she said anything. I assured her that under no circumstance would we mention her name and told her to keep in mind that Freeman's insults constituted overt sexual harassment for which we would hold him accountable once she completed her probationary period.

While I didn't speak with the women who had asked for nurses' passes, I found a few of the seven stewards who had dogged Freeman. I wrote in *Fighting Times*, "I want you guys to know you are really acting like stewards should. Second shift doesn't mean second class, and even if the first shift chief [Gathings] won't do anything, we got enough militant stewards, in collaboration with Fighting Times, to fuck up Freeman!"

Second place for Scab of the Month in that issue was from Department 836:

Mickey Haights[,] a [supervisor] in the drilling area of 836[,] was nominated for his performance when he told a Black woman that he would find a more "degrading" job for her when she refused to sweep the floor. His bid for glory ended when the Chief steward threw the broom into the repair hole.

The issue was settled when the Division head agreed that people in 836 build cars and maintenance sweeps the floor.

Haights having so flippantly insulted a Black woman was squarely within the company's culture of institutional racism. It is doubtful Haights would have hurled the same affront at a white worker. Additionally, Haights's ordering a worker assigned to drilling to perform maintenance work violated distinct job classifications. A fundamental union principle rested on strict demarcation of job classifications to preserve and protect individual jobs. If metal workers could be ordered to perform maintenance, maintenance jobs would be rendered redundant.

The Scab of the Month for the final issue of 1979 was also from Department 836:

> Once again the Body Shop line in 836 was the scene of people's anger being turned into action. On Nov. 14 [workers] on 1st shift stopped work for 20 minutes to get some safety problems taken care of and to get the [supervisor] off their backs.
>
> Dave Rutchik the SCAB [supervisor] for this month has had something like this coming for a long time.
>
> On Tuesday November 13 ... people on the line ... presented some safety complaints [to Rutchik and the general supervisor]. Included in these complaints was the fact that the bucks that the body sides ride on did not all have wheel guards.... Without wheel guards a person's foot could easily be crushed.
>
> On Wednesday when people came in, none of the safety problems had been taken care of. The word started to pass ... that 9:30 was the time for sticking together and taking action.... At 9:30 ... everyone gathered in the aisle.... Nobody went back to work at 9:40....
>
> Several stewards and the Chief steward came down and backed the people up. Maintenance was called and the wheel guards were welded on right then and there....
>
> Rutchik spent most of the rest of the week in the office. He was given a "vacation" the next week.

In December, we also ran a letter written about Freeman by a crew of second-shifters:

Line workers and stewards dubbed Stevie Freeman "Scab of the Month" for misogynist attacks on women, racist tirades, and physical attacks against Black workers, plastering pumpkin-head stickers on every available spot, including the back of Freeman's shirt. Petitions, job actions, and collective harassment by stewards forced management to discharge Freeman.

Dear Fighting Times

We read about Stevie Wonder [Stevie Freeman] in the last paper. We have a little we would like to add in.

1. He fired one employee because she got injured on the job and coded off.

2. He always refuses to get a steward when we ask.

3. He tries to avoid his employees when they ask to go to the nurse. He usually tries diagnosis [sic] what is wrong, maybe he thinks he's an M.D.

4. He's put extra work on a job when it's not on the [job] assignment.

5. He refuses to let any of us see our [job] assignments.

6. He threw an air gun at his employees because he didn't know what else to do with it.

What will this guy do next?

Dave Mattson drew Freeman's face as pumpkin head on top of a white shirt with the AMC logo above the pocket. And we made these into hundreds of round stickers that had the words "Scab of the Month" and "Stevie Wonder." We reprinted the caricature in *Fighting Times* with this caption: "Hundreds of these round stickers were plastered around dept. 838. Some found their way onto Stevie's desk and the back of his shirt."

When I walked through Freeman's section as I left the plant, I saw that stickers were plastered *everywhere*, and everyone was chattering about how Stevie couldn't walk ten feet without having one surreptitiously plastered on his back. The very act of defiantly slapping stickers all over the place empowered people, but not enough to tame Freeman—at least not yet.

The myriad complaints against supervisors created an abundance of material for *Fighting Times*.

On November 28, fumes from paint in Department 837 grew so intense that a worker went to the nurse with nausea, burning eyes, and a splitting headache. The nurse called for Safety. Safety concurred that the air was dangerous to inhale.

Belts on the exhaust fans had been slipping, preventing outside air from being pumped into the "penthouse." At 2:20 p.m., following chief Rich Hughes's lead, workers walked out. After half an hour of not a single car being painted, the company provided penthouse workers with face masks; work resumed with iron-clad guarantees for a permanent repair.

In 836, a probationary employee failed to receive an emergency bathroom break despite waiting forty-five minutes. When he couldn't wait a second longer, he urinated on the spot. Despite the worker being probationary, his fellow workers walked off the line in protest. People held strong until his supervisor, Don Torkelson, pledged that this type of incident would not reoccur.

In 838, a supervisor directed a repair worker to drill a hole in a car body, which he refused to do since it wasn't on his job assignment. Management suspended the repair worker—but also the chief steward, for "directing the workforce." For every union member in the department, regardless of degree of union allegiance, discharge of a chief steward crossed every line. Some started yelling, exhorting others to stop work. Word circulated that repair workers assigned to work overtime had suddenly experienced an obligation to take care of personal business. At the buzzer, every repair worker downed tools and left. The next day, suspensions of the repair worker and the chief steward were reduced to verbal reprimands with a thirty-day review.

In some cases, drawing attention to a supervisor's bad acts had the effect of taming or mitigating unacceptable behavior. In other cases, with the most reprehensible supervisors, such attention fed their needy egos, encouraging them to act even more deplorably. Rutchik proved to be a recidivist, exhibiting the behavior of a petulant child.

836—Scab . . . Deported

A couple of months ago people on his line sat down to get some safety problems settled. Every time Rutchik turned around he was written up for [doing union members' work]. The people on the line stuck together and showed their hatred for Rutchik by averaging about 25 less cars on days than on 2nd shift.

The transfer [deportation] of Rutchik should serve as a warning to other flunky [supervisor]—the people will not stand for your mistreatment and b.s. terror tactics.

The struggle against Rutchik encompassed a few lessons. First, not only those directly impacted by Rutchik joined in the resistance, participating in concerted action to write him up whenever he picked up a welding gun or repaired a defect. It turned into a feeding frenzy, since the company had to remit an hour's pay to a grievant every time Rutchik lifted a finger to perform union work.

Second, workers in Rutchik's section fought back by withholding their labor. The twenty-five fewer completed car bodies meant line workers were slowing down. The slowdown imposed a direct cost on the company by requiring repair workers to put in overtime to clean up repairs.

Third, widespread anger generated in the department reached a boil after management fired Mike Istvanek for allegedly pushing Rutchik. Mike had asked Rutchik for his steward at 11:00 a.m. When Rutchik didn't respond, Mike again demanded his steward, which led to Rutchik clamping his hands over his ears and hastening off like a petulant, spoiled child.

As Rutchik darted from Mike's work area, he tripped and fell. To the astonishment of all, Rutchik curled into a ball on the floor until his general supervisor ordered him to get up. At 3:20 p.m., ten minutes before shift end, Mike was sent to the office and discharged for "pushing" Rutchik. Eight eyewitnesses, however, testified that Rutchik tripped and was not pushed. By waiting till ten minutes before the shift ended, the company preempted a grievance-based disruption of production.

Fourth, 836 stewards asked the caucus to produce a sticker—"HEY RUTCHIK YOU STINK / REHIRE MIKE!" Pressure from the union in Department 836 and the agitation stirred up by hundreds wearing stickers and posting them widely pressured management to drop Mike's discharge to a thirty-day suspension.

While Rutchik's deportation grabbed top billing, a black box on the front page of the February *Fighting Times* awarded Scab of the Month to former general supervisor Bernie Neu, from the Motor Division, who had earned a reputation as a hothead and bar brawler.

Bernie is an EX-general [supervisor] as he recently got busted down to day shift [supervisor] after his infamous pre-Christmas antics. It was common knowledge that Bernie was out to pick up a woman.... He was quoted as saying, "I don't know who or what, but I'm gonna get a piece of a— tonight."...

Later that night Bernie was discovered partying.... Bernie claimed he was on business; but as far as we know there's no motors being produced in bldg. 40.

Word circulated that Bernie intended to retaliate. Rumor had it I was in his sights.

On a freezing winter day, with gray gloom blanketing the late afternoon, I headed to my car.

I froze. "What the fuck? Where's my windshield!" Slowly walking around the car shocked the chill out of me. Not a glass shard remained in any window. Fucking Neu had exacted revenge. I never found out for sure whether Bernie had done that, but he certainly matched the profile.

We didn't see it coming in May 1980, when AMC charged Tod Ohnstad, John Drew, and me with violating the National Labor Relations Act (NLRA). AMC argued that the printing of "Scab of the Month" by three stewards violated the NLRA.

But three months later we reported:

Scab of the Month Lives
N.L.R.B. Drops Charges!

AMC's legal attempts to stifle SCAB OF THE MONTH have failed. Their charges against Local 72, and John Drew, Tod Ohnstad, and Jon Melrod were dismissed on June 30, by the National Labor Relations Board....

We have one word of wisdom for the company—AS LONG AS THERE ARE SCABS WORKING FOR YOU, THERE WILL BE *SCAB OF THE MONTH.*

The lesson we drew from the NLRB charge was that *Fighting Times* was definitely piercing management's vulnerable underbelly.

Of course, there were consequences yet to come. In September, four supervisors, an ex-supervisor, and Wohlgemuth Jr. filed a civil lawsuit against Tod, John, and me. They claimed $4,180,000 in damages caused by *Fighting Times* engaging in "defamation."

Rather than fear the suit or let ourselves be intimidated, we wore it as a badge of honor. In October we reported:

[Supervisors] Sue For $4.2 Million

Steve Freeman, David Rutchik, Donald Phipps, Donald Panzlau, Bernard Neu, and hourly employee Leonard Wohlgemuth (son of 828 Superintendent Frank Wohlgemuth)... hired a Racine law firm to [sue *Fighting Times*].

Ex–Scab of the Month Steve Freeman is only asking for $1,850,000 in damages. The complaint dated 9-12-80 alleges that Fighting Times caused him to undergo "severe psychological strain... an inability to sleep... an ulcer of the stomach." Another popular ex-Scab, David Rutchik is asking for $1,150,000 because, the complaint alleges, Fighting Times caused him to... "consume excessive amounts of alcohol" among other terrible things.... Whoever is actually behind pulling this suit together is after one thing, the destruction of the people's right to complain about or criticize unjust [supervisors]. [Bernie Neu's claims were dismissed for failure to submit to discovery.]

Taking the lawsuit in stride, we barely blinked. None of us, after all, had close to $4 million, so the suit seemed utterly absurd. Plus, we considered the newsletter to be factual and truthful. The lawsuit alleged that we had harassed, intimidated, ridiculed, and vilified supervisory personnel. But we considered the newsletter an exercise of free speech protected by the First Amendment. We opined in the newsletter, "The intention of the suit is clearly to silence our free press. Unfortunately TELLING THE TRUTH COSTS."

Irrespective of the lawsuit, we intensified the campaign against Freeman. Together with second-shift stewards, we drafted a "Stop Stevie petition." Each steward passed the petition around, signing up almost the entire shift.

Pumpkin-head stickers proliferated, as did grievances and a well-substantiated complaint to the reactivated Fair Employment Practices Committee (FEPC), which included John Drew.

Fighting Times reported:

838 Supervisor Stevie Freeman has been found guilty of blatant sexual and racial discrimination by the Local 72 FEPC. The FEPC was

called to 838 to investigate charges against Freeman after hundreds of people signed a STOP STEVIE petition....

The petition spelled out the charges against Freeman:

1. Daily harassment of his people

2. Calling a Black union brother a "lazy M-F nigger"

3.Addressing union sisters who requested nurses passes as a "bunch of pussies"

[The FEPC] *recommended that* [Freeman] *be disciplined by management.*

[The FEPC] has been in Dept. 838 investigating Freeman[,] and new charges keep coming in. One report says that Freeman pointed his fingers like a pistol at two Black women and said "There's two dead blackbirds."

Although most designated Scab of the Month were low-level management, we weren't shy at calling out top brass. April 1980, Werner Jean, director of manufacturing operations in Detroit, mailed a letter to every employee's home. The rather incendiary letter lodged McCarthy-like charges linking *Fighting Times* to "handbilling programs" engaged in by other "Communist groups." Werner Jean had thrown down, so we hit back.

Dear Werner Jean,

We [feel] compelled to respond to your letter... addressed to "All American Motors Employees." In that letter you... referred to "publications that are passed out to employees at the plant gates." We... assume you were referring to the *Fighting Times....*

[You] write, "Lately however the handbills have increased in their inflammatory remarks against individuals and the company."... If your [supervisors] do nothing [evil], then there is nothing to fear. But if they act like scabs, peeping toms, racists and sexists, they'll see their names in print....

[You] write that "similar handbilling programs have been used by Communist groups at other major industrial employers."... [Let's] make it very clear. The UWO is open to all Local 72 members of various political beliefs.

Lastly, you write, "needless to say that the authors have neither the sense nor the fairness nor the courage to identify themselves." Most employees see us face to face everytime we hand out *Fighting*

Times. <u>But</u> for future reference, we have chosen an editorial board so anyone in the shop can submit a letter or an article:

John Drew steward 836, Jon Melrod steward 838, Tod Ohnstad steward 2838

In closing[,] Werner,... we hope you'll read the future issues of *Fighting Times* because THE TRUTH HURTS[,] DOESN'T IT?

CHAPTER 21

Climbing the Union Ladder

With the 1980 contract in the rearview mirror, I turned to the upcoming elections in mid-October. I had a couple of years as line steward and department chair under my belt and felt stoked to go one on one with Gathings for chief.

As line steward, I had listened to frequent complaints against some stewards and Gathings as chief. Many on the line resented seeing stewards off their jobs on "union business," sometimes for up to seven and a half hours a shift, but spending minimal time actually representing workers.

As a steward, I began each day by walking my section, checking in with every individual. I routinely followed up on every grievance, keeping the grievant informed as to the status of their complaint. I considered every grievance consequential, as it represented a personal wrong experienced by the grievant. When a grievance was baseless, however, I did not hesitate to own the responsibility to inform the individual that the complaint had no merit.

While Gathings's performance over the preceding year had been lackluster at best, he commanded a following among conservative workers, particularly among repair workers. Many repair workers were motivated by racking up overtime hours, and Gathings doled out overtime as a reward for loyalty.

Gathings responded with vengeance, spreading his view that the September strike, for which he blamed the UWC, had been unauthorized, too militant, and risked scaring away Renault. My response, honed over a few years, was that Renault had already slated production for Kenosha and that to agree to a substandard agreement would put us in a perpetual bidding war with other UAW locals, with Renault playing "Which local will agree to concessions to land new work?"

I articulated four tangible goals:

1. Ensure proper placement of [workers on the correct job]

2. Actively pursue all grievances
3. Make department meetings responsive
4. Strong[ly] [enforce] the contract

The election turned into a showdown over whether Gathings and vestiges of the Gillette clique still had juice, or my groundwork had persuaded people that I had the chops for the chief's job.

I walked the lines, explaining my four goals person by person: "This election shouldn't be about who you like or don't like. Political innuendo shouldn't determine your vote as some people are talking trash about me. If you want to know what I believe, just ask me. In terms of the election, I believe in the four action points in my flyer."

My election advantage sprang from the dedicated team of activists, including half the elected steward body, who felt vested in my campaign. Each took dozens of campaign stickers, affixing them on shirts, walls, and workstations.

Elections took place over two days, first for ten line stewards and then for chief. Only 162 people voted on day one. Gathings racked up 96 votes versus my 113—too tight a margin. I needed a resounding victory if I planned to shake things up and take charge.

I walked the line, appealing to *every* department member. I urged that a high turnout would send a message to management that the status quo under Gathings was history.

Encouraged by positive feedback, my confidence ran high. Most Blacks retained fresh memories of the racial showdown I had championed against Gathings's bigoted talk. Women were supportive, as I had vigorously struggled against sexism, particularly when it came to calling out supervisors like Freeman.

The election was not just about picking up most votes, however. Crucially, it tested what I had been espousing since I hired on in 1972. I wanted to prove that an upfront political leftist who stood at the gates selling the *Worker* and organizing to march against the KKK could be elected chief steward, representing more than eight hundred people in Department 838.

A whopping 324 people cast votes, all but 25 department members, double the total of the previous day! Counts were 123 votes for Gathings and 201 for me. I won by the margin I needed to feel confident I had a mandate for militant reform.

Pinning on the chief's silver button had been a dream. Now that I had won decisively, I needed to make good on my election promises. I approached department head DellaSanta to schedule weekly grievance meetings.

I was a bit apprehensive. DellaSanta adhered to the old-school boss persona. He had assiduously avoided personal contact with me as a steward, making it abundantly clear he wanted nothing to do with me. As chief, however, I stood on par with him—stewards dealt with supervisors, and chief stewards dealt with department heads.

"Hey DellaSanta. Guess you heard I won the chief's election?"

He gave no sign that I was even there and stood coldly erect. Maybe he hadn't heard me. "DellaSanta, I'm chief now. To get off to a good start..."

Without bothering to answer, he abruptly walked off. *Shit!* I thought, *this is gonna be tougher than I thought. I can't even get the fucking guy to look me in the eyes.*

I thought about my path forward. All that really mattered to a department head was the smooth, uninterrupted running of their department. DellaSanta didn't really give a damn about my politics, he just didn't want disruption. I needed to play that card.

A day or two later, I found DellaSanta standing at the top of the stairs to the glass office. I walked up. It would be just him and me at the top; he had nowhere to run.

"Look, DellaSanta, I understand you're not happy I got elected chief, but we gotta live together. You want the department to run smoothly, right?"

"Yeah," he said after a pause.

"Okay. I got no issue with that. I can promise I'll get the schedule of repair workers working overtime to you every day, so you've got a full crew. Employee moves will be done right so you don't have to waste time and money moving people around to correct union mistakes. But you gotta meet me halfway. For starters, we need to meet on grievances *every single week*. If the grievance is shitty, I ain't afraid to pull it; if it's got merit, I plan to push hard. We gotta get some ground rules or it's gonna be a shit year."

"Okay, Melrod, what day and time? Gathings dumped you with a lot of trash grievances. I guess they're yours now."

"Got it. See you Thursday afternoon at one?"

I deployed my first chief stewards report (an innovation I had promised) to counter DellaSanta's earlier rebuff. I reviewed the circumstances of a serious accident, instructing individuals to shut down the line in the event of a safety breach. A worker shutting the line—disrupting production—on one's own volition was anathema.

ACCIDENT

[O]n November 19 Randy Hansen...was seriously injured...when he was pinned between 2 bodies that jumped the line....An undogged car [one not properly attached] that jump[s] the track...can cause slack in the chain and result in serious injury....

If you see an undogged car...you should shut the line off. It could save a union brother or sister from serious injury.

I also reported on the backlog of grievances Gathings had dumped on me. "All grievances that were submitted prior to Thurs. Nov. 20th [the day I took office] have been met and processed."

Gathings had left me with thirty-two unresolved, problematic grievances. The path of least resistance allowed a chief to push contentious grievances to the board members' step. By resolving twenty-seven out of thirty-two, I signaled a new regimen for processing grievances *within the department.*

I also wanted to establish my availability as a rejoinder to frequent complaints about Gathings' lack of accessibility: "I by no means want these printed reports to replace face to face contact. Anytime you wish to speak with me about a problem or concern please notify your steward and I will be available."

In November, just a month after I was elected chief, AMC laid off the second shift, slashing production in half. Local 72 had 5,952 members working and 3,500 on indefinite layoff. AMC announced a $156 million loss for 1980.

AMC, with Renault pulling the strings, sought to reopen contract negotiations to wrangle concessions. AMC management set out to enlist Ray Majerus's and the international's collaboration. In the *New York Times*, Majerus committed: "Negotiations [will] begin at the earliest possible date."

Like a dancing duo, George Maddox, AMC VP of manufacturing, and Majerus met in December to review giveback proposals, which would undermine seniority in the staffing for a new model. Employees were to be chosen not solely by seniority [the preexisting rule] but rather "on the basis of seniority, qualifications, and work record, including attendance"—a breach of the past practice.

Echoing Charles Nash, Maddox, almost half a century later, threatened to "lock up the plant" if Local 72 didn't cave in to his concessions.

In January 1981, with a bleak economic outlook in Kenosha and nationally, the Local 72 executive board headed back to the bargaining table. An overlooked provision in the Working Agreement provided that the 1980 contract remain open to possible revision for six months.

The board came under intense pressure to bring the new Renault Alliance model to the plant with a guarantee of jobs and to avoid givebacks. Luckily, Majerus absented himself, leaving negotiations to the board.

In early February, the board announced a tentative agreement. The board agreed to minor staffing modifications, guaranteeing two thousand jobs to build the Renault Alliance at Lakefront. The Alliance was a lifeline for AMC and Kenosha. As *Fighting Times* summed up, it was "a tribute to the long-standing sentiment in Local 72 against concessions that the proposed agreement, even with the modifications, remains superior to anything [elsewhere] in the UAW."

The membership voted: 3,613 yeses and only 252 noes.

Back in August 1980, I had written a letter to the International Metalworkers Federation (IMF) in Europe hoping to establish contact with the union(s) at Renault. I mailed the letter, having no idea whether it would ever arrive at a receptive destination.

Six months later, we received the IMF's response, accompanied by a fifty-page profile of Renault. The UWC set out to educate ourselves and the broader membership about the world stage on which we were a new player.

Most Local 72 members recognized AMC as their class antagonist, whose regard for our futures and livelihoods was limited to how much we added to their profits. Renault, however, was a new overlord and an international one at that. We took seriously educating the rank and file as to what it meant to face an international class antagonist. Importantly, we hoped to instill understanding that our futures were now inextricably intertwined with a worldwide workforce.

We distilled the fifty-page profile into a three-part series. The first part described Renault's past and planned growth, and its increasing use of automation.

From the IMF profile, we extracted a succinct analysis of the Renault empire, including aggressive expansion plans for the US market. A quick synopsis: Renault grew from eighth-largest automaker worldwide in 1978 to seventh in 1979, producing over two million vehicles, employing 120,000 worldwide. Renault's projected strategy was to advance to fourth largest in the world by 1985, predicated on US market penetration.

As AMC's Kenosha facility was one of the most antiquated in the United States, the caucus set out to raise awareness of Renault's technological innovations that would seriously impact our jobs.

While automation in the abstract meant technological advance, without a plan, few, if any, of its benefits accrued to the displaced workforce, at least under the rules and laws governing displacement of workers under hardball capitalism.

In March 1981, *Fighting Times* ran the second in the series, pointing to the need for international union cooperation. "When Renault comes to Kenosha, the U.S. will become the 25th country where Renault vehicles are built," we wrote. We printed a chart detailing assembly of Renault vehicles in Europe, Africa, North and South America, and Asia. In a dramatic reorientation, we asked Local 72 members to view their jobs in the context of twenty-five overseas countries—the Renault Empire.

Before printing the third in the series, we fired a shot across Renault's bow by tagging Maurice Fertey, president of AMC Canada, as Scab of the Month. Fertey, before arriving at the Ontario plant, had served as general manager of Renault Canada. A Renault lifer, Fertey had served in Africa, Australia, the Netherlands, Scandinavia, and Turkey.

Scab of the Month Pres. AMC Canada

Maurice Fertey, the new President of AMC Canada[,] recently made the news by shooting off his mouth about how more of our work in Kenosha would be going to Canada....

Fertey was quoted as saying that the Brampton plant was to become the only producer of Concords and Senior Eagles, once production of the [Alliance] began at Lakefront. [T]his would mean that several hundred seniority employees here would be denied work [in Kenosha] while hiring was going on in Canada.

We laid out the very different approach to political action engaged in by unions in Europe. While most unions in the United State have reduced politics to voting for candidates belonging to a major political party, the European model entails direct action, often by flexing muscle in the workplace and on the streets.

Renault Couldn't Do in France What They'd Like to Do in Kenosha
For years the unions and the labor movement in Europe have marched, [gone] on strike[,] and voted in mass for legislation that would protect the rights of workers. [A]ll Common Market countries in Europe have established varying degrees of protective legislation[,] with France having about the best.

According to French law, Renault could not pull off what they are trying to do with our jobs in Kenosha. . . . [We detailed French government requirements for corporate-paid compensation, relocation, and training for those laid off.]

Meanwhile, Renault impacted Local 72 in real time. Lakefront was being retooled for Renault's front-wheel-drive Alliance. Renault's planned technological changes seemed futuristic and promised to eliminate countless jobs. Our lives were soon to be turned upside down by Renault, and the international hadn't uttered a word about what French ownership might mean. The international's interest in Renault ceased when Majerus lost his bid for a corporate board seat. We were left to figure out for ourselves the broader implications of Renault's partnership with AMC.

We did, however, increasingly experience Renault's drive to squeeze out greater productivity. *Fighting Times* published a stark warning:

Beware of IE
In times of slow sales IE [industrial engineering] does their best work—cutting costs. Already IE is working at eliminating every extra body and adding to the number of people laid off.

If you see IE stalking the lines remember the contract offers you some protection. Article 16 Section 4 reads [that] . . . the operator and steward or Chief Steward will be *notified 24 hours in advance of any timing or logging or observation of an employee.*

In conjunction with the *Fighting Times* alert, we produced stickers: "PROTECT YOUR JOB! BEWARE OF IE! ROBOTS NEXT?" All three Building 40 chief stewards, including me, met to discuss management moves to ratchet up productivity. All agreed to mobilize our steward bodies to distribute warning stickers. Chief stewards unleashed a force of twenty-five to thirty line stewards to promote the "Protect Your Job" campaign.

Whether tactically or by happenstance, the boundary line between the caucus and the official union structure in Building 40 blurred, particularly when it came to fighting IE. No one asked, "Why are the stewards handing out stickers printed by the UWC?" It seemed natural and seamless, although I'm sure there were those who questioned the overlap.

Traditionally, repair workers only executed repairs marked by inspectors on tickets. Normally a repair worker grabbed the ticket and fixed noted defects. Word passed to me that a repair worker Leroy needed me urgently. He and his steward were in an animated discussion when I arrived.

I told the supervisor to get Leroy off the line so I could meet with him and his steward.

"What's up, guys?"

Steward: "Chief Doxteter [known as 'Doc'] told Leroy here to eyeball the car to make any repairs he sees."

I asked: "What about the inspector up the line? Isn't she marking repairs on the ticket?"

Steward: "That's what's fucked up, chief. IE notified the inspector her job is being eliminated. Doc is instructing Leroy to do the inspector's job. It ain't on Leroy's job assignment to eyeball car bodies searching for repairs."

Me: "Leroy, whaddya you think?"

Leroy: "Chief, I ain't no inspector. My code is repair. I work off the repair ticket. I don't got no time to inspect *and* repair. That's bullshit."

Me: "Leroy, I'm with you, bro. They're trying to eliminate inspectors. This is Renault's productivity agenda. I'm telling Doc 'no way.' You with me?"

Leroy: "If you got my back, Chief."

Leroy was a high-seniority Black guy, originally from Milwaukee, and a solid union brother. We had known each other for years and had a bond of trust. Leroy grew up in the Local 75 school of combat unionism, whereby the union called the shots and members abided by the union's instructions. If asked, he'd hold the line despite threats of discipline.

Me: "Hey, Doc, whaddya doing? You know it ain't Leroy's job to repair without a ticket."

Alcoholism had long ago gotten the better of Doc. He was thin and sickly, and in the morning his hands shook from the prior night's binge. Doc didn't want hassle from the company or the union. All Doc hoped was to make it to retirement.

"Melrod, you know me. I'm ain't against the union. IE told me to notify Leroy to eyeball repairs. I told IE that Leroy needed an inspection ticket, but IE ordered me to give Leroy twenty-four-hour notice. IE's calling his job 'seek and repair.' I knew shit would hit the fan when you heard."

Me: "Look, Doc, it ain't gonna happen. You can tell whoever you got to tell that Leroy's code is repair and that means working off the ticket. Ain't no such code as 'seek and repair'! Tell your boss he can get that changed in the next contract."

Doc: "Chief, I still gotta give Leroy notice. My job's on the line."

Me: "Okay, Doc, get it done, but he's gonna do the job like he always has."

Doc: "Leroy, I'm here to officially notify you that at this time tomorrow you're expected to fix all repairs—with or without an inspection ticket."

Me: "Leroy, the contract only requires you to perform work within your code. Tomorrow do your job like you always have and no more."

Once Doc had walked off, I checked with Leroy.

"Bro, sure you're down for this? It's gonna be a fight."

I put in a call to the board member who represented my department. I rarely saw Dick O'Brien. He was strictly a by-the-book guy and couldn't be counted on to color outside the lines.

"Dick, this is Melrod. We got us an issue. The company is trying to eliminate an inspector and have repair eyeball repairs without a ticket."

"Okay. I'll be up tomorrow. We might need to file a grievance."

"Nah, that ain't gonna work. If we file a grievance my guy's gonna be forced to do the job, and the inspector is gone for sure. I told my guy it ain't his job to work without an inspector."

"Well, Melrod, I don't know if I can support you on that."

No words of solidarity from my board member. Admittedly, I was a bit worried; but I had drawn a line and couldn't and wouldn't back down.

Next day, I headed over to Doc's section.

"Hey, Leroy, you with me? We still in this together?"

"Whatever you say, Chief."

"Okay, brother, do your job like you always do. If there ain't a ticket, just step back and let the body pass. Any hassle from Doc—holler for me."

I checked back a couple of times during the day, and Leroy was standing watching cars go by. Doc, to avoid a confrontation, had instructed his utility worker to pick up repairs for Leroy.

I couldn't have found a better soldier than Leroy. Back in Milwaukee he had hung with the group of militant Black stewards and head stewards. If the union asked him to take a stand, it would take a lot to scare him off.

CLIMBING THE UNION LADDER

We settled into a day-to-day stalemate. Every day, Leroy sat down on a barrel for eight hours. I'd check on him a couple of times a day just to make sure he held strong. At stake was an important principle. I knew we were out on a limb, and at times I really worried about Leroy's job. I also worried about my job, but it was difficult to fire a chief steward, which required approval from Detroit. I figured we could always back down if it got too hot or if the pressure got to Leroy.

After a few weeks, the company grew sick of putting up with Leroy and me defying them without repercussions. The general supervisor issued us both "direct orders," instructing Leroy to perform all repairs. We listened and let him walk away, sticking with our program.

Eventually, Russ Wing, the powerful department head, pulled me aside. Even though Wing was a company lifer, we had established an understanding. We were straight with each other and both respected each other's word.

"Look, Melrod, you best stop messing around. You're risking Leroy's and your jobs. I don't want to fire you or him, but you better get with the program."

"Russ, you know if you fire me the department goes down. That ain't what you want. Not with Renault watching."

"Melrod, serious advice: don't cock the gun unless you're willing to pull the trigger."

Shit! I thought. *Wing is serious.*

I knew I was in a pincer when I spotted Rudy and Sylvester. I had never seen Sylvester in 838, so I knew things had gotten real. Rudy hadn't gone back on the board yet and was the local's substance abuse counselor. Regardless, he carried more weight than Sylvester, at least with me.

Rudy just sat for a while, not saying a word. I had come to hate his pregnant pauses. You knew Rudy was thinking and about to hit you up. I also knew I was pretty far out on a limb.

"Jon"—damn Rudy's voice always sounded like we were having a death-bed conversation—"the company informed the full board that they're not gonna put up with your repair worker sitting down on his job. I'm told both you and he refused a direct order?"

"But, but Rudy—there's an important union principle. They want my guy to do inspection work."

"Jon, I admire your principles, but there's a time and place for every fight. You're not gonna win this one. Not by yourself, and you're putting another man's job at stake."

"Shit, Rudy, I know that."

"You gotta give this one up before it goes too far."

I remembered advice my mentor and friend Fletch had shared when I became chief: "You can't win every battle."

"Yeah, Rudy, I guess I hear ya."

I asked Doc to get Leroy off the line.

"Leroy, we been fighting this code issue for almost a month. How ya feeling about it?"

"Chief, I gotta be real. I had your back when they fired you in Milwaukee. You got my vote when you ran for chief down here. But truthfully, brother, we're in a messed-up place. You're the only Jewish guy in this factory, and they'd like to run your ass outta here for good. I'm an old Black man hoping to soon retire from this plantation. Like my mama used to say to my brother and me when we screwed up, 'You two fools are like BBs rolling around in a box car.' I think it's time to call it quits before they fire our asses and we're outside looking in. No disrespect, brother."

"No problem, Leroy. I hear ya."

I had campaigned on the promise of making militant changes in how the union operated. Had I failed? The thought plagued me. Out of the blue, a woman whom I barely knew handed me a typed letter:

Dear Jon,

I've been meaning to write you a letter of appreciation for a long time now but have been procrastinating....

Jon, I don't know how anybody else feels, but I appreciate you as our Chief Steward! Let me tell you the ways I love you:

1. I love your informative monthly business letters.
2. I love your friendliness and ability to stay humble.
3. I love the fact that I have never heard any slanderous remarks about you.
4. I love the way you get the job done, professionally and compassionately.

Jon, I can honestly say that I like everyone in 838, maybe some a little more than others but then that's part of being human, isn't it. So, keep up the good work and I've enjoyed working with you on dayshift!

Eloise McCabe

Reading Eloise's letter wiped away feelings of self-doubt I felt over backing down on the inspection issue. As both Rudy and Fletcher, my two main mentors, had counseled, "You gotta know when to fold 'em."

CHAPTER 22

Mr. Bill Comes to Kenosha

The steward body hatched plans for a party at the union hall, to bring together the many diverse people in Department 838, many of whom had minimal contact with each other outside the plant. Most workers go their separate ways, but we hoped to create social bonds to reinforce the in-shop collectivity of factory work and bring together people in a social setting to ameliorate racial and sexual antagonisms. We also planned to use the party to ratchet up our campaign against Stevie Freeman.

A wide swath of department members volunteered to cook, sell tickets, and decorate, with some signing up to act in a guerrilla theater performance based on a TV character popular at the time, Mr. Bill on *Saturday Night Live*. Mr. Bill was a figurine clown and a parody of children's claymation shows. Each episode opened innocently but turned dangerous for Mr. Bill, leading to him being crushed or dismembered, while squealing "Ohhh noooooooooooo!"

We substituted Freeman for Mr. Bill. JoAnne Haley suggested using a half dozen of her kids' Hot Wheels cars to replicate the section of the line Stevie supervised. A small crew created a skit with Stevie (Mr. Bill) as the protagonist.

The hall filled with hundreds, not only people with ties to 838 but also folks I'd never seen. It dawned on me that I alone had responsibility for the night from beginning to end.

Time arrived for the skit, and 838 workers assembled around six Hot Wheels attached as if on an assembly line. Then they mimicked working on the little cars with hammers and screwdrivers.

Enter JoAnne with a sign around her neck: "Stevie Freeman." She nastily harassed workers, repeating Freeman's most egregious harangues. The crowd simultaneously laughed and booed with abandon.

For the final act, workers ganged up on Freeman, pushing him to the ground as Hot Wheels cars ran over him. Freeman/Mr. Bill yelled,

"Ohhh noooooo!" And the crowd echoed, "Ohhh noooooo!" Creatively, we harnessed a pop culture spoof to fuel our anti-Freeman campaign.

The party continued with dancing and a lot of drinking. Soon after midnight I put out the word that people needed to leave. I felt lucky. The night had gone down with no bad shit jumping off.

Then there was yelling from the departing crowd: "Melrod! Melrod! Come quick! Fucked-up scene in the parking lot!"

I rushed out into the darkness. Shadows of indistinguishable bodies appeared totally entangled, as I collided with a melee of flailing fists and knives slicing the air. Everyone yelled in Spanish, making it difficult for me to decipher what was going down.

I picked out Ernie Olivares from 838 and his brothers Joaquin and Ramiro, along with Pedro Longoria, also from 838, trading punches and wrestling with some Latino guys I didn't recognize. Ernie and Pedro, best friends, had been born and raised in the tight-knit Latino community. I had been an outsider. Over time, walls crumbled, and we established a solid rapport. Not infrequently, Ernie, Pedro, their families, and Jessie Sewell gathered in my postage-stamp backyard for Mexican red beef barbacoa.

I attended my first quinceañera at an Olivares family celebration. Their support for me in the union, and for Fighting Times, derived more from our friendship than from political commitment. Intense loyalty defined our relationship.

When I jumped into the melee, I acted without caution, plunging into the midst of whaling fists, yelling for Ernie and Pedro to cut the shit and back off. It took a while to command everyone's attention. Slowly the fight broke up. I quizzed Ernie and Pedro.

"Why'd you guys have to get rowdy? You know that makes us look real fucking bad!"

"Melrod, we're from Piedras Negras. Those motherfuckers are from Eagle Pass. They been calling us wetbacks all night. They're pochos from across the Rio and don't even speak Mexican. We don't take their shit."

"Damn, you guys, head home. Fuck. This was a good night till now!"

I headed home and by 2:00 a.m. had finally crashed.

The phone ringing at 7:00 a.m. reminded me that I was still alive. The phone kept ringing, a sign I'd best pick it up as the caller wasn't gonna quit.

I tried to sound like I had just woken up perky and fresh. "Hello."

After seconds of silence, I said to myself, *Shit, it's gotta be Rudy. Why does he always take so long to start speaking?*

"Jon, you up?"

"Sure, Rudy. What's up?"

"I heard your department had a shindig last night."

"Yeah, we did."

"Sylvester just got off the phone. There's a burned car in the lot. Cops told Sylvester someone musta thrown a firebomb into it. Know anything about it?"

"Nah, not really, Rudy. We had a little altercation, but I got everyone out, and we shut the hall with no damage. There wasn't no burned car."

"Well," he said, and then he paused again. "There is now. Sylvester wants you at headquarters to clean up your mess."

"Will do, Rudy. Thanks for the heads-up."

Driving to headquarters I mused, *Damn, this is gonna be bad. I can already hear the haters talking about the damn radicals in 838. Can't even hold a party without everything going haywire.*

When I arrived at the parking lot, you couldn't miss the burned car. It looked bad—the shell of a charred body. I asked cops there what had happened; they had no clue.

When I got back home, my head pounding like a bass drum, I called Ernie.

"Ernie, what the fuck went down last night?"

"Hombre, we left when you told us. Not sure what you talkin' about."

"Fuck, Ernie, there's a torched car. You don't know nothin' about it?"

"Nah, bro. Don't know shit."

Ernie had invoked an impenetrable code of silence: "Thou shalt never snitch." I hung up.

The party had been a success, demonizing Freeman had been cool, but I knew Monday would be twenty questions about the torched car.

In August 1981 Lakefront shut down to retool for the Alliance. The size of Department 838 jumped to over eight hundred, over four hundred per shift, producing Eagles and Concords. The migration from Lakefront offered me the opportunity to represent many new members of local 72. I issued the following in my chief steward's report:

> Brothers and sisters,
>
> I would like to take this opportunity to welcome . . . Lakefront to dept.
> 838. I realize for many of you to move to Main Plant has been a major

hassle and has meant a change in jobs and/or the switch to another shift.

We spent many hours in the weeks before vacation [trying to] avoid any added inconvenience by placing people on the wrong jobs. Although the contract did not call for it, we worked to place as many Lakefront people who had been relief, bench group, or floaters in their same group.…

Now that we are *all equally members of 838* it will be the *responsibility* and *obligation* of the union to fully represent *everyone*. In order to promote unity I appointed the 3 highest vote receivers from Lakefront to 3 open steward spots on nights. In addition, I felt it fair to appoint the highest vote getter from Lakefront, Tod Ohnstad, as Acting Chief on the second shift. I am happy to report that all the elected 2nd shift stewards from 838 unanimously supported this unity with 2838 [the Lakefront department transferring in] and pledged to work together for all the people's benefits.

From jump street, I promoted fundamental union principles of transparency and unity. Frequently, as when we transferred from Milwaukee, departmental unions responded to an influx of new people by favoring those already in the department.

Well in advance of the transfer, I persuaded the department head that I should be allowed to assign transferees respecting seniority and prior job experience, placing workers from 2838 on jobs similar to what they held at Lakefront.

The upside for management was that the department would avoid weeks of production chaos as people retrained. The plus for workers from 2838 was that they would fill jobs in 838 similar to those with which they were already familiar.

Particular job categories—relief, bench group, repair, and utility—were considered desirable. Had I wanted, I could have filled those jobs with friends and loyalists already in 838. Instead, I spent days reviewing jobs and job categories people had held at Lakefront, assigning these people to the same or similar jobs in 838, using seniority as the determinative factor.

Similarly, I could have appointed loyalists to open steward positions. I opted instead to appoint high vote getters from 2838; luckily that included Tod as assistant chief.

The November 1981 elections came and went without much suspense. I ran on the simple platform of asking people to judge whether I had fulfilled my previous four campaign pledges.

People must have believed that I had, since I ran unopposed. Of ten stewards elected, seven were caucus members or solid allies. The three holdovers from the Gillette days had been defanged and relegated to being backbenchers.

The imprimatur of my tenure turned on my monthly chief steward's report, which I distributed as I walked the lines, stopping to chat and answer questions.

Looking over my files reminds me of the many ups and downs, twists and turns, and challenges. Every day of factory life is challenging. At least with a union, in our case a strong one, workers are afforded a degree of protection from the ravages of working on a monotonous assembly line.

Selections from some of those monthly reports:

December
Additional Phones
After numerous requests we have gotten another phone installed by the steps along the South Wall.

January
Local 72 [Ice] Fishing Derby
Sun. Feb. 15, at the Wonder Bar in Twin Lakes. Food will be served . . . , a country western band will play. . . . See your steward for tickets.
[If there are two sacred events in Wisconsin, one is deer hunting during Thanksgiving week, and the other is the winter ice fishing derby. All a good Wisconsinite needs is a .30-06 for deer, and a jigging rod and reel and ice auger to open a hole in the ice to drop a line and sinker.]

March
G&H Strikers Fundraising Dance
As most people know[,] the G&H strike is in its 5th month. This is nothing but a union-busting attack and needs the full support of all union people. We are selling tickets for $2 to help sustain their strike fund. As a G&H striker said recently, "The fund has saved many strikers from losing their homes or having their gas cut off, as well as keeping food on the table for the kids." So far we have sold approximately 100 tickets in bldg. 40. We can do better!

April

John Zdanowicz

On April 1st Jonsey (181 man in Sec. 107) suffered a heart attack. . . .
$160 was generously donated by the members of 838 to help him out
during his hard times. He was *very* grateful to receive our help and
"Thank You" cards from him are posted on the time clocks.

Strike Vote

At the April 11th Membership Meeting Pres. Sylvester asked support
for a motion to schedule a special meeting for the purpose of a
strike vote. He reported that there are numerous unsettled grievances. . . . Of course, the loss of jobs at the Kenosha plant is included
as one of those major grievances. . . . The motion was passed
unanimously.

May

838 Softball Team

Final preparations are being made for the department softball team.
[In order to fill out the roster for the second team, I was drafted to
play right field, where balls go to die.]

July

G&H

A total of over $6000 was collected for the strike fund, including
$313 in dept. 838. THANKS AGAIN!

While my reports may appear mundane, such a small but consistent effort at keeping people informed paid huge dividends in building a
cohesive departmental union, the most basic democratic forum on the
departmental level.

Every March, *Fighting Times* ran an article celebrating International
Women's Day, focusing on the struggle against sexist discrimination and
for the liberation of women. In Department 838 we had one of the highest
concentrations of women workers in the plant, yet historically leadership
of the departmental union had been the province of men.

Once I became chief, I set out to integrate the steward body by encouraging women to run and assisting them in doing so.

Initially activated by the anti-Freeman campaign, Joanne Haley gravi-
tated to the UWC and became a regular at the gates distributing newsletters.

On her first run, Joanne was overwhelmingly elected steward. Once she broke the barrier, other women followed.

Cathy Meiers involuntarily found herself in the middle of a racist incident when Gathings shamed her for kissing a Black man. After 838 members rallied to bash Gathings, Cathy was motivated to run for steward and was elected in 1979.

The Gathings incident sparked other young women to see themselves as having a voice that needed to be heard. Many had come to the department meeting to support Cathy. Their condemnation of Gathings for racist and sexist behavior opened a floodgate of dissatisfaction felt by women.

Donna Coleman, a friend of Cathy's, also attended the meeting. Overcoming her hesitation to speak in public, she trashed Gathings. Donna became a regular at the gates handing out *Fighting Times* and ran for and was elected alternate steward.

I set aside time to mentor the newly elected women, helping them with the skills required to write and argue grievances and building their confidence to confront male supervisors, who typically expected women to be nonthreatening. I instituted weekly meetings of the steward body, where women stewards raised issues such as the shortage of women's bathrooms or the lack of sanitary napkins, issues typically never addressed.

Lula Smith, a middle-aged, Black, single mother who happened to be my neighbor, bumped into 838 on a cutback. Lula had expressed interest in becoming active in the union. Encouraged by her drive and always looking for opportunities to diversify the steward body, I appointed her steward until she was officially elected.

I worked closely with Lula, who always carried a clipboard for taking copious notes. After I left the plant in 1985, the international drafted Lula onto the regional staff to represent a host of small UAW locals. I fondly remember that after my diagnosis for terminal pancreatic cancer in 2004, I received a heartfelt letter from Lula explaining that she had recruited her church congregation to pray for my recovery.

In the summer of 1981, thirty-nine years before the murder of George Floyd, twenty-two-year-old African American Ernest Lacy died after being arrested by Milwaukee cops while walking to the local convenience store. Two cops held him down and handcuffed him while a third jammed a knee on Lacy's back, constricting air flow. Complaining he couldn't breathe,

The author with trim department worker John Neal, author of the MLK article and member of the *Fighting Times* editorial board.

Lacey became unresponsive. Rather than transporting him to the hospital, the cops loaded him into a police van, where he died.

Lacy's death sparked community outrage and a call for measures to restrain Milwaukee's notoriously racist police. Marches and protests were organized to demand justice and prosecution of the cops.

The Local 72 FEPC, with John Drew's participation, invited Howard Fuller, then the leader of the movement for justice for Ernie Lacy, to speak at our Martin Luther King celebration in January 1982. In *Fighting Times,* we sought to expose Lacy's murder as systemic brutality by police against Milwaukee's Black community. We tied the Lacy campaign for justice to the struggle advocated by MLK, illustrating that the struggle for justice was far from over:

> "Let Justice Run Down Like Waters, and Righteousness Like a Mighty Stream"
>
> —MLK

Make King's Birthday a National Holiday

On January 15, the birthday of Dr. Martin Luther King will be celebrated by freedom loving people around the world. From the Montgomery, Ala. Boycott of 1955 that started the fight against segregation in the South to the open housing marches in Chicago, King was part of a mass social movement that opposed injustice. Recent incidents such as the killing of Ernie [Lacy] by Milwaukee police show that King's struggle is not yet won.

This year... marchers will present petitions to Congress with 2 million signatures calling on them to pass a law making Dr. King's birthday a national holiday. Here in Local 72... we will be getting a paid day off in honor of Dr. King on the Monday after Easter. *Our Local is the first in the UAW to win this day off to honor King's contributions to our society* [emphasis added]. The Local 72 Fair Employment Practices Committee is planning a memorial program... to honor King and highlight Local 72's efforts to win a paid day off.

CHAPTER 23

UWC Crosses the Ocean to France

O ut of the blue, a barely coherent letter, postmarked Paris, France, arrived in the UWC post office box. After repetitive readings and a bit of decoding, we realized that the caucus had been invited to an international meeting of Renault workers in the fall of 1981. While we weren't exactly clear from whom the invitation had come, whether from the official union at Renault or rank-and-file internationalists, we were interested.

The caucus set out to raise funds, $1,000 to cover costs for two delegates. Caucus members chose me, as 838 chief, and Tod, as assistant chief, to attend. In truth, crossing the Atlantic to meet with delegates from all over the world was a bridge too far for other caucus members, many of whom had barely left Wisconsin, let alone the United States.

Caucus members and supportive stewards initiated a raffle, soliciting ticket sales. While a conference of Renault trade unionists in Paris seemed a bit far afield, people supported our attending, particularly with Lakefront being retooled for a Renault vehicle.

Joanne Haley and other 838 stewards ran a weekly 50/50 raffle, with names written on dollar bills as the raffle tickets. To raise additional funds, we busted out merchandise sales—blue T-shirts with the UWC logo, yellow T-shirts with "A WOMAN'S PLACE IS IN HER UNION," and blue nylon UWC jackets with gold trim.

With quite a few UWC activists having been elected steward, and a few as chief stewards, caucus members with union positions had access to countless people. Any stigma once attached to identification with the UWC had largely disappeared. Soon hundreds were wearing UWC T-shirts and jackets.

The international, still mired in 1950s McCarthy-like thinking, rabidly eschewed contact with socialists or communists, making collaborative relations with French unions impossible since French unions were defined by political affiliation. The two major unions were associated with left parties—the CGT with the Communist Party and the CFDT with socialists.

In response to the many questions being raised, we published some of them along with answers:

Why Is the U.W.C. Going to France[?]

Q: Who invited the United Workers Caucus to France?

A: We received our invitation from Roger Sylvain who is the head of the Central Works Committee of Renault-France[,] which is made up of representatives of Renault workers in France....

Q: Is the UWC going to France to party or will Local 72 members find out what happened at the meeting?

A: We pledge to bring back a full written report and a slide show to all interested Local 72 members.

We didn't really know what we were doing or what awaited us in France. When Tod and I deplaned at the sprawling De Gaulle Airport, we wore our UWC jackets, hoping we'd be recognized, as there was no prearranged meetup, and we had no address in Paris. Serendipitously, we bumped into a conference representative picking up another delegate. After explaining as best we could, as neither of us spoke a word of French, that we had come for the world conference, we squeezed into a tiny Renault headed into Paris. Feeling lucky, we were dropped at a small hotel where rooms had been booked in our names.

The following is from the twelve-page *Fighting Times* summary written by Tod and me and edited by John Drew.

The Conference convened in Billancourt outside Paris. Billancourt is the home of the oldest Renault plant where 15,000 worked. The Comite Central D'Entreprise (Central Shop Committee or CCE)... is the umbrella organization of the four different unions that represent workers at the Renault Plants in France. The CCE is made up of 20 elected delegates from the 13 Renault plants in France....

Delegates were present from Renault plants in Spain, Portugal, England, Colombia, Mexico, Turkey, Zimbabwe, Ivory Coast, Morocco, Madagascar and several [locations] in France. We were introduced to Roger Sylvain, President of the CCE[,] who was pleased that we were able to attend from the USA.

Roger Sylvain, head of the whole show, embraced us in a big French bear hug, kissing us on both cheeks. I wasn't sure Roger had even known of our planned attendance.

At the opening session, I looked to the rear and observed a bank of translators. We were provided headsets for simultaneous translation, as if at the UN. We had been preaching international worker solidarity, and here we were living the dream, surrounded by a full complement of Renault workers speaking half a dozen languages.

Following the introductory session, we were bussed to lunch at the nearby Flins plant, where twenty thousand were employed. After touring Flins, the delegation met with Pierre Eelsen, director general and second-ranking executive at Renault.

Tod and I laughed at the absurdity. We had no idea who Roger Sylvain had explained we were, but I had been delegated by the CCE to pose questions to Renault's second in command about the future of production in Kenosha and the United States.

I found myself in the seat that, by protocol, should have been occupied by Sylvester as Local 72 president or by AMC Director Ray Majerus. Majerus had drooled over the very thought of hobnobbing with Renault corporate elites. If only he had seen Tod and me, wearing UWC jackets, waiting to query Monsieur Eelsen.

My nerves were in my mouth as I formulated questions. The following are two questions posed to Eelsen and his answers:

> Q: What responsibility does Renault feel for the laid-off workers [in Kenosha] and does Renault intend to utilize unused capacity in Kenosha?
> EELSEN: The utilization of capacity requires the success of the R-9 ... and there will undoubtedly be at least one more car which could be produced after the R-9 [Alliance] in the US and that should insure capacity ... which will be equivalent to what Kenosha knew normally. Normally[,] that is to say 4 or 5 years ago.
> Q: Will future production in Kenosha be tied to contract concessions?
> EELSEN: It is a very productive plant, so I don't think we'll have any scraps on that angle.... The question of productivity is not uninteresting. But it is certain from indications we have received that it is no problem.... So, I don't think that there will be any problem with the future of productivity of AMC.

I had looked Eelsen squarely in the eye and posed probing questions about the future of Renault's plans for Kenosha and the US auto market, to which he responded with remarkably detailed answers. I'm sure Eelsen would have been shocked had he known that Tod and I were two rank and filers, unauthorized by Local 72, who had sold T-shirts and raffle tickets to get to Paris.

One of the conference highlights was a presentation by unionists from Third World countries where being a union organizer meant having the courage to put your life on the line. As we reported, "Representatives from Argentina and Chile were unable to attend because ... they were not allowed to leave their countries. However, delegates from Colombia, Turkey and Morocco did attend and spoke of [life-threatening] government repression."

As Renault had already begun retooling for the Alliance in Kenosha, we requested a visit to the plant producing the same model. Special arrangements were made to tour the ultramodern plant in Douai, in northern France.

With no one in management overseeing us, we snapped photos of Renault's state-of-the-art technology. It was a dose of hard reality to glimpse the future in this high-tech facility, vastly dissimilar to anything in Kenosha. Robots were already widespread in modern auto plants, but they were new to us then. Our photos included shots of the newest Renault welding robots, at the time more advanced than those being used in Japanese factories. (We used the photos and others to create a comprehensive slideshow upon our return.)

As recounted in our conference summary, the six thousand Douai workers were the most militant in Renault's thirteen-plant system, with the CGT being the most widely supported union based on its militance and success in securing worker protections. When our host, the youthful top in-plant CGT rep Jean Pierre, introduced himself, he sported a button on his lapel of Vladimir Lenin, leader of the 1917 revolution in Russia.

We attributed the high level of combativeness to the young workforce and the young, pugnacious union representatives. In fact, just prior to our tour, a series of rolling departmental strikes, plus two plant-wide walkouts, had seriously disrupted production. As a result, protections had been won against layoffs due to automation.

Back in Kenosha, we reported on the mechanics of each department and how drastically the Alliance reconfigured the ratio between robots and humans. By offering a peek into our future, we provided Local 72 members with their first concrete information about Alliance production.

This report addressed a far-reaching, dramatic transformation of the Kenosha production facility and its impact on Local 72 members' lives.

Fall 1981: First World Conference of Renault workers attended by caucus members Tod Ohnstad and author. There were fifty-seven delegates in attendance from eleven countries.

That it was produced by a rank-and-file caucus rather than the official union constituted an indictment of the UAW's failure to confront changes rendered by new technology and a complete failure to embrace international solidarity.

We learned from the union leadership in Douai that Renault's number-one hit man, the future US executive VP and member of the AMC board of directors Jose Dedeurwaerder, held the distinction of being one of Renault's most notoriously anti-union managers.

Alarm bells rang as we got an earful from both French and Belgian Renault workers about Dedeurwaerder:

- Dedeurwaerder received his education under the brutal military dictatorship in Argentina in the 1970s, when he began his career with Renault.
- Upon transfer to our sister plant in Douai, he stated: "It will be the union or me." Between 1976 and 1980, he refused to attend meetings with the union.
- Between 1978 and 1980, he initiated a new absentee policy, which was unheard of at the plant. During these two years three hundred people were fired for absenteeism.
- He installed steel doors to his plant offices. When the union health and safety committee went to investigate, they were disciplined for being in the office area.

Before Dedeurwaerder departed for the United States, the CGT union paper wrote:

"Good Riddance Dedeurwaerder"
What a pitiful image of our country and of Renault enterprise will Dedeurwaerder be as an ambassador to the U.S. We would like to warn the workers of American Motors ... Monsieur Dedeurwaerder ... is a representative of the most reactionary, anti-democratic tradition of the bosses class. You will certainly have trouble with Dedeurwaerder.

We already knew we would receive a nasty reception from the international when word got out that we had met with a global group of Renault union leaders. On the other hand, shame on them for not embracing international solidarity and union cooperation. Tod and I concluded, "Fuck it! We're here representing the *membership* of Local 72; those are sufficient qualifications."

Before the conference concluded, two press releases were issued. One was in conjunction with the shop committee at the Douai plant, in which we agreed to develop "further exchanges permitting a better knowledge of the workers of the two countries." The other was a joint statement by the fifty-seven trade union delegates from eleven countries. It promised, "Delegates will [seek] the harmonization of the terms and conditions of work of Renault workers in the world based on those offering the best improvements."

Returning to Kenosha, Tod and I pulled together a slideshow. We previewed it at a Department 838 meeting. Lest anyone doubt that rank and filers will participate when they find it relevant, the 160-frame slideshow played to a full house at union headquarters.

Even the board felt compelled to accept our offer to present the slideshow to the fifteen of them. The elected top leaders of Local 72 listened to Tod and me describe scenes of Renault factories and summarize interactions with the second-ranking executive at Renault. I can only imagine, with glee, how uncomfortable it must have been for them.

CHAPTER 24

Renault Returns for Another Bite of the Apple

R enault rang in 1982 by seeking greater concessions, proposing a scheme of takeaways dubbed the "Employee Investment Plan" (EIP). The EIP, stripped of its obfuscating veneer, pressed Local 72 members to "loan" the company 10 percent of our wages and benefits for the next year and one-half.

In dollars and cents, the EIP would cost each Local 72 member $2.22 an hour in 1982 and $2.64 an hour in 1983. In year one, the "investment" would total about $1,800 per person (equivalent to more than $5,000 today.) In addition, the EIP "loan" included the loss of five vacation days, three paid casual days, and the MLK holiday (before it even kicked in).

The purported "repayment provisions" provided: (1) cash or stock with 10 percent interest, (2) repayment to commence in 1984 if auto profits topped 4 percent, (3) otherwise, repayment to commence in 1986.

The "investment" to be pilfered from our pockets totaled $150 million. At 10 percent interest, AMC would have to repay $165 million, which it hoped to finance by setting aside $100 per vehicle, requiring Renault to sell 1.65 million cars. *Fighting Times* pointed out, "At a rate of 200,000 sales per year it would take over 8 years to raise the needed cash. We would be repaid, maybe in 1994."

Backdrop for the EIP was the nationwide tanking of auto sales and US automakers' demands for givebacks. In *Fighting Times*, we linked the Kenosha slowdown to the nationwide recession: "Since Ronald Reagan took office a little over one year ago, an average of 6000 workers have joined the ranks of the unemployed every business day.... For auto workers the rate [of unemployment] went from 15.8% to 21.7%."

The UWC condemned the international's serial concession agreements. Over and over, we warned that granting concessions in exchange for the promise of jobs equaled false assurance without real returns. Under the headline "Do Wage Cuts Guarantee Jobs?" we wrote, "The bottom line is that the number of jobs in the auto industry is determined primarily by the number of sales[,] and right now the industry is selling the fewest cars of any time since 1959! Now AMC is coming back for more, even though the Renault agreement… said they would not seek to reopen the contract unless the changes were to '[a]ccommodate added work.' The 10% Investment Plan in its present form *does not guarantee one single job in Kenosha.*"

Despite understanding our argument, most were of two minds. Concessions do not guarantee jobs. We all had seen that Chrysler workers were paid $2.50 an hour less than workers at Ford and GM and were $1 an hour behind on benefits. Yet, of the 100,000 Chrysler workers who voted to accept concessions, only 57,000 remained on the job.

On the other hand, the unknown is intimidating. With management incessantly hammering that the EIP was essential for Renault's survival, and with the international parroting company propaganda, quite a few were willing to accept concessions in the mere *hope* of securing their jobs.

Advocating that the membership refuse to consider the EIP would have opened us to accusations of having a death wish. Rather than advocating that members reject the EIP out of hand, we shifted the narrative to address the bottom-line issue of job security.

In anticipation of the membership meeting to consider the EIP, we wrote: "If the Local 72 membership votes at this Saturday's union meeting to enter into further discussions with the corporation, job security in Kenosha should be the #1 priority. We must have guarantees of future product lines in Kenosha, more investment in the Kenosha plant, and guaranteed future levels of employment."

On January 16, one thousand apprehensive members packed head-quarters. Members turned out in large numbers, in fear of losing their jobs, but were not willing to write the board a blank check. Most of the board read the people's pulse accurately, putting forward the following resolution, which the membership overwhelmingly passed: "Direct the Executive Board to participate in the meetings on the employee investment program, keep-ing in mind that we want commitments and guarantees that the end results will be advantageous to our members and the Kenosha [plant]."

Then more bad news rocked the plant: fifteen hundred additional layoffs, with the termination of second shift in Building 40. Over half the layoffs resulted from the transfer of Kenosha production to Canada. The biting irony of job loss to Canada was that the Ontario UAW local refused to participate in the EIP, making a mockery of the international's "concessions equal jobs" charade.

Job losses mounted in Kenosha, and meanwhile public reports surfaced that foreclosures had tripled. The register of deeds issued a statement that it was the worst year ever seen, with as many as six foreclosures a day.

Negotiations between US locals and AMC stalled repeatedly because of Local 72 opposition to the EIP. Meanwhile, GM and Ford demanded deep contract concessions. Facing the same push for concessions by the international, the UWC allied with GM and Ford activists and local officers opposed to them.

Opposition to concessions had been initiated by a few local leaders, including Peter Kelly, unit chair of GM Local 160, and Al Gardner, president of the tool and die unit at Ford Local 600. Prior to GM and Ford council meetings, I traveled to Detroit to meet with Pete and Al, along with activists from a few other UAW locals. We formulated strategy to oppose concessions.

On January 8 in Chicago, the opposition launched our pushback with a handbill distributed by Gardener's tool and die unit: "Hell No! We are being asked to give concessions so Ford can use the money to finance their global plans.... Concessions mean you'll be financing our own layoffs, it will not mean jobs are saved."

To the international's chagrin, delegates strolled the lobby of the Palmer House wearing large yellow buttons that read "STOP THE CON-cession GAME." Reflecting the widespread growth of anticoncession sentiment, speaker after speaker lambasted international president Fraser for advocating that contracts be reopened.

Gardner chastised Fraser, "If we give the companies concessions now, they will automate much, much faster, and we'll see more people laid off. It's poor car sales that are causing Ford's problems and not high labor costs."

Kelly added, "The gains made by organized labor have been a safety net for all Americans. Working cheap never saved a single job. If we make concessions, the competition can too."

Fraser tore into the opposition: "Brother Gardner, I'm not gonna get mad, I'm gonna get even. And the next time you raise your whatever... I'm gonna cut your ass up."

Despite the well-organized opposition, Fraser secured, just barely, a voice vote authorizing talks. Even though Fraser secured his vote, a national UAW opposition consolidated for the first time since the early days of the union, when Walter Reuther drove out the radical, independent-thinking opposition in the 1940s.

The opposition convened a few weeks later in Flint, Michigan, to plan ongoing strategy and form Locals Opposed to Concessions (LOC). Even though reopening the Ford and GM contracts didn't equate to our EIP battle, I attended the Flint meeting, where 152 dissidents gathered from thirty-seven locals, mainly from Michigan.

When Fraser put the question of reopening on the floor of the GM Council, LOC forced a roll call vote. In a stunning rebuke, 43 percent of delegates voted not to proceed with negotiations.

The March 20 *New York Times* reported, "Negotiations in January on a contract that would have linked union concessions to lower car prices broke off because of resistance among the rank-and-file union members." Fraser realized that if he could barely rally 50 percent of the council leadership to approve talks, there was no way he could convince the GM membership to accept takeaways.

With concessions at GM stonewalled, the UAW international pivoted to Ford to extract a two-year extension contract full of givebacks. I penned a letter to *Kenosha Labor* (delivered to every Local 72 member's home) expressing the UWC's critique of the Ford contract:

> Dear Editor:
> The new Ford contract is being hailed by some as a major break-through in job protection programs.... But a close look reveals the loopholes in the fine print that are so large you could drive a Mack truck through.... Ford workers will be giving up $9000 in wages and benefits over the next 31 months.
> What did Ford workers lose?
> - 60 cents off cost of living increases for 18 months ($1800 lost)
> - Two 3 percent annual raises (1982 and 1983 given up)
> - Paid personal holidays and Christmas Bonus Holiday given up
> - NO PENSION INCREASE DURING THE LIFE OF THE TWO YEAR EXTENSION
> What did Ford workers win???
> - "Plant Closing Protection"—which is so weak that it puts NO RESTRICTION on plant closings due to the loss of volume, consolidation of operations, or production changes....
> - "Outsourcing Limitations"—The language merely states that Ford will give the union 60 days notice "where practicable" before

making a decision on future outsourcing.... When and if Ford notifies the union of an additional outsourcing decision, the union will have the opportunity to bargain on reducing wages or changing work rules to cut costs and keep the work in their plant. That means a bidding war between local unions is written right into the contract....

- "Guaranteed Income Stream"—provides only 50 percent to 75 percent of base pay.... No protection for under 15 years [or] anyone already laid off....
- "Lifetime Employment"—Ford will pick two plants where it will not lay off any in the top 80 percent of the seniority ladder. Ford can choose any two of its 94 bargaining units, some with as few as 30 workers....

The "historic Ford Agreement" WILL DO NOTHING to protect UAW members' jobs, WHILE IT WILL CUT PAYCHECKS BY 10 PERCENT!...

YES—WE NEED REAL JOB SECURITY AND A GUARANTEED LEVEL OF EMPLOYMENT FOR AMC WORKERS IN KENOSHA but... NO—WE DON'T WANT OR NEED THE FORD SELLOUT!!!

After tying a bow on the Ford sellout, Fraser and Majerus flew to Milwaukee for a March 10 GM council meeting. Hoping to kill two birds with one stone, they scheduled a meeting with the Local 72 executive board about the EIP. If Majerus and Fraser expected smooth sailing after jamming through concessions at Ford, they were mistaken.

The Local 72 executive board presented a counterproposal to the EIP, predicated on job security commitments. The international countered that Local 72 needed to restructure its proposal before negotiations could proceed.

The caucus, meanwhile, navigated between outright rejection of the EIP and—out of respect for members' fear of losing jobs—staying at the table but holding out for real job security provisions.

Local 72 up against AMC & Int'l
Job Security Still #1 Priority

The company and the International claim that cutting our wages is the only way out of this mess.... But giving AMC $2.30 an hour will not generate one job or sell one car in the midst of the worst sales slump in 20 years.

AMC claims the 10% is needed for further product development. The question is future product development where? In Torreon Mexico where Renault is building the engine plant? In a site outside Kenosha where the 3 door and 5 door will be built? ...

Any tentative contract that includes the Employee Investment Plan should be voted up or down based on how it satisfies the need for jobs for Local 72 members.

The Local 72 board had caught the international off guard by submitting an EIP counterproposal.

With most of UWC's activists laid off, I needed allies for the "No EIP" campaign. Rudy and other high-seniority chief stewards like Charlie Underwood joined the stand against givebacks. I collaborated with a broad, diverse group of in-shop activists to form what we called Committee for Job Security and a Decent Contract.

On March 31, before a tentative EIP agreement had been voted on, the company stole outright all unused casual days, unilaterally rescinding that provision of the contract. Shock waves reverberated, as many expressed outrage that the company had reneged on existing benefits.

For the first time since my 1973 discharge, I physically felt the weight of the current situation. All younger people had been laid off. The seniority date for eligibility to work stood at June 1972, just one month after my hire date of May 1972 (although being chief entitled me to super-seniority status). Over 50 percent of the membership stood in unemployment lines or had exhausted benefits.

Gloom descended over those still working. No longer were we orchestrating midnight walkouts. We were struggling to cap overtime to force management to recall laid-off members one or two at a time. No longer were a half dozen stewards dogging Freeman; we were fighting IE's unrelenting efforts to squeeze more work out of fewer people.

Regardless of the challenges, caving in to the company and the international remained unacceptable. The committee drafted a petition protesting the theft of casual days and demanded that the board suspend negotiations pending their restoration. It felt lonely as I sought allies to pass the petition. Most immediately signed, glad that they were not alone in opposition.

The international, without local authorization, prepared a "Proposed EIP Highlights" that purported to summarize the tentative agreement. Not conceding an inch to the international, our committee prepared an eight-page document headed "Analysis: AMC Tentative Agreement 1982–85."

I struggled to enlist volunteers to distribute the document. When I couldn't find activists in other areas of the plant, I sneaked out of 838 on "union business" and planted copies in far-off canteen areas and departments, where I asked random folks to assist with distribution.

The document noted: "There are some serious negative items in the settlement that will set Local 72 back more than just the $8–9,000 we will be investing." On job security we acknowledged:

> The letter in the contract on work placement which states that Toledo, Milwaukee, and Kenosha will not be played off against each other in a bidding war for new work is a step in the right direction. The letter on plant closing protection is also a step forward....
>
> The tentative contract falls short because it does not satisfy our need for job security on two counts:
>
> 1. There is no commitment for new models to replace the AMC line.
> 2. There is no commitment that the components we are producing such as axles, pistons, etc. will stay in the plant or be replaced by new products.
>
> On those grounds, *the agreement should be voted down* and the Board sent back to implement the membership motion of January 16—"KEEPING IN MIND THAT WE WANT COMMITMENTS AND GUARANTEES THAT THE END RESULTS WILL BE ADVANTAGEOUS TO OUR MEMBERS AND THE KENOSHA FACILITIES."

At the ratification meeting, debate was heated, contentious, and split. Most in the hall were high-seniority workers desperately afraid of losing the only job they had ever held, from which they had always assumed they would one day retire.

Taking the floor, I implored members to vote no and send the board back to secure concrete employment protections.

Along with thousands of others voting at trailers positioned at plant gates, I cast a no vote but with trepidation as to the future. Unlike other Local 72 members, I had options. I could seek a career outside the factory, as I had my diploma from Madison. But along with others I had devoted my life since May 1972 to transforming Local 72 into a model of union militancy, rank-and-file democracy, and progressive political action.

Having personal options not available to others brought no comfort. The people I worked with were friends and neighbors. We worked together, partied together, breathed the same air, and shared the same dreams. I wondered if my life's path was soon to be cut short. I'm sure others felt the same trepidation but without seeing any alternatives.

In Kenosha, eight of the thirteen executive board members, including Rudy, rejected the international's position. The EIP barely squeaked by, with 52 percent voting yes. Almost one-half of the membership rejected the company's position that future production in Kenosha depended on our willingness to take a $10,000 hit rather than on the ebb and flow of the auto industry in a chaotic and irrational capitalist marke.

AMC/Renault most likely never intended to pay back the "investments." Folks in the shop, however, took the company at its word. People *demanded* a running tally of how much we were "lending" the company each pay period. After a lot of grousing and sharp criticism of leadership, my July 1982 chief steward's report read: "Many people have been asking when our paychecks will begin showing the amount of each individual's 'investment.' According to the payroll office as of Aug. 13th or Aug. 20th the dollar amount should begin showing on our weekly payroll checks."

It should come as no surprise, however, that AMC/Renault did not pay back EIP monies in 1984 or in 1986. In 1989, after Chrysler acquired AMC and Rudy had been elected Local 72 president, he would negotiate repayment of the EIP as part of a plant closing agreement.

CHAPTER 25

Taking on the International: One Member, One Vote

T od Ohnstad, John Drew, and I had fought to break into the Local 72 standing committee structure, yet major challenges stood in the way of motivating committees to action. After Sylvester's election as president, he appointed me to the local's education committee (EC). The EC had been fairly moribund, here and there sponsoring a few, very few, programs.

My first EC meeting felt like I had landed in alien territory—strictly male, strictly white and high-seniority. All but me belonged to the inner sanctum of the standing committee system.

To push the EC toward a more activist stance, with a program I thought would pass scrutiny, I designed a seven-week Labor School. The curriculum was designed for motivated rank-and-filers and stewards. It opened with a session on the history of UAW Local 72, including its radical roots. Other sessions addressed labor law, robots and new technology, health and safety, contract interpretation, and collective bargaining with multinational corporations like Renault.

Distribution of the sign-up form went well: activist stewards and caucus members took charge, handing out hundreds of forms, primarily in assembly departments. I felt confident that people were hungering for knowledge and would willingly participate. Detractors on the EC, of course, expected "Melrod's little project" to crash and burn.

To everyone's surprise, including mine, 213 people registered. I chaired each class and expounded at will, as no one could criticize the Labor School due to the numbers enrolling.

In the introductory class, I recounted the role of radicals, socialists, and communists in the battle to beat Mr. Nash by unionizing the first auto plant in the country. When a later session focused on multinationals, I took the opportunity to rail against multinational corporate greed and its adverse impact on the international working class.

My enthusiasm soared as lively discussions unfolded, particularly among active shop militants. Labor School concluded with a graduation ceremony, including the award of a completion certificate, handed out by Sylvester, which attendees took as seriously as any school graduation. *This is how a democratic, empowered, politically progressive rank-and-file-based union operates*, I thought with satisfaction.

In my December 1982 chief steward's report I said, "I am happy to announce that... more people from 838 successfully completed the school than any other department." I then listed names of thirteen department members awarded graduation certificates.

Admittedly, I didn't move any on the EC to the left, but I had initiated a program to politically influence 213 active members, banking on their future roles in the local.

Before the 1982 holiday shutdown, rumors circulated that the company might discontinue the Eagle, a model produced by Department 838. After shutdown, we learned that without enough orders to sustain both Canada and Kenosha, we had lost the Eagle to Canada.

I delivered the devastating news in my January report, but life's routines continued. I also announced the annual ice fishing derby, with festivities at Eddie's Wonder Bar.

In March 1983, I announced the total shutdown of Building 40:

> This will be [my] last report as Chief Steward....
> On Mon. March 14 [we] will reluctantly be bumping into a "Renault" department. We've all heard the horror stories of running on the job and have seen the so-called "rules" the company issued in 2838. I remain confident of one fact—those of us who have worked together in 838 have learned our unionism and our contract rights.... (I do mean <u>all</u> [of us] as I bumped a job on the line in 2838 along with the rest of our department members.)

The loss of the Eagle hit like a body blow, particular as Sylvester had announced in February that no plans existed to retool Building 40. The department felt like a morgue as I walked the line handing out my last report. I looked back at unhappy faces, a few with tears running down their cheeks. Lives were rupturing.

As the final Eagle ran by each worker, its passage left a deep foreboding.

Regardless of individual politics, we all shared the same needs and desires for a decent job and to be treated with dignity. We had, to the extent possible under a profit-driven system, achieved that goal over the preceding few years in 838. In an instant, we were collectively descending into the unknown at the five-story Lakefront plant, the late 1800s home of Sterling Bicycle and Simmons, the mattress manufacturer.

Despite the shutdown, we pulled together a slate of five to run for delegate to the Twenty-Seventh UAW Convention in Dallas in 1983. Our slate consisted of John Drew, Kojak, Tod, Lula Smith, and me. We settled on an election platform with direct relevance to our members.

The slate agreed that we could register the most impact by raising the issue of "one member, one vote." Top UAW officers were not voted in by the membership but chosen by convention delegates. The insider Administration Caucus dominated the convention, tilting the outcome of any delegate vote toward the status quo. (In 2022 this autocratic system would be changed under court supervision to direct elections by the membership as we had advocated.)

In conversations with other UAW activists (many in Locals Opposed to Concessions), we proposed a nationwide One Member, One Vote campaign spearheaded by Local 72. The slate drafted a model resolution mandating the election of international officers and regional directors by membership vote. We planned to circulate the resolution throughout the United States and Canada via other delegates who shared our desire to democratize the union.

Rudy supported the resolution and enlisted Sylvester. The twelve hundred in attendance at the February 1983 membership meeting voted *unanimously* to endorse our One Member, One Vote resolution.

We handed out our first campaign flyer at the plant gates:

Vote for UAW Convention Delegates

The five of us are running for delegate because we feel that the upcoming Convention ... [is a place] where important business affecting our membership takes place ... [It is] not a vacation in Playland. ...

If elected we will work with other delegates from Local 72 who believe in the same issues we do. We will work to make Local 72's position in favor of One Member—One Vote, an issue on the Convention floor.

The key distinction between our campaign and that of other candidates was that we ran on issues. The number of candidates who ran—thirty-five—and of members who voted was testament to the interest we generated in a typically ho-hum affair.

We hit the campaign trail with a vengeance. We printed posters to hang in the shop and taverns. We stamped out thousands of buttons: "Vote Melrod #2" and "Vote Drew #33." We printed thousands of cards laying out our platform.

There existed a long-standing tradition that candidates freely walked the lines handing out election materials. John Drew and I set out with an ambitious plan to canvass every department. On March 23, we walked the line in Department 830 in the Motor Division, careful not to interfere with production but at the same time to hand everyone a card or leave one on their workbench. Superintendent Bill Mattox spotted us and ordered us to leave the plant. After I told Mattox he'd have to get someone to throw us out, he scurried to call Labor Relations. We departed before his return.

Later that morning we got busted again, this time in Department 820. General supervisor Rick Fox told us, "Get off the line and into the aisle." We refused but again left by the time Fox returned from conferring with Labor Relations. Regardless, Labor Relations instructed that we be issued five-page disciplinary warnings.

Through countless similar election interactions with management, a clear pattern emerged: when pushed, push back. We considered it important for folks to observe that supervisory personnel were not all-powerful and could be defied. Importantly, people perceived that if management came after us, it must mean we had something important to say. We turned the warning into a campaign message.

> Why did AMC's Labor Relations Department process 5 page warnings…on only 2 candidates out of 35 running for delegate on a charge of "interfering with production in Department 830 and 820?"…
>
> This Wednesday don't let the company interfere in the delegate election. Use your vote to send a message to management to keep their hands off UAW politics.

Of thirty-five candidates running for ten delegate positions, John Drew and I were elected delegate, and Tod was elected alternate. As John noted, our election as delegates constituted an "enormous milestone" since this was the first time UWC members had won a plant-wide election.

When the Local 72 resolutions committee met, we planned a nation-wide strategy for spreading the "One Member, One Vote" campaign. We enlisted Sylvester's agreement to write a letter on Local 72 stationary to be mailed to every local president, recording secretary, and delegate chair in the UAW. With fifteen hundred UAW locals, each mailing (of which we did three) constituted a massive undertaking, but it was financially possible with the local's coffers.

The international threw up a roadblock. The only way to reach locals required the purchase of mailing labels from the international. The mailings and overall expenses, including a lot of paid time out of the plant to get the mailings done and make phone calls to every local in the country and Canada, would cost Local 72 nearly $100,000, a prohibitive amount for any but the largest locals.

Sylvester's first letter described our membership's unanimous approval of a "One Member, One Vote" resolution and for a roll call vote at the convention. Sylvester also informed local leaders that several locals had already passed the same resolution.

Local 72 delegates chose John Stencil as the delegation chair. Stencil constituted a great choice since historically he had balked at international intervention in the local and didn't give a damn what Majerus or the international thought of him. Rather, he enjoyed messing with them.

I was chosen cochair of the "One Member, One Vote" delegates' meeting planned for the first night of the convention. With Stencil nominally chair, I hoped to keep focus on One Member, One Vote without backing into an inflammatory debate centered on my political views.

Right before delegates left for Dallas, Local 72 sent out a final letter to all fifteen hundred locals over Stencil's signature as delegation chair of our eight thousand–member local:

> Our local has been very encouraged by the initial response which has
> included endorsement by a number of large locals who have initiated
> their own letter writing campaign in support of "One Member/One
> Vote." At this time we anticipate a lively debate at the Convention,
> assuming of course that we are able to get the "One Member/One
> Vote" discussion onto the floor.

Roughly one hundred delegates crammed into a small room to discuss the resolution. Stencil called the meeting to order, handing the gavel to me to guide the discussion. I reported that we had gathered firm endorsements from thirty-eight locals. We had turned One Member, One Vote into a lightning rod for dissidents nationwide. Locals that had suffered from the concession drive by GM, Ford, and Chrysler were eagerly looking for a way to hold the international accountable.

When floor discussion turned to One Member, One Vote, Bob King, chair of the constitutional committee, read a long recommendation advocating the existing system. "There is real danger that our elections would be neither free nor fair [under a One Member, One Vote system]," he concluded.

International president Doug Fraser (later in the proceedings to be replaced by Owen Bieber as president) opened debate, and he conducted a fair debate. Eighteen delegates rose to support King's motion to defeat One Member, One Vote. Thirteen spoke in favor of our resolution.

I frantically waved my hand to be recognized, as I worked up the courage to speak to twenty-five hundred delegates, knowing a couple hundred international staff members were bad-mouthing our efforts.

Stencil, whom Fraser didn't recognize, succeeded in being called on and then made a handoff.

Delegate John Stencil, Local 72, Region 10: Mr. Chairman, I would like to yield the floor to Brother Melrod, who's from...Local 72 also.
Delegate Jon Melrod, Local 72, Region 10: Fellow Delegates, I rise to speak against the motion. Local 72, whose 10 delegates have a combined seniority of 276 years and 185 years of union representation, plead guilty to the accusation [made by] some of the previous speakers. Yes, we were prompted by somebody to bring this [motion] to the convention floor—*the 8,000 members of our local union.*

Fraser, in a *Detroit News* article, pointed out the virtues of the delegate system as practiced in 1946. At that time, Walter Reuther beat out the incumbent R.J. Thomas by 114 votes. We say right on to the delegate system as practiced in 1946. Unfortunately, there hasn't been a real election for president since....

Those of us advocating the one-member, one-vote system say that democracy must be [restored] in our union. Decision making must begin with the rank and file's right to vote for our international officers....

I request that the brother chair poll the delegates when the question is called to see if they would wish to have a roll call vote on this question. Thank you.

The author speaking at the 1983 UAW International Convention in support of the One Member, One Vote resolution that would democratize the election procedure to allow the membership to vote for international officers. (In 2022, under court supervision, the UAW membership voted to implement One Member, One Vote.)

> Unnamed Delegate: I would like to call for a roll call vote. [A chorus of boos from delegates followed.]
>
> President Fraser: Under the rules it takes 700 delegates to have a roll call vote....
>
> All those in favor of a roll call vote please stand.
>
> [After counting:] I would say about 150.
>
> While those of us supporting One Member/One Vote believed we had tallied in excess of 150 votes, perhaps as many as 500 in favor of a roll call, we had hit an impenetrable wall.

The media quoted Fraser: "It took us two months of the hardest work we have ever done before a convention to beat one member/one vote." Despite having lost, Local 72 and our allies had given the international a run for its money and perhaps laid the groundwork for the change to democratic voting that would finally come in 2021.

Back in Kenosha, I now worked second shift at Lakefront. I handily won the election for steward.

One day, suddenly a loud commotion. People were yelling at an IE man to get off the floor, as no one had received twenty-four-hour notice, and IE was contractually prohibited from observing second shift.

The volume of those harassing the IE man ramped up, reaching a fever pitch. I felt powerless working on my job as people became increasingly infuriated. I dropped my tools and walked.

"Hey, you gotta get off the floor," I told the IE man, Ed Erickson. "People are unhappy, as you can see, and, by contract, you're not supposed to be here."

Erickson was the most union-friendly IE and was only walking a few feet through the work area.

"Jon, I gotta walk this way to get to my office," he said. "What's the big deal?"

"Sorry. That can't happen."

I had inched closer to where our faces were mere inches apart, our bellies just about bumping. As Erickson continued to protest, I belly-bumped him backward. Seeing the confrontation get physical, the temperature rose, and people were increasingly in an uproar.

Erickson refused to go back down the stairs, and I refused to let him pass. He became quite indignant as, from his perspective, he planned to just pass through. I had dug in, however, and wouldn't back off.

Then people began to chant, calling for everyone to walk off the line. When I looked over, the forty or fifty people on the line had walked off, letting cars run by workstations, work undone. Curious, people moved around us, forming a large scrum, now blocking Erickson's path in either direction.

A supervisor shut down the line and called General Supervisor Albee, who made a beeline toward me and the congestion, now a full-on work stoppage. Albee threatened every form of discipline, including imminent discharge for failure to abide by his "direct order."

Tod, chief on nights, stepped up to Albee, and the two argued back and forth, with Albee continuing to loudly harangue. The stalemate seemed to go on forever, although it probably lasted only a few minutes. Eventually, after a few more rounds of threatening Tod with time-off penalties, Albee coerced and cajoled people back to work, and the line resumed.

No way would management permit such rampant insubordination to go down without issuing discipline. Collectively withholding labor is too great a threat to the corporation's control of the workforce to get a free pass.

Tod bargained to reduce severe time-off penalties to five-page written warnings, to be reviewed and removed in thirty days—rather minor discipline for halting production.

CHAPTER 26

Save *Fighting Times*: Defend Free Speech

The September 15, 1980, headline in the *Racine Journal Times* blared, "3 at AMC Sued for $4.2 Million."

The defamation suit had been filed by four supervisors and the son of a superintendent. The litany of allegations asserted that Tod Ohnstad, John Drew, and I had "damaged" the plaintiffs by publishing false articles that caused severe emotional distress as well as loss of reputation and damage to their careers.

Early in the winter of 1983–84, as if manna had fallen from the sky, we fortuitously gained incontrovertible evidence of what we had suspected: AMC was surreptitiously financing and directing the litigation. The pivotal discovery occurred almost by happenstance. On a cold winter day, Rudy Kuzel (at that time still the substance abuse rep) serendipitously observed a seemingly inconsequential occurrence that a less-discerning person would have ignored.

Rudy noticed a management secretary being handed a list of employees and asked for their addresses. The seemingly innocuous query sparked Rudy's curiosity. "Why," he wondered, "were all the addresses being requested those of workers who had lodged complaints against infamous Scab of the Month Stevie Freeman?"

As Rudy explained in an extensive October 1983 *Chicago Reader* interview, "I suspected that they [those whose names were on the list] were going to be subpoenaed. My first reaction was [that] they [AMC] shouldn't be doing that kind of thing. It's a misuse of corporate funds."

Rudy relayed his suspicions to Local 72 president Sylvester, and the two confronted the director of manufacturing, Gil Austin, demanding to

---

For an archive of upwards of two hundred published articles written before, during, and after the defamation trial described in this chapter, see https://www.jonathanmelrod.com/archive.—Ed.

know if AMC was financing the lawsuit. Austin responded that he doubted it but agreed to find out. In an ensuing conversation, Austin showed Rudy a memo revealing that corporate Industrial Relations counsel Alex McCloskey had authorized AMC to pay plaintiffs' legal costs.

As David Moberg of the *Chicago Reader* wrote, "Kuzel knew from past conversations that Maddox [VP of manufacturing] and other managers disliked Melrod, Drew, and Ohnstad, whom they considered communists.... Maddox said, 'the company wanted to stop all the derogatory articles [in *Fighting Times*] that were filled with lies... and the company would look like heroes for coming to the assistance of the plaintiffs.'"

Moberg continued, "Kuzel [grew] more outraged.... 'The main thing they're after is to quash that paper [*Fighting Times*] and to stop the printing of the truth about supervisors.... The whole theory of the labor movement is that as one person you can't stand up to the corporation, but you have to act together—an injury to one is an injury to all.'

"'Maddox... said that he [was] going to get Melrod because he [Melrod] is against everything that America stands for.... Maybe George Maddox's America is where corporations can limit the right to free speech.... But that's not my America, and it's not Jon Melrod's America.'"

Next, Rudy acted in a manner atypical of many in leadership of the labor movement, who generally feared young, outspoken militants and political radicals. He swore an affidavit that attested to facts indicting the company for surreptitiously funding the litigation: "On five separate occasions, management employees, and high level executives of the American Motors Corporation, have disclosed to me that said corporation has signed a written fee agreement to pay the law firm of Foley, Foley... all legal fees and expenses for the representation of the plaintiffs in the case of Freeman et al vs. Melrod et al."

Armed with Rudy's March 25 affidavit, John, Tod and I headed to the National Labor Relations Board (NLRB) to file an unfair labor practice charge. On April 27, regional director Joseph A. Szabo filed charges alleging that AMC had engaged in an unfair labor practice by financing and orchestrating the lawsuit. Szabo wrote, "The 10-year history of AMC's repeated and continuing efforts to squelch Melrod's protected activities, and to exact retribution against those employees supporting Melrod, evince a continuing campaign of harassment and discrimination culminating in the lawsuit." Szabo said, "We are suing them (AMC) for suing the other guys [Drew, Ohnstad, and me]. And if they don't stop suing the other guys, we'll keep suing them until they do."

For Alex McCloskey, instigator of the secret agreement pledging financial support for the litigation, the manic drive to get rid of me was both personal and, at its core, highly ideological. As McCloskey's assistant Richard Dodd told Szabo, "McCloskey undertook a vendetta against Melrod in the early 1970's.... When Melrod resurfaced in Kenosha after having been laid off in Milwaukee, McCloskey raised hell with McCracken [AMC VP] about the 'idiots in Kenosha' who hired Melrod.... McCloskey vowed, '*I'll get him if it's the last thing I do* [emphasis added].'"

According to Dodd, "McCloskey had a reputation in the corporate department for his vendetta against Melrod.... McCloskey [is] an ultra-conservative type, who sometimes circulates petitions for the John Birch Society.... McCloskey explained the basis for his crusade against Melrod, 'we've got to get rid of the Communists.'... McCloskey thought Melrod was a Communist... something to do with Melrod's involvement with SDS.'"

The board held that AMC be "ordered to drop its support for the litigation by instructing [plaintiffs'] attorney Wyant to withdraw the legal action." The board set a July 12 trial to hear the complaint that there was reasonable cause to believe that AMC committed an unfair labor practice.

The three of us and our supporters were elated! Before the civil trial even commenced, it looked like the First Amendment gods had shined the light of justice and righteousness on us.

But the Reagan-dominated Supreme Court soon squelched that prospect. In a unanimous decision, the Supreme Court ruled in *Bill Johnson's Restaurants, Inc. v. NLRB* that the board *could* throw out a libel suit but *only* if the suit was known by the litigant to be frivolous. After the *Bill Johnson's* ruling, the NLRB couldn't enjoin an action unless it was "frivolous *and* retaliatory." *Bill Johnson's Restaurants* thrust our litigation back into state court.

Our deepest support came from Local 72 rank and filers. We would designate a plant gate and mobilize a gaggle of supporters wearing UWC jackets, to form a cluster that everyone heading into work would have to traverse. We displayed a large board with rows of yellow "Save the Fighting Times" buttons and gave one to all who contributed to our legal fund. Hundreds wore buttons in an ongoing show of solidarity and resistance to the company. The litigation had morphed from a court case into a solidarity movement involving thousands.

Letters and pledges of support arrived from across the United States and around the world. The Comité de Groupe Renault sent $100, arriving via money order with a message of solidarity. *Racine Labor* reported,

"The libel suit has incurred the wrath of worker representatives on the [Renault] Board.... Roger Silvain, representing the largest union [CGT]... sent a blistering letter to company officials denouncing the harassment of the Fighting Times."

Other letters were equally passionate:

Dear Brothers,
I'm a laid off steelworker so I can't contribute what I'd like to for your very important fight. You have fought to preserve free speech for all of us. Keep up the struggle.
Linda Stovall, Homestead, PA

Dear Jon Melrod, John Drew, and Tod Ohnstad,
Truly an issue of free speech in the workplace, we are proud to stand on the side of those defending this basic constitutional right.
National Association of Letter Carriers, Branch 436, Racine WI

Dear Tod, Jon and John,
Things certainly look grim for you all, but as I see it you just can not lose this one. Surely the American public will not allow this to happen. What are the International Unions doing about it? Or do they want to crucify people such as you?
All the Best, Sid Turney, Coventry, England

Supporters organized fund-raising parties in Milwaukee, Chicago, and New York.

As the trial date grew close, I felt increasingly uneasy, plagued by concerns over the preparedness of our legal defense. Our costs could easily run into six figures. I lay awake worrying not only for myself but also thinking how life-altering a loss would be for my best friends and fellow caucus members, Tod and John.

While I had always prided myself on being fiercely independent, I wasn't too proud to know the time had arrived to seek help. I sought legal advice from my father, knowing that one of his law partners, Warren Kaplan, was an outstanding libel and First Amendment attorney. Warren dropped all matters, personal and legal, and boarded a plane from DC to Milwaukee to prepare our legal defense.

With his beat-up suitcase, two gray suits (soon to become very wrinkled), and a photo of his sons, Warren moved into the small empty bedroom in my home on a working-class street in Racine. Without missing a beat, he took command of not only preparing legal arguments but also turning John, Tod, and me into a fact-gathering squad, working hard to compensate for having lagged. Every day we worked our eight hours in the plant and afterward remained at Warren's beck and call, as he sought to shape up and then fine-tune our defense.

Warren made it crystal clear, in a way that left us reeling from our negligence, that our defense preparation had been sorely lacking.

We tracked down some sixty-five fact witnesses and interviewed each. We located AMC workers, current and laid-off, who had been harassed by plaintiffs; we located former AMC supervisors who didn't condone the racist and sexist behavior of the litigants; and we even found the disgruntled former, wife of lead plaintiff Steve Freeman.

Whether we were ready or not, the high-stakes trial opened in a Racine courtroom on October 31, 1983, with Judge Dennis J. Flynn presiding. Warren, with a lifetime of courtroom experience, impressed on us the importance of jury discretion, meaning that the jury observed *everything* that transpired in the court, including our daily demeanor.

We took full advantage of the class composition of the Racine jury pool. The jury selected had a similar makeup to workers at AMC. The twelve consisted of nine women and three men: a teacher, a clerk, a supply technician, a homemaker, two machinists, the manager of a women's apparel store, a postal clerk, a welder at J.I. Case, a waitress, a secretary, and two retirees. Pretty close to a jury of our peers.

The trial opened, but before jurors even stepped into the jury box, Judge Flynn laid down a marker revealing his pro-company class predilection. Warren advanced a motion seeking to enter evidence that AMC had financed and orchestrated the litigation: "Your honor, AMC pressured and encouraged these plaintiffs to bring this suit. The information on who is paying for the litigation is thus relevant."

Judge Flynn, aware that the issue of financing would take center stage, had prepped well. Quoting both state statutes and prior case law, Flynn ruled, "As a general rule in Wisconsin, credibility of a witness cannot be attacked by raising such issues as who is financing a lawsuit.... The issue of who is financing the suit is a collateral issue to the dispute between the parties."

Hmm, I thought. *Looks like we're facing six plaintiffs, and one is on the bench having donned a black robe.*

I thought, *We have to appeal directly to the jury. We've lined up witnesses for everything we published. Let's hope that none are too intimidated to retell the story as it went down in the shop and later appeared in* Fighting Times.

The unfolding courtroom drama drew widespread media interest. The *Milwaukee Journal, Milwaukee Sentinel, Racine Journal Times, Kenosha News*, and both Kenosha and Racine labor papers covered the trial daily. Underscoring the national importance of the issues at stake, the *Wall Street Journal, New York Times, Los Angeles Times, Washington Post*, and *Chicago Tribune* also reported on the proceedings. (Much of the following dialogue derives from press coverage.)

I awoke on the morning of October 31 filled with apprehension. I had never been sued before, much less had I been sued for $4 million. After Warren and I donned our courtroom attire (a sports coat and tie for me), neither of us had much to say.

Tod, John, and I sat on the courtroom's scuffed wooden benches, directly behind Warren and Al Ugent at the defense table. Attorney Ugent, our co-counsel, had represented me in 1983 when I had been arrested on a United Electrical Workers picket line blocking scabs from entering a struck plant. As a longtime UE lawyer, Al seemed a reliable choice to assist Warren.

Instructed by Warren, the three of us jumped to attention as the jury, walking single file, heads not turning, entered the jury box. I studied each juror, hoping to discover a sympathetic ally, but their faces revealed little. The game had yet to begin.

The plaintiffs' attorney Judley Wyant opened, arguing that his clients were "victims of a campaign of harassment, intimidation, ridicule and vilification directed against supervisory personnel at AMC, and the union activists [the three of us at whom he was pointing] were trying to get them fired.... The five plaintiffs claim that *Fighting Times* articles interfered with their jobs, presented them falsely, and caused them mental and emotional distress."

Wyant, not required to stick to facts in his opening, painted the three of us as horrible, callous union bullies, who, without justification, set out to undermine and disparage clean-cut, white-shirted, nice-guy supervisors. A few jurors glanced at us quizzically.

Kaplan and Ugent kept their powder dry. The jury didn't have to wait for our attorneys to argue our case before making up their minds about who

"*Fighting Times* Three" (left to right: John Drew, Jon Melrod, Tod Ohnstad) in Racine, WI, courtroom on trial for defamation with alleged damages of $4.2 million. American Motors surreptitiously funded and orchestrated the litigation to quash the voice of the irreverent *Fighting Times* newsletter. (*Racine Journal Times* photo)

were the good guys and who were the bad guys. As I later learned, jurors formed a clear picture early in the trial of what had transpired, and it didn't comport with the one Wyant sought to paint.

Wyant called to the stand Robert Fesko, AMC director of employee relations. In the organizational chart, Fesko ranked near the top for Wisconsin operations. Whatever Wyant's intention in calling Fesko, his strategy went awry. Through deft cross-examination, Ugent flipped Fesko into an unwitting witness for our defense, linking him and top corporate management to the supervisors' lawsuit.

Ugent's questions and Fesko's answers established that Alex McCloskey had pulled the strings, the same McCloskey who had vowed "I'll get [Melrod] if it's the last thing I do."

Excerpts from the court proceedings:

Q: In the field of industrial relations, where you are an expert, is it proper to refer to workers or employees as lazy niggers?
A: No, sir.
Q: And if one of your supervisors referred to an employee as a lazy nigger would he be working for your company for very long?

A: We would take a look at the reason that this was said, why it was said, talk to the employee.

Q: So, are you telling us that there are some circumstances where a supervisor could refer to a Black employee as a lazy nigger and still keep his job?

A: There would be circumstances where he could do that.

Q: Do you have any knowledge whatsoever as to whether or not American Motors Corporation has given any kind of encouragement to Mr. Freeman to start this suit?

A: I had discussions with Mr. Freeman after his determination to [file the lawsuit as] to whether or not he would be interested in pursuing this.

Q: Why did you do that?

A: I was instructed.

Q: Who instructed you?

A: Mr. McCloskey.

Q: In other words, you sat down with him (Freeman) and you said, 'Are you interested in starting a lawsuit against Mr. Melrod, Mr. Ohnstad, and Mr. Drew?' and that was it?

A: Yes sir.

Q: Now if you didn't know about all those things that Mr. Freeman was accused of, wouldn't you consider it a good thing if the Fighting Times called these things to your attention?

A: Yes.

Q: Have you ever sent a letter thanking Fighting Times for calling those things to your attention?

A: No sir.

Q: Can you recount a single false fact ever published in the Fighting Times about Mr. Freeman?

A: I can't tell you a single false fact, no.

Q: In other words, you don't know anything that's false that was published in Fighting Times, do you? ...

A: No sir.

Q: And you've made a very thorough investigation, haven't you?

A: Yes.

As a pugnacious Ugent examined Fesko in a steady, rapid cadence that allowed no time for hesitation, my eyes riveted on the jury. Racine was a solidly union town, and our jury consisted of working-class men and women, many of whom punched a time clock. While it was hard to read their faces, none could mistake the David-versus-Goliath scenario unfolding before them.

Next up, Dave Rutchik, often called Space Ace in the plant, swore to tell the truth and nothing but the truth. Early into his testimony, Rutchik stumbled. Under cross-examination, he admitted that Mike Istvanek never pushed him and that he (Rutchik) simply fell, as suggested in *Fighting Times*. Warren maneuvered Rutchik into testifying against himself and upholding the veracity of *Fighting Times*!

As grounds for damages, Rutchik claimed that the emotional distress experienced from criticism of his in-plant behavior "exacerbated his marital problems." Blaming us for his marital problems opened the door to questions about other possible causes. Judge Flynn ordered the jury removed from the courtroom, and cross-examination regarding Rutchik's marriage continued:

Q: You claim to have marital problems?
A: Yes sir.
Q: Is it possible that your self-described marital problems are a result of your drug use?
A: I plead the Fifth.
Q: Are your marital problems connected to your sale of marijuana or other illicit drugs?
A: I plead the Fifth.
Q: Do you smoke marijuana during lunch break?
A: I plead the Fifth.

Stuck in the witness box, Rutchik looked like a deer caught in the headlights, as he gazed pleadingly at Wyant, then the judge, and then back to Wyant, hoping for an off-ramp. None appeared.

In response to Rutchik repetitively pleading the Fifth, Warren brought to the judge's attention a line of court cases establishing that the law bound Flynn to dismiss Rutchik as a plaintiff. "Your honor, based on uncontroverted case law, I move to strike plaintiff Rutchik."

While I might have felt a twinge of guilt nailing Rutchik on the benign issue of smoking pot, all's fair in love and war, especially in a war he started. With the jury excused from the courtroom, the questions, motions, and discussion concerning the legal impact of Rutchik's reliance on the Fifth continued, after which the judge recessed the trial.

On November 10, the *Kenosha News* reported, "Wednesday afternoon, the eighth day of the trial, Racine Judge Dennis J. Flynn granted a motion by the defense to strike Rutchik as a plaintiff because he continued invocation of his Fifth Amendment right to not make incriminating statements against himself, preventing the defense from questioning him on his alleged marijuana use.... Flynn simply told [the jury] that Rutchik's claim 'had been dismissed for legal reasons.'"

The *Los Angeles Times* printed a surprising mid-trial admission by Rutchik: "American Motors signed an agreement with me that they would pay my legal fees and expenses." You can bet the bank that every juror read and discussed Rutchik's uncensored revelation that AMC had paid his legal fees. You can also rest assured that Rutchik's dismissal by the judge left an indelible impression on the jurors and badly tarnished the remaining plaintiffs.

Soon it came time for Freeman, who had hatched the lawsuit and first discussed the litigation with Fesko, to take the stand. While I had felt somewhat sorry for Rutchik, as he seemed a lost soul, I bore no empathy for Freeman. I had been an 838 steward and chief steward during Freeman's petty reign of unmitigated terror.

I had interviewed the women he'd molested and the Black workers whom he'd racially disparaged. I had collaborated with the steward body to provide stickers depicting Freeman as a pumpkin head, branding him Scab of the Month. My beef with Freeman was personal, and I felt no sympathy for this racist, misogynistic, power-hungry boss.

Wyant sought to have Freeman present the case from his own perspective:

Q: How did you react to the articles about you in the October, November and December issues of Fighting Times that were highly critical of you?
A: Those articles contained mostly erroneous information. The effect was to make it very difficult for me to effectively manage my people. People were laughing at me. My ability to get along with subordinates definitely decreased.

As Freeman sought to appeal to the jury, explaining that he was just trying to be the best supervisor he could, he broke down crying (crocodile tears). He had only been on the stand for about an hour, but Judge Flynn called a recess.

When questioning resumed, Freeman couldn't recall if he had called workers "lazy pussies," but he did recall twenty-four or twenty-six workers in his section raising their hands at the same time to ask for passes to see the nurse. "I can't say for sure that I did not say that [calling them pussies]. I was frustrated."

"It was really hard for me. Whole groups of stewards followed me around telling my employees they didn't have to listen to me. One even pressed a knife to my stomach. Using obscene language, he threatened to remove my genitals if he caught me doing union work again."

Then the time arrived for Ugent and Kaplan to decimate Freeman, piece by piece, lie by lie, until any facade of false humanity or feigned decency had been stripped away.

Joanne Tank, a night-shift steward, described an incident she witnessed. One of the women she represented had just returned from sick leave. "I was observing her as she was having trouble keeping up with her job, having been off work for a while. Freeman had been hassling and berating her to keep up on her 'fucking job.' I watched in shock as his glare turned piercing. He picked up a heavy air gun and threw it right at her, scaring her to death. I went to the chief and immediately filed a grievance."

Sam Picchietti, a steward, testified: "I had the impression he felt we were just animals."

Lisa Moreau had transferred to first shift to escape Freeman's misogynist behavior toward her. Warren called Lisa to the stand:

Q: Could you describe for the court [an incident that was written about in *Fighting Times*]?
A: Within a couple weeks of Steve becoming my boss, he repeatedly brushed up against me. I never had any problems before or after with people brushing up against me while I did my job.
Q: Was it a tight squeeze by your work area?
A: Not at all. There was plenty of room for a man Steve's size [two hundred pounds] to pass by without touching me. Every time he walked past me, he brushed up against my behind. I told him I didn't

like it. I said that I was a respectable person, and I didn't have to work under conditions like that.

Q: Did Freeman listen to you?

A: No. I went to his boss, Frank Stella, to complain. Mr. Stella told Steve to apologize to me and to stop his actions that bothered me. But Freeman didn't listen. When Stella left, he kept touching me.

Q: What happened next?

A: Freeman told me, in these exact words, "I can brush up against your 80-year-old ass anytime I want and all I have to do is apologize."

Wyant stepped in to pursue cross-examination:

Q: Ms. Moreau, Steve Freeman is a very enthusiastic person who swings his arms when he walks. Isn't it possible that he may have unintentionally brushed the back of his hand against your backside?

A: Like I said—I'm a respectable person and I don't have to work under those conditions; he touched me on purpose.

Kurt Christensen and Carolyn Hiegert, both of whom worked in Freeman's department, testified about an incident at a nearby tavern. "We saw Steve sitting alone in the bar. He was new, so we asked him to join us for a drink. After a while he was looking into the back room and said to us, 'do you put up with that?' We didn't understand until he explained that down south where he came from, people wouldn't tolerate a white woman dancing with a Black man."

Hiegert continued, "On one particular warm night Freeman came up to me. He said, 'Let's go to my place and get naked. It's the kind of weather for that.'"

I felt it important that Sarah Santiago testify, but she was very shy, and deeply humiliated about an incident I had reported in *Fighting Times*. To persuade her to testify, I guardedly reminded her that she would be standing up for herself but also for the other women Freeman had harassed with impunity. Reluctantly, she agreed to take the stand.

In a barely audible voice, Sarah struggled to recount the incident. With jury members leaning forward, straining to hear, she described asking Freeman for a piece of chewing gum. "He told me I could have one if he could see my ... [inaudible]," Sarah strained under the pressure to squeeze out Freeman's words.

Judge Flynn instructed, as Sarah squirmed and blushed, "Ms. Santiago, please speak loudly enough for the jury to hear, and you must use Mr. Freeman's words as you heard them."

A: He said that I could have a stick of gum if he could look at my breasts. I then said, "What?"
Q: Did he respond?
A: Yes. He said, "Oh, I mean your hair." He laughed and snickered, but I was very embarrassed. I was afraid that my husband might find out.
Q: Ms. Santiago, did you have other conversations with Mr. Freeman of a personal nature?
A: Yes. I asked him if I could leave work one day as I had just been informed that my ex-husband had kidnapped my three children.
Q: How did Mr. Freeman respond?
A: He refused to allow me to leave.

Following Sarah, we called LaFonda Griffith who testified: "One night, Freeman came up to me and another Black woman. He formed his fingers into the shape of a pistol and said, 'Bang, bang. There's two dead black-birds.'" La Fonda continued, "Another time he told me that I was a good worker, but [the] only thing wrong with me was that I was flat-chested."

I had collaborated with a night-shift steward and caucus activist, Sharon Holmes, to write a number of articles about Freeman. Sharon had been active as a steward, pushing back against Freeman's egregious mistreatment of the people she represented, particularly the women. Freeman sought to retaliate against Sharon in a not-so-subtle manner.

Freeman's fellow line supervisor, James Prevec, described Freeman's interactions:

I was walking through Freeman's section, and I happened to see him intentionally standing in front of Sharon, purposefully interfering with her so that she couldn't install parts on the cars. I watched Sharon trying to navigate around the 200-pound Freeman, as she became increasingly frustrated. I got so damn pissed, I grabbed Freeman and slammed him against a car; I told him to cut that stuff out, and I meant it.

I don't feel he had any respect for the people around [on the assembly line]. On one occasion, a Black employee who worked for Freeman came to me with a complaint that Freeman had called him a "lazy nigger." I asked Freeman if he had said that. He just looked at me and walked away.

When asked about *Fighting Times*, Prevec responded that we had criticized him twice. "I've always found the allegations in *Fighting Times* are somewhat accurate. The wording is strong, but the facts were there."

Warren had tracked down Freeman's ex-fiancée Carol Vansell, who had moved out of state. Warren telephoned to ask if she would testify. Not only was she happy to talk to Warren about Freeman, but she was also like an uncapped fire hose. All the sordid details flooded out, as Warren scribbled on a yellow legal pad. Warren convinced her to fly back to take the stand.

When Warren called Carol to the stand, a hush descended over the courtroom. The coiled cobra stood ready to demonstrate that Freeman's instability and errant behavior existed long before *Fighting Times* articles ever appeared.

The jury had been looking bored after days of endless testimony. Now they sat up, taking out pads and pencils.

Q: [Ms. Vansell, did] Steve Freeman ever engage in violent acts in your presence?
A: Many.
Q: Could you recount one such incident?
A: Steve had a business raising beagle puppies. After one litter, he let me keep the runt rather than put it down.

At this point tears began streaming down Carol's face as she recalled an incident she was about to describe in painful detail. She could barely continue. Judge Flynn instructed the clerk to provide her with tissue.

Q: I'm sorry to have to ask you, but can you please continue?
A: One day, Steve and I got into a heated argument. It turned ugly, and Steve was furious. He picked up my puppy as I tried to grab it. He held it out of my reach. I screamed for him to put it down. The look in his eyes was wild.
Q: Please continue.
A: Steve stepped on the puppy's head. He tore the puppy's body away from the head. It snapped my dog's neck.

Dead silence descended over the courtroom like a dark cloud. I glanced at the stenographer; she was silently sobbing, her shoulders shaking with emotion, her fingers no longer clicking the keys to record witness testimony. I heard quiet sniffling from the jury box and saw at least two jurors in tears. The always cold, stern Judge Flynn gazed out at his once orderly judicial kingdom, waiting to move on as he gaveled the courtroom back to order.

Warren continued:

Q: I'm sorry that this is so difficult, but I have to ask, were there any other occasions during your relationship with Steve when he lost his temper?
A: Too many to list.
Q: Would you mind recounting other incidents that come to mind?
A: One time, after we had a heated argument, I went into our garage. Steve followed me, still yelling. Suddenly he grabbed a lawnmower blade that was hanging in the garage and swung it, hitting me in my head. I don't know how much later, but I regained consciousness while lying in a pool of frozen blood.

Carol's testimony ran counter to Freeman. Referring to the same incident, Freeman claimed that he bumped into the lawnmower blade while getting into his car and that it had grazed Carol. One glance at the jury box revealed their disdain for Freeman and their distrust.

Q: Ms. Vansell, there was testimony earlier that threatening phone calls were made to the house you shared with Steve?
A: We received a couple of angry calls. In one instance, I answered the phone and a man whose voice I didn't recognize told me that I better warn Steve to stop harassing his wife or he would kill Steve. On two occasions women called complaining that Steve had harassed them at work.
Q: It sounds as if your relationship was marked by violent arguments. Are there any other instances that come to mind?

Before answering, Carol needed time to compose herself. The jury had never been so riveted. Twelve jurors avidly hung on each word.

A: After a particularly bad argument, Steve really flipped out. He grabbed his shotgun, put it to my head, and threatened to kill me. Another time, Steve wanted to have sex, but I didn't. We quarreled. Afterwards, I took a bath. In a rage, Steve broke into the bathroom.

He grabbed my head and held it under the water. I thought he was going to drown me.

Q: Following these incidents of abuse, did you decide to end the relationship?

A: Yes. I'd finally had enough. I called some friends to help me move. The problem was that Steve's sister was our landlady. When she saw me moving my stuff, she called Steve. He pulled up while I was packing. We argued about who owned what. He forced me to leave all my belongings, including my clothes and medicine.

Questions regarding Freeman's character ended on that note.

I was mentally prepared when Wyant called me to the stand. I looked forward to sparring with him after his bullying of our witnesses. After I was sworn in, I turned my gaze to the twelve jurors. It was to them I planned to testify. The following is a brief synopsis of my testimony:

Q: Mr. Melrod, are you the editor of *Fighting Times*?

A: Yes, one of the editors. Many of the articles are written by people in the shop who experienced unfair or discriminatory treatment. Sometimes we assisted them in writing articles about their complaints. We also encouraged people to write letters that we printed.

Q: Mr. Melrod, my question called for a yes or no answer. No need to deviate from my questions with long, drawn-out responses.

A: I'll do my best, but I need to fully explore the questions and answers so that I provide the jury with the most thorough responses possible.

Q: Let's proceed. Mr. Melrod, do you know Steve Freeman, one of the plaintiffs?

A: Not know, but I've had occasions to speak with people who've been harassed in one manner or another by Stevie while he was their boss. I assisted the stewards with drafting a petition to protest some of Freeman's more egregious racist and sexist behavior.

Q: Your honor, please instruct Mr. Melrod to be more responsive and not deliver a speech.

Judge Flynn: Mr. Melrod. You are to respond directly to the questions Mr. Wyant is asking without editorializing.

Q: Did you have occasion to write articles in *Fighting Times* about Mr. Freeman?

A: Yes, many. Every time we heard about a complaint regarding Freeman, we dug up information to report on his malfeasance. We wrote about Freeman in four successive issues in an attempt to correct problems in Freeman's section.

Q: Mr. Melrod, can you tell the court if those articles were always accurate and factual?

A: Of course, that is the purpose of *Fighting Times*. We take our responsibility to report accurately very seriously. In our statement of "Who We Are" we are very clear that...

Wyant: Objection, your honor. Mr. Melrod is editorializing.

Flynn: Sustained. Mr. Melrod, I again instruct you to provide direct answers to Mr. Wyant's questions.

Melrod: I forget, your honor. What was the question again?

Wyant: I hadn't asked one. Your honor was sustaining my objection.

Melrod: Okay. Mr. Wyant, proceed.

The jury appeared to be enjoying the verbal sparring. From my perspective, I was getting the better of Wyant; I hoped the jury shared my assessment.

Q: Mr. Melrod, let's try to proceed in an orderly fashion. I will ask the questions, and you will provide the answers.

A: That's just what I've been doing.

Q: Okay, then. It is your testimony that you are always factual, is that correct?

A: One hundred percent.

Q: I have in my hand a sticker that I'd like you to identify. Did you manufacture that sticker?

A: Yup.

Q: Why?

A: The stewards and workers on the second shift, particularly the workers of color and the women in Freeman's section, were having serious, ongoing problems with his rude behavior.

Q: So you thought manufacturing stickers would help that situation?

A: It seemed to be pretty effective. That's why we're here today, isn't it?

Q: I'll ask the questions. I'm holding in my hand a sticker that you manufactured. Is it an accurate picture of Mr. Freeman?

A: No. Actually, it's a caricature.

Q: So it's not an accurate picture of him?

A: As I said, it's a caricature of Stevie Freeman, you can read his name on it.

Q: If you are so factual, and if you always tell the truth, answer whether Mr. Freeman has a [pumpkin] stem coming out of his head as portrayed on the sticker.

Wyant happened to be standing in the line of sight between me on the witness stand and Freeman, behind him. Before answering, I paused to allow the jury to concentrate on my answer.

A: Well, Mr. Wyant [pause], could you please move out of my line of sight so I can see whether Mr. Freeman has a stem sticking out the top of his head. [The courtroom, including the jurors, broke into boisterous laughter. After a minute, Judge Flynn established decorum by pounding his gavel repeatedly.]

Q: Please continue with a direct response to my question.

A: Like I said, it is a caricature. He does look like a pumpkin, so I guess the answer is yes.

Laughter again erupted, as Judge Flynn repeatedly banged his gavel. I caught a few smiles on the faces of the jurors. I had set out to humanize myself, while making a mockery of Freeman, who had been badly tarnished in the jury's eyes.

Once the laughter and snickering quieted, Wyant resumed.

Q: Let's try to proceed. Mr. Melrod, does the *Fighting Times* ever participate in political events, let's say in Milwaukee?

A: Yes, whenever the opportunity presents itself.

Q: I have here a poster announcing a protest against President Carter and his energy policies. One of the sponsors is the United Workers Organization. Is that the same as the United Workers Caucus?

A: Basically.

Q: Is that your phone number on the poster advertising rides to the anti-Carter event?

A: Correct.

Q: I'm holding up a copy of the *Fighting Times* with the very same phone number. Is that also your phone number?

A: Yes.

Q: Could you please read off a list of organizations sponsoring the anti-Carter demonstration.

A: Socialist Party of Wisconsin and the Communist Party/Marxist Leninists....

Q: Stop right there, please. So are you telling this court that the United Workers Organization sponsored a demonstration with the Communist Party?

A: Objection, your honor! [I loudly objected despite having no standing to do so.] This is nothing less than a crude, bald-faced attempt to return to the days of Wisconsin's infamous Joseph McCarthy's red-baiting, which...

Judge Flynn's gavel banged down again. "I'm going to ask the jury to excuse itself from the courtroom," he said. After they had left, he told me to proceed.

A: This is nothing but a cheap attempt to try to prejudice the jury against us by raising the specter of communism in the exact fashion as the contemptible, discredited Wisconsin senator Joseph McCarthy. McCarthy stood in Congress with a blank sheet of paper claiming boogey men and communists had infiltrated the government. Of course, the paper was blank. Today, Attorney Wyant follows in McCarthy's footsteps intending to create a similar red scare.

Mr. Wyant is hoping that he can paint us with a brush by association so that the jury will turn on us rather than judge us by the truth and honesty of articles in *Fighting Times*, which is what is at issue in this courtroom.

Your honor, I move that Wyant's questions and political innuendo be stricken from the record.

Judge Flynn: Mr. Melrod, need I remind you that you are *not* an attorney and *not* authorized to interject or make objections. We will proceed, without further interruption from you.

Bailiff, please bring the jury into the courtroom. Mr. Wyant, you are free to continue with your questioning of Mr. Melrod now that he has finished with his uncalled-for editorializing.

In a final attempt to rehabilitate a badly damaged Freeman, Wyant called Freeman's wife, Harriet Freeman. By that time, nothing she could say had any chance of eliciting sympathy from the jury. After days of testimony of sadistic, misogynist, racist, and downright mean-spirited behavior, any prior iota of sympathy had been obliterated. Freeman sat in disgrace as he waited for the day to end.

Another plaintiff to take the stand was Leonard Wohlgemuth, who, by the time of the trial, had been promoted from line worker to supervisor. He denied our assertion that he had benefited from favoritism in being assigned desirable jobs because his father was assistant plant superintendent.

Wohlgemuth's denial of favoritism might have been believable if he hadn't been such a smug, self-righteous twenty-five-year-old. I pictured myself as a juror observing an arrogant, pompous young man and wondered if I would believe anything he said. His early testimony surely raised the eyebrows of the working-class jurors.

When queried as to whether seniority should determine priority in job placement, Wohlgemuth responded, "Seniority has *nothing* to do with it. You can work here fifteen years, but if you can't tie your shoes, you're no good." When asked about his father exercising favoritism to help him advance, he replied, "I see nothing wrong with a father helping his son if the son deserves it."

The jurors didn't look impressed by Wohlgemuth's answers. I couldn't help but think that jurors were saying to themselves, "Oh yeah, just forget the seventy-eight hundred other workers whose father didn't hold a high management position."

Donald Phipps, a sad-looking, sickly figure, a man who had consumed way too much alcohol, might as well have been testifying in our defense. Warren introduced a portion of Phipps's Ford employment file that established that he had been terminated twice by Ford for absenteeism and for exhibiting a poor attitude.

In *Fighting Times*, we had accused Phipps of being a sexist and a racist. On cross-examination, Ugent pushed Phipps into a corner:

Q: Mr. Phipps, on any occasion, in your capacity as line supervisor, did you ever tell a female employee in the repair department that she needed a broom rather than tools to do her job?
A: Well, I will say that I believe that men are better suited for work in the repair department than women.

Q: Can you please enlighten the court as to the basis for that observation?
A: Yes. Women are more adept at working at home than in a factory, or at least in the repair department.

From the look on a few of the women jurors' faces, the article in *Fighting Times* criticizing Phipps's misogynist attitudes had just been confirmed.

We recalled Robert Fesko, director of employee relations. Asked whether it was a common occurrence for supervisory personnel to be discharged for acts of misconduct, including accusations of racist and sexist behavior, he responded, "In my four years overseeing employment relations, it was unprecedented for Local 72 to insist that a foreman be fired. We have now done so twice within six months. We fired both Steve Freeman and David Rutchik."

Over the two weeks of the trial, we went home encouraged on some days, and on others we felt like we were losing. We were emotionally exhausted, but there was no way off our judicial roller coaster until the final gavel.

On November 17, fourteen long days into our courtroom drama, Wyant rose. "Your honor, we're seeking permission from the court to allow Steve Freeman to drop his claim 'with prejudice.'" As the *Kenosha News* described, "Warren Kaplan, one of the two defense attorneys, looked surprised, yet elated. The three defendants, still uncertain about the meaning of Wyant's words, sat looking incredulous."

Freeman had been seeking $1,850,000 in damages, twice as much as the total sought by the three remaining plaintiffs. As John Drew told the reporter from the *Racine Journal Times*, "All I gotta say is something is wrong somewhere when a guy can put us through all this trouble and expense for three years and just walk away."

Our archnemesis had been decimated and vanquished. Freeman had forever forfeited his right to file another claim against us. We now faced a motley trio of Leonard Wohlgemuth, Donald Phipps, and Donald Panzlau.

Leaving the courtroom, we were all smiles. Our legal liability had decreased to $980,000.

When next the trial resumed, Wyant rose to make a motion on behalf of his remaining plaintiffs:

"Your honor, respectfully, I move the court issue a directed verdict in favor of plaintiffs Wohlgemuth and Phipps." He made no mention of Panzlau, whom he seemed to have dropped as a client.

A directed verdict would allow the judge to rule on a specific issue, as a matter of law, removing decision making from the jury. We had long considered Judge Flynn to be blatant in his bias for AMC and hometown lawyer Wyant. Now, in a legal coup d'état, Flynn might usurp the jury's power by robbing the twelve men and women of their voice in determining our liability and destiny.

As an apprehensive silence descended over the courtroom, we all focused on Judge Flynn.

"In response to plaintiffs' motion for a directed verdict, considering all the testimony and evidence entered into the record, a reasonable juror could only conclude that four statements about plaintiffs Wohlgemuth and Phipps were false and that those two plaintiffs were therefore defamed, although other statements about the two were true."

What the fuck? I wanted to jump up and rip into Judge Flynn's face. He knew that David was about to whip Goliath's ass when the jury deliberated; rather than let the process play out, he directed a verdict. We had been robbed by the so-called system of impartial justice.

Based on witness testimony about the *Fighting Times* report on the reasons for Ford's firing of Phipps—the source for which was Darlene Janovicz, a worker under Phipps's supervision—Judge Flynn ruled that we had relied on unconfirmed rumors. Despite the seriousness of Flynn's holding, John Drew and I couldn't suppress our laughter. *That* was the best Flynn could come up with? On that one, we admittedly could have been more thorough in checking our sources.

Flynn also took issue with reporting that "this kid [Wohlgemuth] made relief with absolutely no experience or qualifications." Flynn asserted that our statement that Wohlgemuth possessed "absolutely no experience" did not meet the requisite standard of truthfulness. If we had said that Wohlgemuth had a "virtual lack of skills," that would have passed legal muster.

Flynn's verdict that we defamed Phipps and Wohlgemuth hit like a ton of bricks. We sat in stunned silence, unable to fathom how the "jury of our peers" system could have been steamrolled by Judge Flynn, with his procorporate bias. We walked out of the courthouse into the chilly fall air, none of us uttering a word. We each headed our own way, there being little to say.

I bypassed dinner, preferring liquids (gin and tonics) to solids. During the night, I periodically woke to the sounds of Warren pacing the floor, talking to himself.

In the morning, Warren looked exhausted, but the germ of a strategy had formed. He telephoned a junior counsel in DC, instructing him to head to the library for some intense legal research. Like a man possessed, I heard him rehearse a script for Monday.

Our fates now rested on what had transpired on November 17. Discussion turned to how the jury would be instructed as to how much Wohlgemuth and Phipps should be compensated.

It came time for Warren to present the arguments he had prepared.

"Your honor, under the standard articulated by a long line of Supreme Court decisions, the jury can, and should, award damages *only* for additional suffering that would not have been incurred had the truth been told."

In other words, if Wohlgemuth and Phipps experienced no more suffering from the *Fighting Times* articles that "defamed" them than they would have suffered had the articles been true, the jury could opt to award no damages.

A lower court judge like Flynn is loath to be overturned by a higher court. A common ground for reversal is when a judge is found to have committed an error when submitting jury instructions. Flynn felt compelled to allow Warren to draft an instruction that the jury could consider awarding zero damages.

Tuesday, after closing arguments, Warren and I waited for a phone call that would alert us that the jury had completed deliberations. Finally the phone rang, beckoning us to court. The bailiff led the nine women and three men into the jury box. I thought I detected a hint of a smile on a few jurors' faces. For anyone on trial, the seconds between the jury returning a verdict and the head juror standing to read the verdict are an eternity.

The twelve men and women found that neither of the two remaining plaintiffs deserved any monetary damages. The bottom line was that *we were totally vindicated.* The jury awarded zero monetary damages, as Warren had so dramatically implored in his closing argument.

The *Kenosha News* reported, "The defendants and friends shrieked and jumped for joy when the verdict was announced. Jurors later said they were pleased for the defendants."

The *Los Angeles Times* reported, "Melrod, Drew and Ohnstad said they felt 'vindicated' despite the judge's negligence ruling and stressed that they would continue to publish their newspaper.... 'The paper will be more popular than ever,' Melrod predicted. He said that the company sponsoring the lawsuit had 'made us the biggest heroes in the plant.'"

One of our supporters called in to the second-shift chief stewards to spread word that we had won. When stewards took the word out to the lines; spontaneous cheers, hooting, and hollering drowned out the hum of air guns and the crackle of welding guns.

Jurors Dorothy Hackler and Jean Spranger told the *Los Angeles Times*, "The jury did not believe that either Phipps or Wohlgemuth were personally injured by the articles." Juror Hackler said, "I do think the paper is a necessary item in the factory to wake up the company to things that are happening."

John Drew aptly concluded, "AMC picked up a big rock and hoped to crush us with it but dropped it on their own foot. AMC's sadly misused front men Freeman, Rutchik, Wohlgemuth, Phipps, and Panzlau and were unable to get the jury to award one single penny."

On Friday, July 27, 1984, in a large font extending across three columns, *the Kenosha News* headline read, "NLRB rips AMC action in libel case."

Joseph A. Szabo, NLRB regional director of the Milwaukee office, wrote, "What should Melrod have done that he didn't do? The short answer is nothing. Again, AMC wants Melrod to be punished for being so stupid as to not assume that AMC was conniving and backhanded."

Szabo even acknowledged that the ten-year history of AMC's conduct against me might be hard for the Washington Labor Board to accept as having really happened. "It is hard to imagine a large corporation devoting so much of its energies to such a hopeless effort."

After Szabo's sizzling brief, AMC agreed to pay our lost wages, and Warren's and Ugent's fees: a total of $238,000. Pursuant to the settlement agreement drafted by the board, the company agreed to cease and desist from

- prosecuting, financing, sponsoring, or controlling "any non-meritorious and retaliatory" lawsuit against any employee.
- interfering with, restraining, or coercing Melrod, Drew, Ohnstad or any other employee in the exercise of their protected rights, including publication of the *Fighting Times*.

All in all, it had been a grueling battle, plagued by countless emotional lows but also exuberant highs. Folks in the shop had stuck with us by wearing "Save the Fighting Times" buttons and turning our defense into a shop-wide crusade. Hundreds donated multiple times at the gates. Most rewarding, virtually no one who had been the subject of an article or had written a letter to *Fighting Times* backed down or allowed intimidation to silence them. Not a single soul abandoned us out of fear of company retribution.

AMC, one of capitalism's Fortune 500, had thrown everything they had at the three of us. They thought they could break us, but we were stronger than ever, and AMC had made us heroes. We took pride in having slain Goliath or at least laying him low for the moment. Now we could head back to work to pick up where we had left off.

CHAPTER 27

Time to Lead Local 72

For the January 1984 *Fighting Times*, published two months after the verdict, we produced an expanded, sixteen-page edition, including a summary of legal highlights by John Drew under the heading "NLRB Complaint Pending, AMC Can't Stop Free Speech in the Plant."

We branded the disgraced Robert Fesko, AMC's Wisconsin director of employee relations, as the first Scab of the Month for 1984.

The issue included two pages of Fesko's trial testimony, epitomized by the following questions from our attorneys:

> Q: In other words, [Mr. Fesko,] you don't know anything that's false that was published in the *Fighting Times*, do you? Can you tell us a *single fact* ever published in the *Fighting Times* that was false or untrue?
> Fesko: No sir.
> Q: And you've made a very thorough investigation, haven't you?
> Fesko: Yes.

With the release of the *Fighting Times*, we assured folks in the shop, *and in management*, that we were back in the game and weren't intimidated or silenced.

In April, we published what turned out to be the last issue. John penned "Judge Upholds Jury Verdict; Victory for Freedom of Speech."

Post-trial, Judge Flynn belatedly issued an order upholding the jury verdict. His order gave us the green light to activate our NLRB charge, which led AMC to settle and cut us a check for $238,000.

The concluding sentence of our last *Fighting Times*: "The final chapter has yet to be written in this story."

With elections for a new executive board scheduled for May, Tod, John, and I were well positioned. We ran in collaboration with a close ally, militant

2836 chief steward Bob Rosinski. Bob's honesty and fearlessness made him a force to be reckoned with.

Rudy announced a run for president of Local 72; he would be unopposed. A Kuzel administration would offer the opportunity to exercise the full potential of a militant, progressive, politically active union. We knew Rudy would never kowtow to the international, and, if the three of us and Rosinski were elected, we would have the opportunity to put into practice our combative, democratic, class-conscious trade unionism.

Unlike in previous campaigns, we encountered little negative reaction, nor did I experience red-baiting attacks. While we certainly had detractors, their voices were drowned out by the many who welcomed our pull-no-punches campaign and militant message.

With the contract expiring on the heels of the board election, we sought to set the terms honestly and strategically for the 1985 negotiations. Bargaining promised to be a full-scale battle. We synthesized our collective experience to develop a succinct, four-point, pragmatic program (with no sugarcoating) to meet the enormous challenges that loomed in Local 72's immediate future.

> Dear brothers and sisters of Local 72:
>
> [W]ith a multinational giant like Renault controlling AMC, the 1985 negotiations could prove to be the most difficult in our history.
>
> ### STAY ALIVE IN '85
>
> - PENSION GUARANTEES—Any new contract must contain language that guarantees Renault's commitment to take care of past and future retirees....
> - SUCCESSOR CLAUSE—[I]n the event of a total takeover [of AMC by Renault], Renault [must] be locked into keeping the same workforce, working agreement and economic benefits we now have.
> - BANKRUPTCY PROTECTION—[Using] bankruptcy as a means of getting rid of a union contract could be appealing to AMC. We need language to protect us from a rip off of this type....
> - PROTECTION AGAINST LOSING WORK AND MID-CONTRACT CONCESSIONS—We need language in the new contract to prevent AMC from moving our jobs out while the contract is in force.

Every day leading up to the vote we tirelessly walked the lines and production areas, leafletted the unemployment office to reach laid-off workers, and attended a retirees' meeting to speak.

The election results were an impressive affirmation of our strength and of Rudy's. Rudy's unopposed candidacy stood as proof that a life-long, politically progressive, hard-core, pragmatic union militant could stand as the Local 72 president.

I chalked up 2,529 votes running against three candidates, with the nearest challenger receiving only 903 votes. John polled 2,303 votes, while Tod polled 2,319 votes. Rosinski netted 2,503 votes in a runoff. Local 72 now had a solid bloc of four young, militant, progressive board members out of fifteen, and the rest of the new board were, on the whole, loyal to Rudy. Eleven years after setting my sights on climbing the ranks of Local 72 leadership, I achieved my ultimate goal—winning a position on the all-powerful executive board (equivalent of the bargaining committee in other locals).

Wisconsin journalist and historian Eric Gunn wrote that Rudy and the new board took office at the most critical time in Local 72's storied history: "As of July 1, 1984, the AMC's Kenosha operation employed 2,500 people, with another 6,500 on layoff. Additionally, there were 12,500 retirees—a total of 21,500 men and women whose lives were directly tied to the plant. On average, every one of those people accounted for at least one family member, Kuzel recalled in a 2003 interview, 'There were 43,000 people whose wages, insurance, and pensions were dependent on what local 72 did.'"

Rudy's leadership really made a difference, especially when I had to duke it out with Superintendent Mattox, who earlier had interfered with our campaigning for convention delegate.

The new board sent stewards through the plant to take up a collection to support a local nine-week strike by UAW 960 against the Macwhyte Wire Rope Company. On a Friday night, Mattox suspended Russ Gillette, at that time chief steward in the ninety-six-person Department 820 in the Motor Division, and two of his stewards, for soliciting strike support funds.

Since I was the board member responsible for a number of departments in the Motor Division, Gillette beeped me to inform me of the suspensions. Board members carried six-inch beepers—cutting-edge technology at the time.

Reaching 820, I demanded that Mattox immediately put the three back to work. Huffing and puffing like one of the three little pigs, Mattox refused. I headed toward the line. Looking back, I let him know, "Mattox, I'm planning to continue the collection right where Gillette stopped, so you'll have to discipline me as well. Don't think you're up for disciplining a board member, do you?"

Mattox made a beeline in my direction, raging, "Melrod, what do you think you're doing?"

"What does it look like? I'm collecting funds for the strikers at—"

"You need to get the hell out of my department. You're interfering with production."

"Listen, Mattox, I ain't going nowhere till I finish collecting funds from *everyone* in 820, and after that I'll head over to 830 (also a department under Mattox's authority). By then I expect you to put Gillette and the stewards back to work."

I had pushed Mattox's buttons; I kept pushing.

"Mattox, you do what you gotta do, and so will I. Do we understand each other?"

"Okay, Melrod, you're subject to discharge pending further investigation."

"Whatever. I'm not leaving till I finish collecting."

"That's it! You're fired. You need to leave the plant."

"Mattox, I told you, I ain't leaving the plant."

Everyone in 820 strained to hear. What better way to relieve Friday night's boredom? I made sure to be loud enough for people to hear. People on the line were having a great time watching the unfolding drama since Mattox had the reputation of being an unassailable jerk.

At the chief's desk, I called Rudy to apprise him of our suspensions.

"Hi, Connie [Rudy's wife], how's your evening? Is Rudy there, please?"

"Jon, he's out walking the dogs. Anything I can tell him?"

"Could you please ask him to beep me when he's home. No rush. Mattox, Motor Division superintendent, fired me and a few stewards for collecting strike funds. Rudy will know about it as the board authorized the collection."

"Sure, Jon. Don't worry. I'll have him call."

I sat at the chief's desk, ignoring Mattox who incessantly badgered me to leave the plant. An hour later, I spied Rudy headed up the aisle. Minutes later, other board members arrived. In sixty minutes, on a Friday night, Rudy had rallied the entire fifteen-member board.

Mattox, confronted by the entire board, called Doug Ross, head of Labor Relations, who soon strode into the plant looking pissed. Past practice dictated that a board member couldn't be fired without consulting Detroit management, as discharge of a board member would lead to a work stoppage.

Rudy broke from our scrum to confer with Ross. Rudy had assured me that no board member was leaving until the company rescinded my discharge, so I relaxed and enjoyed the show. After dealing with Ross, Rudy relayed that the "suspensions" had been withdrawn and said we could return to our Friday-night activities.

Late in 1984, Local 72 received an invitation from the French organization of Renault workers, Comité de Groupe Renault. With our September 1985 contract expiration months off, the board, without consulting the international (which would have certainly tried to block the trip), voted unanimously to send a delegation to strengthen ties with the French union. Tod, Bob Rosinski, and I were selected to meet with the Comité.

We headed to France as an official Local 72 delegation. The front page of the February *Kenosha Labor* read: "Local 72 strengthens ties to Renault unionists." What a difference with Rudy at the helm! We no longer needed to hold out coffee cans soliciting spare change at the gates, as the local picked up the tab.

Kenosha Labor quoted Tod: "'We were able to get a better understanding of the unions in France,' Ohnstad said. 'We also gave them a better understanding of our problems in Kenosha. We were able to get them to agree that it is important for us to struggle for this plant [Kenosha] and for them to support that struggle.'"

Tod's point hit at the core of our mission. Diminishing auto sales and the endemic chaos of world capitalism had pushed the working classes of both the United States and France to protect their own national interests, fighting for a piece of the decreasing pie. Renault had been under increasing pressure from French unions to bring overseas production back to France.

Even our CGT friends had demanded that Renault pull back foreign financial investment, succumbing to a nationalist posture while simultaneously paying lip service to international solidarity. We did our best to promote solidarity to meet the crisis with a unified response.

We posited that the more Kenosha-built Renault vehicles that sold in the United States, the more engines produced in Cléon, France, would be exported. Over ten days, our lobbying efforts resulted in incremental inroads.

We ultimately secured a commitment from the Comité, which said: "[We] agree with your struggle to defend the workers and factory in Kenosha and will agree with the solution you choose. . . . [W]e can try to help you."

Before departing, we were pleased to receive a letter that the Comité had sent to George Besse, the new president of Renault. The letter reinforced the promise of trade union support and condemned Renault management for supporting the litigation against *Fighting Times*.

At the same time that we faced the existential crisis of whether production would continue in Kenosha, Local 72's half-century anniversary took center stage. For months, the board fashioned elaborate plans to celebrate the local's history.

We set Saturday May 11 for the grand event. The threat of a plant shutdown cast a pall of anxiety over every family dependent on AMC. But hardship and the struggle to survive had defined the union's existence since 1933 when the biggest dog, Charles Nash, threatened to lock the gates and throw the keys into Lake Michigan before he'd negotiate. In a full circle after five decades, May 1985 promised to be no different.

John Drew, Tod, and I had devoted months to collecting old photos from the attics of Local 72 members. John composed a booklet, printed in the thousands, recounting the proud history of a militant, scrappy union that had been forged from one of the nation's first documented sit-downs in the auto industry. John's text noted that Charles Nash and his managers had been bitterly opposed to labor organizing, calling the president of the Kenosha Labor Council, Olkives, and others "communistic." "On November 9, 1933," John wrote, "the hundred or so workers in [final assembly] ... sat down in protest.... Nash responded by locking out all 3000 plant workers."

Within a week Nash had caved and recognized Local 19008 of the American Federation of Labor.

The booklet reprinted the first signed agreement with Nash:

April 11, 1934.
TO THE COMMITTEE
Kenosha, Wisconsin
Gentlemen:
The Nash Motors company has accepted in its entirety the statement of the automobile labor board for the settlement of the strike, and also guarantees that every factory worker in the Kenosha plant will receive not less than a 5% increase in wages.
Yours very truly,
THE NASH MOTOR COMPANY

A year later, the AFL held the first convention of a new national auto workers union in Detroit. Local 19008 received a charter as UAW Local 72.

We seized the opportunity of the fiftieth anniversary to forge a stronger bond with French unions. Local 72 issued an invitation to the Comité de Groupe. The response: Pierre Febre, high-profile CGT member and president of the Comité, planned to attend.

Oh my God, I thought. *This should prove interesting!* Not only was Pierre going to be sitting on the dais, but so too would be Victor Reuther, brother of Walter Reuther. While mainstream history remembers Walter Reuther as the golden boy of the UAW, it was also Walter Reuther and his cohorts who drummed out radicals, progressives, and leftists.

Victor would be sharing the stage with Pierre Febre, an old-school, traditional French communist. In fact, soon after deplaning in Chicago, Pierre commented offhandedly to Rosinski, "I would never have thought that I'd be visiting imperialist America before setting foot on the soil of the socialist motherland in the Soviet Union."

Victor had served as the UAW's international director, during which time he had collaborated with the labor movement in many European countries. Leftists and communists were prominent throughout European trade unionism, and Victor certainly had worked with many.

After the 1983 election of Owen Bieber as UAW international president, Victor became persona non grata. Rejecting the international's proconcession bargaining, Victor forged an oppositional path, siding with those of us fighting concessions, which led to his banning from the floor of UAW conventions.

At our anniversary event, Victor spoke before Pierre. "You don't hand the boss a gallon of wine any longer, and you don't carry a basket of fruit, but the corporations still like that system," he said. "They're using it at a much higher, more profitable level now.... The corporations are demanding outrageous tax breaks and incentives as blackmail to locate plants and create jobs ... just like they're trying to do to Local 72 now."

After Victor concluded his remarks, Rudy invited Pierre to the lectern. My heart skipped a beat as I saw that Victor and Pierre's paths would cross on stage. What would be Victor's reaction? As Pierre stepped ever closer to Victor, a broad smile crossed Victor's face. His outstretched arms grasped Pierre in a bear hug. Loud enough for all to hear, including those from the international, Victor greeted Pierre: "Salutations, cher camarade." I smiled.

The author meeting with Victor Reuther (Walter's elder brother who lost an eye in 1940 when a would-be assassin fired a shotgun through his home window) on occasion of Local 72's fiftieth anniversary. Speaking out against the international's concession bargaining, Victor became an ardent voice of the opposition movement challenging the International.

On our fiftieth anniversary we had buried the political animosity that had marked decades of Cold War distrust.

Of course, no celebration of one of the UAW's oldest locals would be complete without a parade of UAW international figures lining up at the mic, but the voices that inspired were those of wise union elders who had struggled to carve out dignity and fundamental human rights when faced with vicious capitalist suppression.

Former Local 72 president Paul Russo, elected by the 1934 sit-down strikers as one of three to negotiate with Charles Nash, reminded, "Mr. Nash told us it was a great mistake to listen to the communists. Nash told us he would throw the plant keys in Lake Michigan, but within a year all our demands were met." That was the strength and militance we were there to celebrate.

CHAPTER 28

Concessions Take Their Toll

My final chief steward's report, written shortly before I was elected to the board, had included stern straight talk that turned out to be prophetic: "Let no one be fooled, no matter who is elected to fill the entire 15 positions on the new Board—we are all in for tough times. The 1985 contract will be a tremendous challenge for this membership, and there will be no heroes on the Board after negotiations. It will take *militant, but responsible* unionism on all our parts to survive in '85."

In the first two years, Alliance and Encore sales were substantial, with 146,000 vehicles sold in 1983, climbing to 169,000 in 1984. *Motor Trend* conferred its prestigious Car of the Year award on the Alliance, declaring, "The Alliance may well be the best-assembled first-year car we've ever seen. Way to go Renault!" Our future looked promising.

Our excitement was short-lived, however. AMC lost $29 million in the first three months of 1985, ending five quarters of modest profitability.

By 1985, the fuel crisis that had juiced Renault sales in 1983 and 1984 ended, along with the popularity of small, fuel-efficient cars. Renault had no larger model to feed into the American market, a major flaw in the multinational's strategy to penetrate the United States.

The mood in the plant darkened as a bleak future was slowly unveiled.

We didn't have to wait for September contract expiration for the looming existential crisis to erupt. In early May, a letter arrived in members' mailboxes propounding fifteen major contract takeaways, pay and benefit cuts, and work rule changes that management demanded be *immediately* instituted to prevent the cessation of auto production in Kenosha. Even the atypical method of notification, mailing directly to homes rather than notifying the board, conveyed management's intent to uproot the foundation of our union-management bargaining relationship.

The threatening letter asserted that the plant would close unless there was unequivocal acceptance of fifteen concessions. What followed was a steady, unceasing drumbeat of ultimatums.

In prior contracts, Local 72 had successfully called the company's bluff, bolstered by the limitation that AMC had no alternative manufacturing site. In 1985, however, Renault posited that it would be cheaper to build the Alliance and Encore in France and ship vehicles to the United States than to pay Kenosha's higher production costs, more expensive than those of the Big Three.

On May 6, under mounting pressure, the board flew to Detroit to meet with corporate management. Election to the board, where I could strengthen the rank and file in its struggle with AMC, had been a long-term goal. Now I felt only deep foreboding as we sat across the table from upper management. The sides faced off, knowing that our fates hung precariously in the balance.

For the first time, I faced AMC's chief negotiator and VP of labor relations, Richard Calmes. Calmes, with comically bushy eyebrows and mustache that projected the appearance of a walrus, opened with an abrupt ultimatum. "Your choice as the Executive Board is to immediately abrogate fifteen existing provisions of the contract, *before* entering into September contract negotiations, or face the closure of the Kenosha facility." In other words: surrender or perish.

The vast power imbalance of industrial capitalism couldn't have been starker. Across from us sat a corporate henchman wielding nearly unlimited power over the livelihoods of thousands of Local 72 members and their families, along with retirees. Calmes promulgated his ultimatum without the slightest hint of humanity or remorse as to the dire consequences of his threatened actions.

After Calmes abruptly departed, a deafening silence filled the cavernous hotel meeting hall. Staring down at the institutional carpet that smelled of stale smoke and was stained by countless spilled drinks, I recalled the cautionary words in my own chief steward's report: "There will be no heroes after negotiations." How prescient that now seemed.

The media quoted Rudy: "There [is] no way that Local 72 could comply with management's demands to abrogate the collective bargaining process and sign a blank check that the company could do anything it wanted without even entering into negotiations.... They [AMC] said [the board] must agree to all these things before we talk. Clearly that option was not possible."

In speaking to the steward's institute, a component of the local's fiftieth anniversary celebration a few weeks later, Rudy ran down the alternatives presented in Detroit: "Some people expect the international to intervene to impose a solution. Ray Majerus [head of the UAW's AMC Department] ... said they would not do that. The next alternative was to work out some kind of middle ground. The company ... [maintained] they did not want to work out a middle ground, they wanted total capitulation. The last option was for the company to go ahead and send out the notices to close the plant."

Had I not sat within feet of Calmes, I might have thought he was simply posturing. I had stared, however, into the emotionless, calculating eyes of AMC's chief negotiator as he issued his ultimatum. I tried to penetrate the icy facade but found no humanity hiding behind it.

I understood all too well the lousy financial situation AMC faced. Perhaps to my detriment, I routinely read the *Wall Street Journal* and *Automotive News*, the unvarnished voices of vulture capitalism. I couldn't hide from the truth of the market-driven economy: Sales of small cars were tanking. Calmes's ultimatum necessitated a response measured by an objective appraisal rather than an emotional fit of fury.

That being said, Local 72 had never in its storied history rolled over in response to corporate intimidation. With Rudy at the helm, we had a fighting chance. Having successfully used the NLRB in the past, we turned to it to push back and slow the company steamroller.

We alleged that AMC had violated the NLRA by foreclosing negotiations while insisting we accept fifteen concessions. While we knew the labor board wouldn't prevent AMC from shutting the plant (and couldn't under US law), we felt it important to signal to the membership that the Local 72 board was not caving in without a fight.

On May 16, local headquarters filled with more than a thousand anxious members. Rudy's decades-long reputation for unblemished honesty now served him and all of us well. Most calm when facing adversity, Rudy stoked no fear but at the same time made no undeliverable promises: "I believe with the support of the membership and fair-minded and reasonable people in the community, the company will have to sit down and negotiate. I'm not trying to kid anybody that it's going to be easy negotiations. I would ask for all of your support."

In a testament to the trust members placed in Rudy, 83 percent voted to authorize the board to "enter into early negotiations to achieve a mutually satisfactory agreement and equitable EIP [Employee Investment Plan] repayment"—tough marching orders but not a surrender. (In 1988, during negotiations to close the assembly and stamping plants, Rudy would secure repayment from Chrysler, which purchased AMC in 1987. The "loan" amount that had appeared on each paycheck was actually repaid—and with 10% interest.)

Local 72 leaders and members in 1985 began calling on community allies to pressure the company. The devastation of a complete shutdown promised to adversely impact the wider community. In a campaign led by Richard Stoffel, pastor of St. Mary Catholic Church, twenty-nine local priests and members of the Kenosha County Clergy Association sent a telegram to Renault's US leader, Jose Dedeurwaerder, imploring that a meeting be scheduled with Local 72.

Governor Tony Earl and Milwaukee archbishop Rembert Weakland offered assistance in resolving the standoff, sending a telegram to Dedeurwaerder asserting that AMC and the UAW's differences were "reconcilable" and adding, "We wish to underscore the seriousness of the consequences to thousands of Wisconsin families if the AMC plants in Kenosha and Milwaukee cease operations."

Corporate spokesperson Lloyd Northard informed the media that no meetings were scheduled. Further, he affirmed that AMC intended to send certified notices to local and state governments of the corporation's intent to close the plant unless there was "last-minute acceptance by the UAW of the concessions." State law required a mere sixty-day notice before a plant closing, a far cry from the restrictions on plant closings our compatriots had won in France.

Despite pressure from a nervous membership and with the company's sword of Damocles swinging precariously close, Rudy remained steadfast. In Rudy's words, acceptance of preconditions constituted "unilateral surrender," an act not in his repertoire. The *Kenosha News* reported, "Both sides indicated they do not plan on changing their stances."

Early evening on May 22, I received a surprise call, long after the close of business, from an agitated Steve Schultz, NLRB field examiner. Schultz asked that the local union board meet with the labor board to articulate our position.

Next morning, Rudy, Recording Secretary Curt Wilson, John Drew, and I drove to Milwaukee. The trip tipped the scales in our favor, as the labor board issued a formal complaint the following day, May 24, charging AMC, Wisconsin's largest employer, with "bargaining in bad faith."

Undeterred, on Saturday, May 25, Detroit sent notices to members' homes declaring that it would begin phasing out Kenosha operations within sixty days and "terminate vehicle assembly operations in Kenosha on or before July 1, 1986. Other operations [were to] be terminated as soon as feasible." Additionally, the company made it known that the Motor Division would cease operations within two years.

The threat of the labor board hauling AMC before a judge, mounting pressure from the clergy, other community leaders, and the governor, plus Rudy's steadfast refusal to accept the company's ultimatum broke the stalemate. In early June, the corporation agreed to talks, and the local's executive board headed to the Milwaukee Hyatt Regency to commence early bargaining, *without preconditions.*

Calmes set June 28 as the day on which an agreement had to be reached "to head off steps to close Wisconsin's manufacturing operations."

No niceties or cordiality masked AMC's intent during bargaining. Day by day, Calmes and team picked apart our working agreement, intending to eliminate provisions that restricted management's freedom to abrogate protections and impose less-restrictive work rules.

Point by point, we argued, hoping to wear management down and retain protections that had made life on the assembly line a little more tolerable. With each session, corporate bargainers repeated the assertion that their offer on the table constituted their last.

Regardless, we painstakingly picked apart their arguments and made alternative suggestions. Most often we hit a brick wall or worse. In response to our position that workers needed the security of knowing what job they had a right to, a company guy countered, "We'll concede that workers have the right to a particular job, just like a cow coming to the same stall every day."

One day ran into the next. We lived on an unwholesome diet of burgers, pizza, and beer. And little by little we watched the erosion of protections held dear for decades. Our 1:35 steward-to-worker ratio gave way to the GM pattern of one district steward for 250 workers.

Arbitration replaced the right to strike over grievances. Our full-time board of fifteen shrank to a GM-type shop committee. Pegged to plant population, the shop committee would include only four to six members. Nine-hour days and two out of three mandatory Saturdays replaced voluntary overtime. With each concession, I swallowed hard and felt a bit of history slip away, as our once-enviable working agreement looked increasingly like that of Ford and GM.

Periodically, Majerus, titular head of the AMC Department, dropped in to observe, a meaningless gesture. We much preferred his absence.

There did come a time, unfortunately, when the board needed Majerus's assistance. Despite every argument we made, despite every angle we played, we were forced to admit that we had pushed back to the extent possible. Begrudgingly, we acknowledged that we were staring at the corporation's final offer.

Having reached that juncture, tradition provided that the local president, Rudy, engage in one last attempt to reach out to the international with a short list of items necessary to "clean up" the final agreement. Rudy, despite despising Majerus, called for a recess to approach him with the few items he said he had to have in order to put the agreement before the membership.

Rudy punched the elevator button for the upper floor, the location of Majerus's ample suite.

The look on Rudy's face when he returned to the meeting hall betrayed his deep disgust. Majerus hadn't even entertained the possibility of the international's securing a few final requests.

On June 28, the day of Calmes's deadline, the corporation's final offer confronted us. Majerus warned, "The international [will] compel the local to hold a vote as authorized by the UAW's constitution on offers rejected by the local leadership." In the *Kenosha News,* he was quoted from the day before, "The final document on the 28th of June *will* be put to the membership for a vote."

For years, *Fighting Times* and I had been loud voices against auto industry concessions. Cold, hard reality no longer allowed us the luxury of being the loudest, most absolutist opposition.

The time came to vote on whether to recommend the agreement. Rudy polled the board. Only John Stencil and Eddie Steagal voted no. John and Eddie were both political opportunists and had mastered the art of beating their chests—looking militant—while dodging the consequences. Knowing that thirteen had voted yes, they could comfortably vote no, claiming to be too radical to compromise.

Their no votes stung, salt in an open wound. None of us, particularly not Rudy, wanted to agree to the rape of our contract. We had swallowed hard and followed the only sustainable path to salvage as much as could be salvaged under the most unfavorable of circumstances.

Watching John and Eddie resort to their typical showboating, I mused, "The hell if I'm going to let them hide behind a no vote and play the super-militant."

I raised my hand. "There is no way we're going to walk out of this board meeting with John and Eddie claiming to be badass, holdout militants," I said. "They ... know the score as well as every one of us. We're not voting on some tentative agreement that we can reject simply to enhance our bargaining position and go back to bargain for a better deal.... The facts are that a 'no' vote *will close the doors*. Calmes wasn't fucking around. He was delivering a clear message. To disregard that message is irresponsible."

I took a breath and continued, knowing a lot rode on what I said next. "Let me be clear," I said. "If Brother Stencil and Brother Steagal don't vote yes to make this a unanimous recommendation by the board, I will be in my basement tonight printing a flyer to go out at every gate tomorrow, and that flyer will be very clear—John and Eddy voted to shut the fucking plant!"

As Rudy would recount many times after the vote, laughing heartily every time, "Melrod, you scared the shit out of John and Eddie with the threat of your letter." Of course, the vote was then fifteen to zero in favor of recommending the contract.

On July 12 Local 72 members ratified a new agreement, sacrificing long-cherished contract provisions in exchange for a modicum of job security, a temporary fix to a systemic flaw embedded in capitalism. In the final analysis, members voted for an agreement best described by Rudy at the ratification meeting, "We decided a job with a Big Three contract is better than no job at all."

The new contract provided for substantial pay cuts softened by increases in pensions and insurance benefits. In terms of economics, the new agreement closely matched GM and Ford, bringing AMC's labor costs in line with the industry standard.

In return, the corporation pledged not to import vehicles from France but to keep the plant open for the remaining life of the Alliance and Encore. Renault agreed to lend American Motors $174 million (in addition to the $545 million it had invested since 1979), despite intense pressure from French unions to concentrate all new investment in France.

It would have been painless for me to advocate a no vote, as I already had locked in plans to leave for California. When the final push came to shove, Tod, John Drew, Rosinski, and I stuck by our principles and asked the membership to accept the agreement. Our honest assessment of the situation was that a Big Three–type agreement was the only hope for keeping the plant open, at least for a while longer. (As it turned out, the 1985 agreement maintained production in Kenosha until Chrysler purchased AMC; Chrysler then continued to build engines in Kenosha until 2010. During the years after 1985, John fittingly rose to Local 72 president and Tod to the shop committee.)

I had accomplished much of what I had set out to achieve when I first walked through the doors of AMC in May 1972. Long gone were the days of handing out flyers as a twenty-two-year-old only to have a bucket of cleaning fluid dumped on my head. Gone were the days of driving a carload of ostensible supporters to the polls, then receiving the votes of only two of my three passengers.

I had assumed I'd be working at American Motors or its successor Renault for as long as autos were manufactured in Kenosha. Now long-term production was deeply in doubt. I turned thirty-five in June 1985, still young enough to pursue another path. As a fallback, I had applied to Hastings College of the Law in San Francisco.

It wasn't an easy departure. After the ups and downs of my life at AMC, Steve Lund provided a nice send-off on the front page of the Sunday, July 21, 1985, *Kenosha News* business section:

An Era Ends at Local 72

Lots of things changed last week when the new contract between American Motors Corp. and United Auto Workers Local 72 went into effect. Paychecks reflected a wage cut. Union stewards were relatively scarce.

And if something went wrong, nobody could blame it on Jonathan Melrod.

Melrod, 35, the leader of the "Fighting Times" trio of labor activists, has taken a leave of absence to go to law school....

It's the end of an era.

For 13 years as an AMC employee, Melrod has been the leading voice of dissent in Local 72 in Kenosha, and before he came here in 1976, Local 75 in Milwaukee. He's been a thorn in the side of union leadership and company management alike.

As a worker, he's been fired for union activities. As a newsletter publisher, he's been sued for libel. As a union activist he's been branded a "commie." He won his job back after being fired. He and fellow "Fighting Times" publishers John Drew and Tod Ohnstad successfully defended themselves in the libel suit.

Melrod's role in Kenosha has almost always been to raise the dissenting voice.

"Dissent has to be the lifeblood of the union movement. Without it, it gets stale," said Melrod.

Racine Labor, a venerable weekly, ran a front-page photo of me wearing my 1973 "FIGHT SPEED UP" T-shirt. The story, "Melrod Leaves for Law School with 7–0 Record [at the NLRB] vs. AMC," included a quote from Rudy: "Local 72's loss is somebody else's gain. He'll always be out there trying to correct injustice. He'll be there, with integrity, caring about people, and trying to help them."

Epilogue

After departing Kenosha for San Francisco, I slogged through law school at the University of California, Hastings College of the Law, a miserable experience that I don't recommend. I then opened an office practicing refugee and asylum law, representing clients from all over the world fleeing political, sexual, religious, and ethnic persecution.

Representing several Spanish-speaking clients led to my experiencing "Rock en español," US-bred Latin indie rock. This inspired my entry into the music industry, first with Aztlan Records and then with Rock River Music.

In 2004, I was diagnosed with terminal pancreatic cancer. A surgeon removed a tumor on the tail of my pancreas. The long, protracted night after surgery was the most tormented of my life. My mind swung continually between the insufferable agony of physical pain and the irrepressible fear of dying.

With each slight movement, a tube painfully tugged, reminding me that only medical intervention kept me alive. I couldn't sleep. My mind replayed my life frame by frame. Over that long, endless, excruciatingly painful night, I persuaded myself that I could, and would, summon the inner strength to find a path out of the mess I found myself in, no matter what the doctors told me.

Ten years later, I was pronounced cancer-free.

In 2014 I became involved in the Philippine human rights movement through then-acquaintance Maria Isabel Lopez. Isabel was active in GABRIELA—National Alliance of Women, and Karapatan, a leading Philippine human rights group. Isabel, who was to become my wife, involved me in meeting and aiding women political prisoners through Karapatan. Karapatan posits that there are close to five hundred political prisoners

---

Due to space constraints, this epilogue has been greatly abbreviated. For more about my battle to beat pancreatic cancer, see www.jonathanmelrod.com.—Ed.

The author and Maria Isabel Lopez meeting with women political prisoners incarcerated on trumped up charges in Camp Bagong Diwa, Philippines. The meeting concluded with the singing of "The Internationale"—the worldwide anthem of oppressed peoples.

being held under false pretense in miserable, inhumane conditions across the country.

Along with Isabel, I also joined in solidarity with the Lumad indigenous people in the Southern Philippines, fighting to protect their ancestral lands from foreign logging and mining interests. Isabel and I both remain active today with Karapatan and the struggle for Lumad rights.

My activist efforts also focused much nearer to home. When a Sonoma County sheriff murdered a thirteen-year-old Latino boy, Andy Lopez, on October 13, 2017, I renewed my dormant bar membership and took on cases representing families of young Latinos murdered by police. One eighteen-year-old murder victim, Yanira Serrano, was murdered by police in Half Moon Bay, California, following a 911 call asking for emergency medical assistance during a schizophrenic episode.

Isabel and I now live in Sonoma County, California.

John Drew went on to be elected president of Local 72 and then worked for the UAW regional office that covers southeastern Wisconsin. Now retired, he continues to be active in labor and political affairs.

Tod Ohnstad served on the Local 72 executive board for twenty years. After that he was elected to the Kenosha Common Council and then to the Wisconsin State Assembly, where he currently represents the 65th District, covering most of Kenosha.

I return to the question posed by my sons: "Dad, after having your intestines cut up and battling pancreatic cancer caused by factory chemicals, would you have made the same choice to work in those factories you've told us about?"

I'm no Don Quixote. When I made the choice to leave Madison to work in Milwaukee factories in 1972, I was one among thousands whose political roots lay in Revolutionary Youth Movement II, the faction of Students for a Democratic Society that believed that the working class possessed the ultimate power to stand up to capitalism and fight for a more humane socialist alternative. I still embrace that philosophy but realize the goal many of us share isn't on the immediate horizon as I once perhaps naively believed.

Of course, the millions upon millions of working people, who face alienating, insecure, life-threatening, and toxic working conditions daily, aren't afforded the luxury of contemplating whether or not to subject themselves to capitalist exploitation. Survival itself necessitates going to work, despite the inherent consequences and risks.

As I look back over what I've written, I'd like to think I lived by a worthy creed. In the United States we are not taught history as it truly unfolded, at least the chapters that were lived by working-class heroes. I'd like to leave my readers with the words of an American socialist who chose jail rather than fight a rich man's war (World War I):

> "To stir the masses, to appeal to their higher, better selves, to set them thinking for themselves, and to hold ever before them the ideal of mutual kindness and good will, based upon mutual interests, is to render real service to the cause of humanity."
>
> —Eugene V. Debs

About the Author

Born into the political and cultural quiescence of the 1950s, Jonathan Melrod grew up in deeply segregated and unequal Washington, DC. Active in the student movement that opposed the Vietnam War and a supporter of Black liberation, Jon embraced the ideology that the working class held the power to radically transform society. He left the campus for the factory in 1972. For thirteen years, he immersed himself in the day-to-day struggles of Milwaukee's working class, both on the factory floor and in the political arena. Despite FBI surveillance and interference, Jon organized a militant rank-and-file caucus and rose through union ranks to a top leadership position in UAW Local 72. After a mass workforce cutback imposed by AMC's joint venture partner Renault, he left to attend Hastings College of the Law in San Francisco in 1985. Graduating cum laude with a JD, he opened a law firm in San Francisco successfully representing hundreds of political refugees. His website, featuring further writing and more, is www.jonathanmelrod.com.

ABOUT PM PRESS

PM Press is an independent, radical publisher of books and media to educate, entertain, and inspire. Founded in 2007 by a small group of people with decades of publishing, media, and organizing experience, PM Press amplifies the voices of radical authors, artists, and activists. Our aim is to deliver bold political ideas and vital stories to all walks of life and arm the dreamers to demand the impossible. We have sold millions of copies of our books, most often one at a time, face to face. We're old enough to know what we're doing and young enough to know what's at stake. Join us to create a better world.

PM Press
PO Box 23912
Oakland, CA 94623
www.pmpress.org

PM Press in Europe
europe@pmpress.org
www.pmpress.org.uk

FRIENDS OF PM PRESS

These are indisputably momentous times—the financial system is melting down globally and the Empire is stumbling. Now more than ever there is a vital need for radical ideas.

In the many years since its founding—and on a mere shoestring—PM Press has risen to the formidable challenge of publishing and distributing knowledge and entertainment for the struggles ahead. With hundreds of releases to date, we have published an impressive and stimulating array of literature, art, music, politics, and culture. Using every available medium, we've succeeded in connecting those hungry for ideas and information to those putting them into practice.

Friends of PM allows you to directly help impact, amplify, and revitalize the discourse and actions of radical writers, filmmakers, and artists. It provides us with a stable foundation from which we can build upon our early successes and provides a much-needed subsidy for the materials that can't necessarily pay their own way. You can help make that happen—and receive every new title automatically delivered to your door once a month—by joining as a Friend of PM Press. And, we'll throw in a free T-shirt when you sign up.

Here are your options:

- **$30 a month** Get all books and pamphlets plus 50% discount on all webstore purchases

- **$40 a month** Get all PM Press releases (including CDs and DVDs) plus 50% discount on all webstore purchases

- **$100 a month** Superstar—Everything plus PM merchandise, free downloads, and 50% discount on all webstore purchases

For those who can't afford $30 or more a month, we have **Sustainer Rates** at $15, $10, and $5. Sustainers get a free PM Press T-shirt and a 50% discount on all purchases from our website.

Your Visa or Mastercard will be billed once a month, until you tell us to stop. Or until our efforts succeed in bringing the revolution around. Or the financial meltdown of Capital makes plastic redundant. Whichever comes first.

Homestead Steel Mill—the Final Ten Years: USWA Local 1397 and the Fight for Union Democracy

Mike Stout with an Introduction by JoAnn Wypijewski and an Afterword by Staughton Lynd

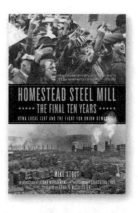

ISBN: 978-1-62963-791-4 (paperback)
978-1-62963-855-3 (hardcover)
$24.95/$60.00   352 pages

Spanning the famous Homestead steel strike of 1892 through the century-long fight for a union and union democracy, *Homestead Steel Mill—the Final Ten Years* is a case history on the vitality of organized labor. Written by fellow worker and musician Mike Stout, the book is an insider's portrait of the union at the U.S. Steel's Homestead Works, specifically the workers, activists, and insurgents that made up the radically democratic Rank and File Caucus from 1977 to 1987. Developing its own "inside-outside" approach to unionism, the Rank and File Caucus drastically expanded their sphere of influence so that, in addition to fighting for their own rights as workers, they fought to prevent the closures of other steel plants, opposed U.S. imperialism in Central America, fought for civil rights, and built strategic coalitions with local environmental groups.

Mike Stout skillfully chronicles his experience in the takeover and restructuring of the union's grievance procedure at Homestead by regular workers and put at the service of its thousands of members. Stout writes with raw honesty and pulls no punches when recounting the many foibles and setbacks he experienced along the way. The Rank and File Caucus was a profound experiment in democracy that was aided by the 1397 Rank and File newspaper—an ultimate expression of truth, democracy, and free speech that guaranteed every union member a valuable voice.

Profusely illustrated with dozens of photographs, *Homestead Steel Mill—the Final Ten Years* is labor history at its best, providing a vivid account of how ordinary workers can radicalize their unions.

"Mike Stout's well-constructed and splendidly illustrated memoir is about a special place and time, but it also serves as a window on a social insurgency that can provide inspiration for future social progress. It is a story of skilled workers who proudly got their hands dirty—an industrial world of crane men, machinists, mechanics, millwrights, laborers, and electricians that once dominated a region—but who also combined working-class culture as writers, poets musicians, cartoonists, and even lawyers. Today, there are new skills and different jobs, but class oppression endures. Greed without end or solidarity forever? The choice remains and the consequences for a sick earth and an imperial world order could not be greater."
—Charles McCollester, chief steward, UE Local 610, Switch and Signal Plant; former professor of labor history at Indiana University of Pennsylvania

Strike! 50th Anniversary Edition

Jeremy Brecher with a Preface by Sara
Nelson and a Foreword by Kim Kelly

ISBN: 978-1-62963-800-3 (paperback)
    978-1-62963-856-0 (hardcover)
$28.95/$60.00   640 pages

Jeremy Brecher's *Strike!* narrates the dramatic story
of repeated, massive, and sometimes violent revolts
by ordinary working people in America. Involving
nationwide general strikes, the seizure of vast industrial
establishments, nonviolent direct action on a massive scale, and armed battles
with artillery and tanks, this exciting hidden history is told from the point of view
of the rank-and-file workers who lived it. Encompassing the repeated repression of
workers' rebellions by company-sponsored violence, local police, state militias, and
the US Army and National Guard, it reveals a dimension of American history rarely
found in the usual high school or college history course.

Since its original publication in 1972, no book has done as much as *Strike!* to bring
US labor history to a wide audience. Now this fiftieth anniversary edition brings
the story up to date with chapters covering the "mini-revolts of the 21st century,"
including Occupy Wall Street and the Fight for Fifteen. The new edition contains
over a hundred pages of new materials and concludes by examining a wide range
of current struggles, ranging from #BlackLivesMatter, to the great wave of teachers
strikes "for the soul of public education," to the global "Student Strike for Climate,"
that may be harbingers of mass strikes to come.

*"Jeremy Brecher's Strike! is a classic of American historical writing. This new edition,
bringing his account up to the present, comes amid rampant inequality and growing
popular resistance. No book could be more timely for those seeking the roots of our
current condition."*
—Eric Foner, Pulitzer Prize winner and DeWitt Clinton Professor of History at
Columbia University

*"Magnificent—a vivid, muscular labor history, just updated and rereleased by PM Press,
which should be at the side of anyone who wants to understand the deep structure of
force and counterforce in America."*
—JoAnn Wypijewski, author of *Killing Trayvons: An Anthology of American Violence*

*"An exciting history of American labor. Brings to life the flashpoints of labor history.
Scholarly, genuinely stirring."*
—New York Times

*"Splendid . . . clearly the best single-volume summary yet published of American general
strikes."*
—Washington Post

Labor Law for the Rank and Filer: Building Solidarity While Staying Clear of the Law (2nd Edition)

Staughton Lynd and Daniel Gross

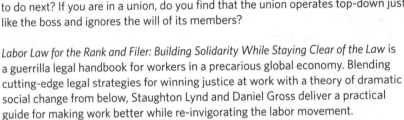

ISBN: 978-1-60486-419-9
$12.00   120 pages

Have you ever felt your blood boil at work but lacked the tools to fight back and win? Or have you acted together with your co-workers, made progress, but wondered what to do next? If you are in a union, do you find that the union operates top-down just like the boss and ignores the will of its members?

Labor Law for the Rank and Filer: Building Solidarity While Staying Clear of the Law is a guerrilla legal handbook for workers in a precarious global economy. Blending cutting-edge legal strategies for winning justice at work with a theory of dramatic social change from below, Staughton Lynd and Daniel Gross deliver a practical guide for making work better while re-invigorating the labor movement.

Labor Law for the Rank and Filer demonstrates how a powerful model of organizing called "Solidarity Unionism" can help workers avoid the pitfalls of the legal system and utilize direct action to win. This new revised and expanded edition includes new cases governing fundamental labor rights as well as an added section on Practicing Solidarity Unionism. This new section includes chapters discussing the hard-hitting tactic of working to rule; organizing under the principle that no one is illegal; and building grassroots solidarity across borders to challenge neoliberalism, among several other new topics. Illustrative stories of workers' struggles make the legal principles come alive.

"*Workers' rights are under attack on every front. Bosses break the law every day. For 30 years* Labor Law for the Rank and Filer *has been arming workers with an introduction to their legal rights (and the limited means to enforce them) while reminding everyone that real power comes from workers' solidarity.*"
—Alexis Buss, former General Secretary-Treasurer of the IWW

"*As valuable to working persons as any hammer, drill, stapler, or copy machine,* Labor Law for the Rank and Filer *is a damn fine tool empowering workers who struggle to realize their basic dignity in the workplace while living through an era of unchecked corporate greed. Smart, tough, and optimistic, Staughton Lynd and Daniel Gross provide nuts and bolts information to realize on-the-job rights while showing us that another world is not only possible but inevitable.*"
—John Philo, Legal Director, Maurice and Jane Sugar Law Center for Economic and Social Justice

Living and Dying on the Factory Floor: From the Outside In and the Inside Out

David Ranney

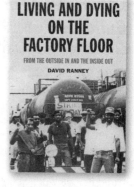

ISBN: 978-1-62963-639-9
$15.00   160 pages

David Ranney's vivid memoir describes his work experiences between 1976 and 1982 in the factories of southeast Chicago and northwest Indiana. The book opens with a detailed description of what it was like to live and work in one of the heaviest industrial concentrations in the world. The author takes the reader on a walk through the heart of the South Side of Chicago, observing the noise, heavy traffic, the 24-hour restaurants and bars, the rich diversity of people on the streets at all hours of the day and night, and the smell of the highly polluted air.

Factory life includes stints at a machine shop, a shortening factory, a railroad car factory, a structural steel shop, a box factory, a chemical plant, and a paper cup factory. Along the way there is a wildcat strike, an immigration raid, shop-floor actions protesting supervisor abuses, serious injuries, a failed effort to unionize, and a murder. Ranney's emphasis is on race and class relations, working conditions, environmental issues, and broader social issues in the 1970s that impacted the shop floor.

Forty years later, the narrator returns to Chicago's South Side to reveal what happened to the communities, buildings, and the companies that had inhabited them. *Living and Dying on the Factory Floor* concludes with discussions on the nature of work; racism, race, and class; the use of immigration policy for social control; and our ability to create a just society.

"David Ranney's is our best account of the New Left's turn to the factory and other workplaces in the seventies. Reading in some parts like a novel, it introduces us to a remarkable cast of working-class characters, while offering a refreshingly critical look at his own experiences. We get compelling views of factory work, including the physical dangers and injuries that came with it, as well as a better understanding of a range of New Left organizing efforts. With the experience of a radical organizer and the insights of a very good social scientist, Ranney writes with particular sensitivity about race relations in the workplace."
—James R. Barrett, author of *History from the Bottom Up & the Inside Out: Ethnicity, Race, and Identity in Working-Class History*

Labor Power and Strategy

John Womack Jr.
Edited by Peter Olney and Glenn Perusek

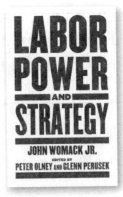

ISBN: 978-1-62963-974-1
$16.95   192 pages

What would it take to topple Amazon? To change how health care works in America? To break up the media monopolies that have taken hold of our information and imaginations? How is it possible to organize those without hope working on the margins? In *Labor Power and Strategy*, legendary strategist, historian and labor organizer John Womack, speaks directly to a new generation, providing rational, radical, experience-based perspectives that help target and run smart, strategic, effective campaigns in the working class.

In this sleek, practical, pocket inspiration, Womack lays out a timely plan for identifying chokepoints and taking advantage of supply chain issues in order to seize and build labor power and solidarity. Interviewed by Peter Olney of the International Longshore and Warehouse Union—Womack's lively, illuminating thoughts are built upon by ten young labor organizers and educators, whose responses create a rich dialogue and open a space for joyful, achievable change. With stories of triumph that will bring readers to tears this back-pocket primer is an instant classic.

"In Our Revolution we shout, 'When we Organize, We Win,' but organize who and win what? Labor Power and Strategy *is a great collection of Womack and 10 organizers debating strategic workplace organizing vs associational or more general organizing at workplaces or in communities. Womack, in a long initial interview and in the conclusion, argues that without organizing workplace chokepoints, we are left with the spontaneous movements that come and go. Several of the 10 organizers essentially argue that the spontaneous can become conscious and long lasting. Grab the book and take up the debate."*
—Larry Cohen, board chair Our Revolution, past president, Communications Workers of America

"In this fascinating and insightful dialogue, the distinguished historian John Womack and a set of veteran labor activists probe the most fundamental of questions: How do we organize the 21 century working-class and give it the power to transform world capitalism? Are workers with vital skills and strategic leverage the key to a labor resurgence, or should organizers wager upon a mobilization of working people whose relationship to the economy's commanding heights is more diffuse? Or can we arrive at some dialectical symbiosis? Whatever the answer, this is the kind of constructively radical conversation essential to the rebirth of working-class power in our time."
—Nelson Lichtenstein, historian and author of Capitalism Contested: The New Deal and Its Legacies